DATE DUE

The American Nightmare

The American Nightmare

Trade Politics after Seattle

Thomas A. Hockin

LEXINGTON BOOKS
Lanham • Boulder • New York • Oxford

LEXINGTON BOOKS

Published in the United States of America
by Lexington Books
4720 Boston Way, Lanham, Maryland 20706

12 Hid's Copse Road
Cumnor Hill, Oxford OX2 9JJ, England

British Library Cataloguing in Publication Information Available

Library of Congress Cataloging-in-Publication Data

Hockin, Thomas A., 1938–
    The American nightmare : trade politics after Seattle / Thomas A. Hockin.
      p. cm.
    Includes bibliographical references and index.
    ISBN 0-7391-0241-9 (cloth : alk. paper)
    1. International trade. 2. Commercial policy. 3. United States—Commercial policy.
   4. World Trade Organization. I. Title.

HF1379 .H63 2001
382'.3'0973—dc21
                                           00-067827

Printed in the United States of America

♾™ The paper used in this publication meets the minimum requirements of American
National Standard for Information Sciences—Permanence of Paper for Printed Library
Materials, ANSI/NISO Z39.48–1992.

This book is dedicated to the late

William Donner
of Columbus, Indiana
and Montreal Canada

and his foundation

The Donner Canadian Foundation who made this book
possible.

Contents

Preface

Why do we labor at the poem?
Out of the turbulence of the sea
Flower by brittle flower, rises.
The coral reef that calms the water.

Archibald MacLeish[1]

This book is aimed at the general public and university students. Some political people might find it helpful as well. It is a review of trade politics in general terms only, but it also advocates some directions for the future..

Woodrow Wilson thought that internationally-minded regimes under the rule of law would slide into international comity. Socialists such as Karl Marx once thought that competitive, freely trading nations would eventually destroy each other's economy. Wilson was too optimistic, just as Marx was too negative. It was Oscar Wilde who said, "I am never wrong. I am sometimes early." This book is about not being so early about the endurance of the WTO and NAFTA as to be wrong.

This book centers on the growth of international and multinational trade obligations. These obligations are producing a fragile yet real and growing coral reef of disciplines on governments and corporations that violate international trade undertakings. As a result, shadows of suspicion descend on the creators of those disciplines, the World Trade Organization (WTO) and the North American Free Trade Agreement (NAFTA). Not only the Seattle protesters but many on the right, the left, conservatives or liberals, resent this growing set of new disciplines. This book is a reflection from a former trade minister, international relations professor and current investment funds association president.

The growth of these restraints – however tentative and novel – are not, in fact, instruments of the right or of the left or of conservatives or liberals, or of Republicans or of Democrats, but of something else. That "something else" we try to untangle in this essay, explication and collection of cases. We observe that it is not only multinational corporations, but a reluctant yet solid desire by governments to build something approaching a rules-based trading system which encourages disciplines to accomplish this. This thrust by governments, not simply by business lobbyists, has powered the advance of the WTO, NAFTA and European Union restraints in the last decade.

Why did sovereign states agree to these constraints? From what this writer has read and experienced in multilateral trade negotiations, this agreement sprung from three suspicions of some adversarial country's unwelcome trade policy or tactic. These suspicions felt by governments and lobbies are worth untangling. They are based essentially on any of Kenneth Waltz's three suspects in his long respected study *Man: The State and War*. One suspect is predatory individual political leaders or narrowly based lobbies; another suspect is unwelcome domestic, political and industrial arrangements in some other nation; another suspect is that trade ministers will misread their international options or, to put it vernacularly, "play international chess badly." The desire to find a refuge from these three horsemen powers this urge that has built a somewhat fragile WTO coral reef to "calm the waters" of contestation in world trade.

These three images are explained in chapter 2. These images of "what one perceives as other countries' failings" dictate ones own analysis and action. As John Maynard Keynes put it long ago, "practical men" see the world through "world views" fashioned by "theorists" reflections whether they know it or not. These three images flow from political philosophers through the centuries. They are not new, but they should not be forgotten. They are used here to untangle and clarify the liberalized trade story and the future dispute-settlement agreements. We emphasize the importance of some realistic "loopholes" from the tightest application of some WTO restraints for a time for nations in some cases but we argue for a growing set of multilateral legal restraints to "calm the waters".

What follows then is not an academic trade specialist's exhaustive treatment of the issues. Mostly, this is a political activist's and a political scientist's reading of the issues. Legal analysis will be focused only on key political questions. For impressive U.S. trade policy histories, see I. M. Destler's *American Trade Politics* and Edward Kaplan's two volumes on *American Trade Policy.*

We will explore the growth – but far from permanent growth – of the WTO and NAFTA undertakings and their dispute settlement instruments. We note their confining effect on domestic administration of trade law. We will see that this confining effect, although significant, is not overwhelming. Room for unilateral responses, both administrative and political, circumventing some of this discipline still can be found.

The nightmare is this: the coral reef of growing multilateral restraints of the WTO and NAFTA against member nations could easily break and be swept away. The consequences of course would be disastrous for world trade, and for the world financial system. Enthusiasts on the right, left, protectionists, internationalists, Republicans or Democrats should wish to avoid this disastrous cycle.

This book concentrates on the WTO, NAFTA and the environmental and labor side accords to NAFTA because these are what this writer sees as the immediate challenges to the international system. Expanding the trade agreements in a new round is also vital, but to do this we must first locate the debate between the "civil society" groups that descended on Seattle in December 1999 and the ideology against them. There is an introductory ideological essay in chapters 1 and 2. What can be done for the civil society's favorite cause, "environmental protection" will be examined later in the book as well. This writer helped negotiate the side accords on this to NAFTA in 1993.

After recognizing the ideological differences around freer trade, we turn to a "process problem" that may be as serious as any ideological divide, or failed expansion of any future round for trade liberalization. We examine as central to the new order the credibility of the new WTO dispute settlement system and NAFTA's. We discover how tenuous the dispute settlement arrangements can be at times. The admission of China to the WTO is explored from a political economy perspective and then from the challenge it will place on the WTO's dispute settlement arrangement. The safety valves that relieve some domestic political pressures will be gently introduced as "political" realities to allow the multilateral pacts to evolve and not suffocate.

This book, then, is a political reading and it questions how much commitment really exists in national governments to these new international disciplines. It observes how tender the commitment to the WTO and NAFTA actually is in spite of their contribution to the settlement of disputes and the liberalization of trade. It concludes that recent American trade policy as a major architect of the new system lacks coherence and therefore contributes to the ambiguity of the international system's future. Sometimes freer trade without multilateral discipline on American sovereignty seems to be U.S. trade policy.

Prime examples of this are analyzed. One example is the endless *Softwood Lumber* dispute in the case of the Canada–United States Free Trade Agreement (1989-94) (FTA) and NAFTA. Another is the failure to implement the "trucking" clause for Mexico in NAFTA. Another is the deployment by the U.S. administration of Super 301 (to usefully transform GATT in the Uruguay Round negotiations) but is still used unilaterally on some sensitive WTO determinations. Another is the indeterminacy of the unglamorous but vital matter of the administration of U.S. trade law. These are some examples of this start–and–stop incoherence.

Ironically, the most positive United States contribution in the past decade may have been the bilateral United States negotiations with China to align that regime with the WTO prior to China's entry to that body. Whether these exertions flow from a totally domestically powered realist strategy or from a voluntarist concern for the WTO's success remain ambiguous.

We will see in this book that the "coral reef" of concrete achievements of the Uruguay Round and NAFTA are not necessarily permanent. The true American nightmare would be to see these restraints dislodged and fall away. Awakening from this nightmare and seeing it in real life would quickly unravel the world trading and financial systems. American interests as well as other national's interests would be seriously undermined.

At present, neither the United States nor any other major power seems to know where the next round, WTO's millennium round, should go next. All agree some momentum must be found and that the voice of other values beside trade, such as those asking for better environmental and labor standards, should also be enhanced. Not long ago Sylvia Ostry, veteran trade negotiator and scholar, described the present predicament by citing the work of German physicist Werner Heisenberg, winner of the 1932 Nobel Prize. She paraphrased Mr. Heisenberg's uncertainty principle "you know where you are, but not where you are going, or you know where you are going, but not where you are".[2]

This book is a modest answer from the perspective of a political scientist and a former politician who has witnessed and been moved by the politics of trade.

This book is not about comprehensive international trade policy or trade theory. Nor is it necessarily (but possibly), about some imminent Armageddon to be triggered by a giant trade conflict. Nor can it replace the huge and advanced scholarship on international dispute resolution. This is a plea for some understanding of political threats and fears that could very soon overload the nascent World Trade Organization, an organization few understand and even fewer have any affection for.

I try, in what follows, to capture a few of the political realities that now impede any unanimous vision of free trade. This book reminds us of Machiavelli's political "necessita" that can trample the best laid plans of well-intentioned internationalists. "Necessita" limned the political ambit of Princes, not their good intentions. What follows reminds us that if you wish to do good you are best advised to keep your eyes open for the array of political impediments.

I wish to acknowledge the insights and research of the following who, over the past six years knowingly or unknowingly, helped me through each chapter: Donner Canadian Foundation; John Millar; Robert Leckey; Christopher Rickerd; Jim McIllroy; Jeffrey Mammon; Ina Sharpley; Tori and Mary Hockin; John Whalley; Jonathon Fried; Adrian Johnson; Jeanette Williams; Lara Tessaro, Josh Bezonski; John Kirton; David Crane; Christopher Thomas; Todd Weiler; John Weekes; John Howard; David Wingfield; Scott Little; Joseph Meehan; Michael Hart; Sylvia Ostry; Gary Horlick; Colin Dickenson; John Mercury; James Baker; Rt. Hon. Brian Mulroney and Hon. Michael Wilson. None are responsible for any of the defects, those are mine alone.

I wish to dedicate this book to political leaders and the dedicated public servants who helped make Canada's and the United States' role in international trade constructive from 1985 to 2000.

Notes

1. Archibald MacLeish, excerpt from "Reasons for Music," from COLLECTED POEMS *1917-1982* by Archibald MacLeish, Copyright © 1985 by The Estate of Archibald MacLeish. Reprinted by permission of Houghton Mifflin Co. All Rights reserved. Boston, 1985.
2. Ryerson University Conference, February 10, 2000, at Toronto.

"The World Economics Forum at Davos, Switzerland, was created to bring business leaders, government leaders, media people, non-governmental organizations and intellectuals together to spark debate and action on some of the world's problems.

In February 2001, in Porto Alegre in Southern Brazil, the World Social Forum was inaugurated. Inspired by Brazilian and French leftists, it was to be, and intends to remain the alternative to, and enemy of, Davos. Its founder Bernard Cassen, senior editor of the radical monthly *Le Monde Diplomatique* is blunt. "We have nothing to say to people at Davos. We know what their line is – we know what they mean by global responsibility." Added Waldon Bello, a Philippino academic and trade activist: "We live on different planets. Here in Porto Alegre we are looking for ways to save the planet; you in Davos, are looking for ways to maintain the hegemony of multinationals across the world."

John Lloyd [1]

Many folks and movements hold aggressively and narrow partisan positions, usually linked to an active political agenda, based on exalting one side while bashing the other.

Stephen Jay Gould [2]

---

[1] John Lloyd, F.T. Magazine *Financial Times,* Feb. 24, 25, 2001

[2] Stephen Jay Gould, *Rock of Ages: Science and Religion in the Fullness of Life* (New York: Ballantine, 1999), 68.

Part I
The Ideas

Chapter One

The Ideological Resistance to the WTO and the Strangely Inarticulate Defenders of the WTO

As the proverb goes, "if you want peace, prepare for war," announced Quebec's public security minister as he announced security measures for Quebec City's Summit of the Americas in April 2001. This summit gathering of the leaders of 34 countries in the Americas aims to create a free trade zone from Alaska to Argentina. [1]

Why such security precautions? After all, America has enjoyed fifty years of rounds successfully liberalizing trade. What is more, the negotiators have enjoyed relative public obscurity. Then suddenly one hundred thousand activists protesting perceived "injustice" descended on the World Trade Organization in Seattle in early December 1999. Ministers to the WTO had hoped to initiate a new "millennium round." instead they called for an adjournment and returned home. What exactly is this "WTO," this surrogate for globalization all about? What briefly does it include?

The World Trade Organization is made up of a number of distinct trade agreements including:

1) General Agreement on Tariffs and Trade
2) Agreement on Technical Barriers to Trade
3) Agreement on Agriculture
4) Agreement on Sanitary and Phyto-Sanitary Standards
5) Agreement on Dispute Settlement Procedures
6) General Agreement on Trade in Services

7) Agreement on Trade-Related Investment Measures
8) Agreement on Trade-Related Intellectual Property

Although this book centers on dispute settlement as the potential Achilles' heel of the WTO, the ambitious reach of its integrated agreements create a large arena for controversy. Here is a wonderfully clear brief summary, compiled by John Whalley and Colleen Hamilton, two of the world's closest economics scholars of some of the most important components of the final Uruguay Round Agreement of December 15, 1993:[2]

> **Market access for nonagricultural goods**. The industrialized countries reduced tariffs on manufactured goods by 38 percent on a trade-weighted average. Tariff bindings for this category of goods were extended. Comparable tariff reductions by developing countries were extended for up to over half of the existing level for other imports. Tariff reductions by industrialized countries were uneven by sector but not insignificant.
>
> The tariff reductions went beyond the objective of a one-third average reduction adopted at Montreal in 1988. The zero-for-zero elimination of tariffs for eight major sectors established a pattern of free trade by sector, which could be pursued further in future negotiations.
>
> **Agriculture**. This sector was brought for the first time within the GATT multilateral trading system. Internal support programs reduced on average by 20 percent from the base level and bound against future increase.
>
> Export subsidies reduced by 36 percent in value and 21 percent in quantity over a six-year period.
>
> Market access for imports based on a process of "tariffication" whereby all nontariff barriers, such as variable levies, quotas, import bans and voluntary export restraints, were converted into a single fixed tariff. Tariffication of Japanese and South Korean rice imports postponed for six years in conjunction with higher initial minimum access levels.

Textiles and clothing. This sector was integrated into the GATT system over ten years and subject to the same disciplines as other sectors. Key provisions pertain to the phaseout of existing import quotas, improved market access in all participating countries and safeguards during the transition period.

Doubts were raised, however, whether industrialized country bilateral quotas will be fully eliminated if imports threaten to grow rapidly. Trade liberalization undertaken by developing countries, particularly in Asia, were unclear.

Services. The General Agreement on Trade and Services (GATS) provides a framework of rules and principles for trade in services and the basis for future negotiations to reduce barriers that discriminate against foreign service providers and deny them market access. The framework agreement includes most-favored-nation (MFN) treatment, national treatment, market access, transparency and the free flow of payments and transfers.

Intellectual property rights. The trade-related intellectual property rights (TRIPs) agreement establishes improved standards for protection of the full range of intellectual property rights and the enforcement of these standards both internally and at the border. Intellectual property rights covered by the agreement are patents, copyright, trade marks, industrial designs, trade secrets, integrated circuits and geographical indicators.

Patent protection is for twenty years from the date of application, covering patents for virtually all types of investment, and limitations are placed on compulsory licensing. Copyright protection was extended beyond literary works to sound recordings, motion pictures, computer programs and data bases, and members are obligated to comply with provisions of the Berne convention.

Trade-related investment measures. The trade-related investment measures (TRIMs) agreement reinforces GATT provisions, whereby no such measures should be applied that are inconsistent with the GATT specifically identifying local content and trade-balancing requirements.

The explicit prohibition on local content and trade balancing requirements addressed the most flagrant trade–distorting investment measures in developing countries, but discouraged the growing tendency in the United States and the EC to consider such actions as well.

Antidumping. The revised antidumping agreement requires public notice and written explanation of actions. The agreement defines the methodology authorities may apply in conducting antidumping investigations, including the definition of *de minimus* margins and negligible imports for purposes of terminating an investigation. Antidumping disputes will be assessed by WTO dispute settlement panels for binding settlement.

As later chapters in this book will explore, the standard of review interpretation greatly limits the ability of dispute panels to challenge assessments by the importing countries and their application of antidumping duties.

Subsidies and countervailing measures. The agreement establishes categories of subsidies: red-, amber- and green-light dealing, respectively, with prohibited subsidies, permissible subsidies subject to countervailing duties if they cause adverse trade effects and permissible subsidies exempt from countervailing duty actions. Export subsidies are prohibited, including de facto export subsidies and subsidies contingent on the use of local content.

Government procurement. New disciplines include the requirement to inform losing bidders promptly of decisions on contract awards and the provision for timely, transparent and effective procedures for losing bidders to challenge alleged breaches in procedures as contained in the agreement. The WTO dispute settlement mechanism is applicable to review disputes, but without authorization to assess trade retaliation.

The critical dimension of applicable scope, however, will continue to be pursued outside the WTO, largely between the United States, the EC and Japan, or through comprehensive regional free trade agreements within Europe, the Americas, and perhaps the Asia-Pacific region.

Safeguards. Temporary import restrictions will be transparent, temporary, digressive and subject to review and termination. Injury determinations more precisely defined and subject to a public hearing and a public report giving an analysis of the reasons for the decision. Safeguard actions are permitted for a maximum of eight years and existing voluntary restraint agreements are to be phased out within four years.

Sanitary and phyto-sanitary measures (S&P). This agreement establishes rules and disciplines for measures taken to protect human, animal and plant life, and health in the areas of food safety and agriculture. Such measures include quarantine procedures, food processing, inspection rules and the establishment of pesticide tolerances. The agreement is intended to prevent the use of S&P measures as disguised barriers to trade.

Whalley and Hamilton also provide a table pointing to the escalation leading up to the Uruguay Round's initiation in 1986 of contingent protection measures by major developed countries in the 1980s. This escalation together with hopes for more trade liberalization prompted the United States, EC and others to initiate the Uruguay Round in 1986. The volume of contingent protection measures flow as a percentage of trade volume was high in terms of the distrust it engendered among many GATT members.

Safeguards	1980	1981	1982	1983	1984	1985	1986	1980-1986
United States	2	6	4	2	6	3	5	28
Australia	1	0	1	2	0	0	0	4
Canada	0	1	2	0	0	1	0	4
E.C.	3	1	1	1	1	0	2	9
Countervailing actions								
United States	8	10	123	21	51	39	30	282
Australia	0	0	2	7	6	3	3	21
Canada	3	0	1	3	2	3	4	16
E.C.	0	1	3	2	1	0	0	7
Antidumping actions								
United States	22	14	61	47	71	65	71	351
Australia	62	50	78	87	56	60	63	456
Canada	25	19	72	36	31	36	74	293
E.C.	25	47	55	36	49	42	40	294
Other unfair trade practices – U.S.	28	19	73	39	33	39	28	259
All categories								
United States	60	49	261	109	161	146	134	920
Australia	63	50	81	96	62	63	66	481
Canada	28	20	75	39	33	40	78	313
E.C.	28	49	59	39	51	42	42	310
TOTAL	179	168	476	283	307	291	320	2,024

Source: J. M. Finger (1990)

As a result of these agreements of the Uruguay Round it is obvious a number of new disciplines have been imposed on national sovereignty. Just as a coral reef can "calm the waters," these disciplines can be seen as advances, at least from the perspective of those seeking an international framework to govern international trade. Although this book will examine how these disciplines are less than total, it is useful to remind ourselves of their essential effect (as detailed by critics of the agreement): [3] Various articles require: all parties to the trade agreement to treat "like" products of member nations as favorably as their own domestic products. Other articles disallow discrimination among foreign producers of a given product; eliminate quantitative restrictions and import and export controls. The Agreement on Technical Barriers to Trade allows challenges against a number of government regulatory initiatives. The Agreement on Agriculture (often considered insufficient by many negotiating nations) does not allow favoritism to domestic food producers, except in limited cases. the Agreement on Trade-Related

Intellectual Property Rights provides a global patent protection regime. The General Agreement on Trade in Services (GATS) demands that foreign and domestic private service providers be eligible for funding and subsidies as public providers.

After reading this list one can see that ammunition is readily available for the "civil society" protesters who wish for potent domestic reasons, for example, of environment, safety, worker protection or culture.

The Dialectic

David F. Sanger notes trenchantly in *Foreign Affairs* (Jan-Feb. 2001):

> No country is happy with a WTO that reaches far inside national borders, orders changes in that country's laws, or authorizes trade sanctions against nations that ignore its rulings. But in fact the system has worked relatively well so far. In most of the handful of cases that the United States has lost before the WTO, the Clinton administration has quietly changed the offending regulations.

Most activist groups involved in "direct action against" the WTO seem more interested in stopping the organization than in negotiating with it. They seem to rest their case on two arguments.

> It's about shifting power and public control away from governments and into the hands of corporations, CEOs and their shareholders and the basic drive for profits.[4]

Explains Brent Patterson, a Toronto member of the Council of Canadians who flew to Seattle on a trip sponsored for the council, the Metro Toronto Network for Social Justice and the Church of the Holy Trinity: What menaces do this so-called "shift of power" threaten to unleash on a wealthy developed country like Canada? A colleague of Patterson's explains.

> The WTO meeting concerns Canadians because it's their education, their health care, their postal service, their water and their environment that's on the negotiating table for multinationals to come and scoop up for profit.[5]

Gene Sharp, director of the Albert Einstein Institution in Cambridge (Mass.) and author of *The Methods of Non Violent Action* (1973) would not describe the Seattle protests as an incoherent or anarchic "acting out." His emphasis on strategic training helps explain why the protesters felt stronger and more organized than protesters of the 1960s.

> If one wishes to accomplish something, the chances of achieving that goal are the greatest if one uses one's available resources and leverage to maximum effectiveness. That means having a strategic plan designed to move from the present (in which the goal is not achieved) to the future (in which it is achieved). This type of thinking should be undertaken by leaders of social and political movements along the strategic way.

He lists 198 techniques for getting attention. [6]

This writer finds the WTO agenda for Seattle read remarkably like the Canada-U.S. FTA agenda of 1987. We should not be surprised that it arouses the same legion of protesters. Unlike North American freer trade, as a result of Seattle, the protesters could feel a part of a community spanning many nations. American and Canadian protesters found activist fraternity in uniting with 100,000 citizens with the same worries from around the world. These groups, now emboldened by Seattle, prepping for UN Conferences on Civil Society, will hardly go away soon. With the Cold War over, it is now safer and easier to gravitate to these anti-free trade groups without being accused in industrialized nations of being a "Soviet dupe."

The proposed General Agreement on Trade in Services (GATS) is written in such a way as to stir up WTO critics. According to one critic it:

> [s]tates quite clearly that healthcare, education and water supplies must be opened up to foreign corporate ownership. The Agreement on Agriculture would control local farm subsidies while the Sanitary and Phyto-Sanitary Standards Agreement (SPS) will guarantee international market access for genetically engineered foods. The revised General Agreement on Tariffs and Trade Financial Services Agreement will forward the cause of unrestricted trade and investment throughout the world. If accepted, the WTO proposals will even forbid democratically elected governments from refusing to accept contract bids from foreign countries on the grounds that they are human rights violators. [7]

Those who believe in "direct action" against the WTO also believe, in almost every case, that the push for global free trade is being fueled by the demands of the financial elite. WTO Director General Mike Moore (himself a former union leader), claimed otherwise in his fervent opening at the Seattle meetings.

> People who march in Seattle will be marching against opportunities for poor people to sell their products and services.[8]

Yet a member of the Toronto Chapter of Canada's Association of Filipino Youth argued one need only look to the last 100 years of "American domination" in the Philippines to see the social devastation, grinding poverty, uncontrolled pollution, dumped goods, financial chaos, civil unrest and political depression brought on by corporate rule. Asked why leaders in developing countries support free trade agreements like the FTA and WTO proposals, he asserted that:

> in any of these third world countries, they have highly class–stratified societies and different cultures, the culture of the elite, landed elite and everyone else. And the elite act as a kind of financial go-between in terms of how foreign corporations operate inside the country. So they have business interests. That's why they would support free trade. [9]

Deflecting critics who see arguments like these as mere "left-wing" propaganda, others point to leading non-left economists like Harvard's Jeffrey Sachs, MIT's Paul Krugman and Columbia University's Jagdish Bhagwati, all of whom conjecture that the devastating financial crises in Mexico, Brazil and Indonesia were caused at least partly by currency speculators and short-term investors. These economists also question whether further deregulation of financial flows will lead to even larger spontaneous currency imbalances.[10]

An Early Experience with the So-Called "Civil Society" in Canada

At the end of the 1980s warnings of this debate surfaced (of all places!) in Canada. Protests against free trade did not begin in Seattle at the end of 1999. This writer lived through much of its fury in the mid-to-late 1980s as an advocate of a Canada-U.S. Free Trade Agreement (FTA). In Canada the FTA was considered in 1986, passed through Parliament in 1987 and became the centerpiece of a national election in

1988. This writer was also part of a trinational negotiation in 1993 that ingeniously muted many of these protests by adding labor and environmental side accords to the Mexico-U.S.-Canada trade agreement (NAFTA). During those negotiations, objectors in Canada disparaged any kind of North American agreement and campaigned to have us do trade agreements only through GATT (now the WTO).

Once the FTA was in place in 1989 (not so long ago), many of these same groups fixated on the GATT to prevent freer trade. In the Brussels Ministerial Round of GATT in 1990, thousands of angry protesters marched through the streets only to be dispersed by police wielding water cannons. The trade talks led the British Broadcasting Corporation newscast four days in a row. This was in dramatic contrast to the opening of the Uruguay Round of GATT negotiations in Punta del Este (1986), which attracted no protesters and only scattered antiseptic news coverage.

To provide cautionary prologue to this new history of anti-WTO protests, let us digress to a personal experience that reveals how the new WTO "millennium round" might be perceived by "civil society" groups.

As cochair of the first-ever Canadian Joint Senate–House Parliamentary Committee to consider comprehensively Canada's trade, foreign relations and defense policy in 1985, this writer remembers beginning by considering two topics. First was the advisability of negotiating a free trade relationship with the Reagan administration that would somehow also protect us from being side-swiped by an administration and Congress angry at tariffs, nontariff barriers and subsidies in Japan, China and Europe. Second, the committee was considering an invitation to participate in the research phase of President Reagan's anti-missile defense scheme, the Strategic Defense Initiative, which provided full ventilation to anti-American groups pivoting on Cold War concerns.

We visited all major cities across Canada and opened our proceedings to self-invited academic experts, lobby groups, researched proposals and ordinary citizens with "axes they wished to grind in public." We also invited experts and groups we desired to hear, using a "guest list" devised in all–party negotiations. Remember, this was the summer of 1985. There was no WTO, no NAFTA. The number of "concerned" interest groups, social groups, farm groups and labor groups who wished to speak against any kind of trade liberalization was huge. Although a Royal Commission report and several studies by academic and business groups supported free trade, those for it were generally silent, inarticulate or fearful of antagonizing those who disagreed. The business community seemed particularly uncomfortable about trying to articulate free trade's advantages in the mass media.

The print media often led the electronic media in covering our committee. The news-gathering press was always more happy to emphasize the potential "plant closings" such a trade agreement might bring, rather than the potential for jobs or for lower-cost inputs. Editorial pages (with the exception of the country's largest circulation newspaper and the government-owned radio and TV stations which were vigorously against) were more coolly balanced on free trade.

It was here one witnessed the forceful manifestation of a controlling theme this writer had published about ten years before.[11] The book questioned the American political science thesis of David Truman (and concomitantly of Macgregor Dawson in Canada) which saw the "black box" of government as a processor, broker and mediator of the "inputs" of independent variables such as groups, interests and opinions outside the black box. This was essentially a "brokerage" view of government. In this theory's description of how governments work; the so-called dependent outputs (political scientists called them "policy" or "allocations of value"), were driven by brokered compromises within the black box by public servants in their domain and politicians in theirs. (This theory has dominated Canadian political science for the last fifty years). I questioned this view by noting how codependent the so-called "independent variables" were on the government itself. These forces weren't as independent as the model posited. In fact, they depended on politicians and the bureaucrats, and the politicians and bureaucrats depended on them. The lobbies were dependent in a number of ways:

i) dependent on partial or full government funding to stay alive;
ii) dependent on the status afforded to them by governments as "intervenors" on issues regardless of the group's size or the solidity of its membership;
iii) dependent on the media's recognition of them as spokespersons for the interest in question.

In other words, the book argued that parties governing with "a status quo interventionist ideology" on behalf of a "non-business" agenda (or any government whose public servants and politicians depend on favorable reception from those groups) are necessarily manipulators of the "inputs" to correspond to their political survival by funding them and encouraging the media to seek them out for supportive comment. This insight, this writer's book dubbed gently the "liberal way." (The pure "socialist way" would be for the state to take over these groups by nationalization). One supposes a "progressive conservative" way would be to not fund any policy advocacy group that could not exist without government funding, and to be skeptical of self-appointed spokespersons for causes that are already supported by government.[12]

The media would then seek out these government funded groups for their point of view on how, for example, "teachers" or "workers" or "environmentalists" or "church members" felt about the issue at hand.

Elected to government after forty-four (out of fifty) years of Liberal rule, our government witnessed the full force of Liberal government-financed interest groups springing from the so-called "civil" society. Invariably, Liberal MPs on our committee knew these groups well and had enjoyed the synergy of political support that comes from funding them uncritically. The New Democratic Party (NDP), Canada's labor-allied party, also knew them well.

Our committee's parade across the country was an eye-opener for this writer, a newly elected MP, and a love-in for the Liberals and the NDP. We, the newly elected Progressive Conservatives, were treated as usurpers of power, insensitive to these interest groups' needs, and soon to be discharged by the voters. We Progressive Conservatives did take some critical distance from the constantly mutating and multiplying phalanx of civil society groups and NGOs (non-government organizations). We thought it our task to assess the cogency of their research and arguments. For whom do they purport to speak? This was a particularly difficult task. For example, at one point in a visit with the primate of the Anglican Church, he was asked how he knew that these "delegations" against free trade from his church really spoke for congregations? He replied in the only way he could: he said the church's mission is to speak out for those most vulnerable in society. Even if there were "two or more sides in a given political debate," the primate joined other church spokespeople in siding with those he felt were most vulnerable.

All in all, over 200 groups visited our committees. Some delivered a little attention-getting theatre. Groups not funded in part by government, especially business groups, were hesitant to appear and when they did appear, they were not schooled in articulate public positioning like the social groups and NGOs who articulate in order to survive.

The media routinely and uncritically sought out these social activist groups and NGOs for opinions. The media did show some skepticism to labor groups because the media knew where labor stood. The media took less critical distance from the NGOs.

Perhaps one should not blame the media slant on *leftist press bias* (whatever that means) as much as on editors demanding that reporters seek out articulate spokesmen from both sides of the barricades.

The cycle of protest rebegan during the Canadian election of 1988, which essentially turned on the question of the U.S-Canada trade agreement. Hundreds of groups "acted out" in ways akin to their Seattle confreres of 1999. The "FTA election" (1988) was the most bitter election of the century in Canada. Almost all the protest modes were carried out with enormous ferocity. Nor was it all extra-parliamentary. After the Progressive Conservatives won the 1988 election, Liberal senators acted out like "civil society" protesters with Kazoo-playing and passive resistance, refusing to pass the bill for months even though the electorate had clearly spoken in favor of the party supporting the FTA.

The WTO Version

Let us now return to the present and to the WTO and NAFTA. "Direct action" protestors are made up predominantly of those who want to alter the WTO because it perpetuates "profit-making global capitalism," which some say is simply American imperialism fostering nothing but a world-wide corporate elite. To live as an advocate of "direct action" is not to be frivolous but to feel passionately for a cause one shares with some others. This cause sees the world as being corrupted by one voice. The voice sees globalization to be as inimical to local particularities such as government programs that define the cultural or environmental essence of one's nation. This cause is hardly anarchistic, in fact, it is more akin to classical conservatism.

This mood worries about the apocalypse of globalization and its three horsemen: globalized trade agreements; global financial turbulence; unfettered global capitalism. At bottom, this mood results in an unhealthy mind-set if it is nihilistic and promotes nothing more than the destruction of the WTO. WTO abolition would solve nothing of course. In fact, it would only add to the indeterminacy that so troubles these "activists." Insofar as this mood locates its demons in a narrow circle of people and ideas it is unidimensional (i.e., the assumption that the destruction of landed, or financial/corporate elite and a capitalist ideology will pave the way to a more tolerable future). These analyses are in need of more dimensions. We will turn to answer these in chapter two and later chapters.

As for the new notion of the threat of globalization, one is entitled to ask how new is globalization anyway? Baron Carl Meyer Von

Rothschild said, "the world is a city" in 1875.[13] He was speaking of the powerful forces of globalization that seemed to be making national borders porous even then. As for novelty of globalization let us not forget that in many respects, the nineteenth century was *more* global than the twentieth. Today, we find globalization's emanations in broadly-based portfolio investments, the entertainment industry, opportunity travel, the Internet and the fact that manufactured goods have parts from many countries. Yet today there is less mobility of labor, of securities investments, of domestic tax regimes and social programs than 125 years ago. "We're still not back to where we were 125 years ago," says Charles Calomiris of Columbia University's School of Business. In that century 60 million Europeans moved to the United States, Canada and Australia. In 1900, 14 percent of the U.S. population was foreign-born, passports were unnecessary and people could travel freely from one country to work or visit. Today it is 8 percent.[14]

In the nineteenth century, goods moved easily across borders. Almost all of Germany's imports were duty-free. U.S. exports were the same percentage of GNP in 1900 as in 1999. The Investors Monthly Fund Report in 1997 suggested in its "capital mobility index" that capital movements as a percentage of economic output are below the levels of the 1880s. Foreign capital financed one of three investments in New Zealand and Canada in the nineteenth century. Now foreign investment comprises only 10 percent of domestic investment in emerging markets.

Alan M. Taylor, of North Western University's economics department, discussed that nineteenth century investors had a larger share of their stock portfolios abroad than do investors today. (Americans may own lots of foreign-made goods but their portfolios tend to be heavily weighted in the United States).[15] For those of us who blithely assume that globalization is unprecedented we should be more cautious. For those who see the WTO to be a juggernaut, invincible and lethal in its imposition of globalized trade, we should remember the astonishing retreat in world economic integration after World War I and during the Great Depression. The same could happen again.

From the "Unappeasables" to the "Pragmatics"

Some of the crowd in Seattle were not of the "direct action" variety. To these "others" we now turn. Clearly there were critical voices involved seeking some practical changes within the WTO context, calling for pragmatic restraints on behalf of the environment, the labor rights movement and cultural particularity. Let's call them "pragmatics."

Unacknowledged here is the fact that there are already countless relevant regulations for those interested in these values in the WTO's disposition of the trade agreement, just as there are *continuously unused and unclaimed* opportunities for developed countries to seek redress against developing countries. To think the WTO is riding roughshod over all these values is to think unclearly, unfairly and inaccurately.

But the pragmatic people yearn to be "inside" the WTO, to somehow be a part of it, to fasten an environmental and labor code to the agreement. Is this possible? One perspective on the matter treats this "fastening" as impossible. But this is not exact; NAFTA has side agreements on both environment and labor. This writer participated in negotiations on both. We will look at how these agreements evolved and trace its relevance as a model in the final chapters.

Another group of protesters was relatively small, but trade analysts and the media make much of them. These are those special interests groups or industrial groups who have been stung by a WTO decision or who fear the WTO will lower the trade barrier they now thrive on. These interests some day will likely disappear from the protest crowds as soon as they win or prolong protection for their own chosen barrier. These groups dominate the formal political debate over an incrementally better WTO.

As for these interests, the Uruguay Round of trade talks established a clean set of rules for trade in a number of goods and service industries, establishing the mechanism for resolving disputes and penalties when the rules were broken. As one trade consultant suggested, the public became more aware of the process as panel rulings began dealing with issues everyone could understand.[16] One can agree with this observation, but the issues are hardly electrifying, sensationalistic or even broad-based. With the exception of bananas, hormone beef and some cultural issues, one doubts these issues produce domestically in the United States or elsewhere a "call to arms" across a wide domestic front against the WTO. For example, one WTO panel decided that the United States could not block tuna from other countries even if the fish was caught in dolphin-killing nets. Another ruled that countries could not block imported shrimp caught in nets that lacked escape hatches for endangered sea turtles.

Of course, those decisions kicked ecological NGOs into action, but was there a broad-based slump in overall confidence in the WTO meetings because of them? One doubts it.

A ruling preventing the European Union from banning hormone-treated beef, in tandem with the transatlantic dispute over genetically-modified food, finally put issues on the trade table that the general public could understand. Still, other than kicking environmentalists and farmers into action, did these decisions seriously undermine the WTO in the public mind? It seems unlikely.

This brings us to the waning influence of these special producer and corporate groups that wish to be sheltered forever behind trade barriers. With the exception of the highly geographic specificity of farm voters or the special self-definition of voters engaged in cultural protectionism and their media advocates, one doubts how sustained and deep public support will remain for those protected by privileged shields. David Ricardo said centuries ago that free trade need not be reciprocal to be beneficial. Consumers in a nation that lowers its own trade barriers are always better off. (This writer remembers how few tariffs were left against the United States *before* Canada negotiated the FTA).

No serious thinker actually believes in the worth of individual trade barriers, even as he doggedly clings to them. Yet he is often obliged to pretend that he does. (This writer remembers when the finance minister of Japan, in dealing in the early morning 1993 Quad negotiations in Tokyo before the Heads of Governments Summit, finally brought in his prime minister and inner cabinet to break an impasse for the impending summit in his capital, in agreeing on lower tariffs for "Brown liquor," from four percent to zero. Could that barrier have been worth anything, let alone a failed summit meeting?)

Essentially, in most cases, the clock is ticking against producer groups that have lost their appeal in the WTO. Generally, their domestic political roots are not sufficiently broad to hold out forever and to denigrate the WTO.

Legitimacy of Some CSOs and NGOs

A metaphor for the dilemma tax payers in North America face with some of these "civil society" groups is the example during enrollment at the University of Wisconsin in September of 1998. A team of students took the university to court. They objected not to the fees for tuition, board and meals, but to the size and composition of the mandatory "student service" fee. They objected to the compulsory contribution to a host of NGOs subsidized by the service fee namely, activist student groups claiming to represent all students under their banners. Many of these paraded in Seattle against the WTO.

Seattle was a whistle-stop for many of these NGOs. One week later, funded in part by these subventions, they joined 300 NGO representatives from 60 nations in a grand Montreal hotel ballroom to the "walk-sock" (WOCSOC) the first "World Civil Society Conference." The topic: Creating conditions for global government. In fact some certainly not all, of these NGOs are government-driven and government-centric themselves; much of their funding comes from national or local governments, or from departments of the United Nations. Private foundations also fund them, as do compulsory university student fees. [17]

Let us pause and commend the non-politically based NGOs. Some NGOs attract universal commendation and considerable funding for their work in disaster relief, refugee aid, education, health care (such as the Nobel Peace Prize-winning Doctors Without Borders) and job training in the Third World's most challenged locations. The problem is that these NGOs and their good works are in danger of being lumped with those NGOs and CSOs (civil society organizations) who now act as if they should enjoy the final call on national and international social and economic policy.

All these groups made their presence felt in the Ottawa agreement to end the use of land mines; the 1998 Rome agreement to establish an International Criminal Court; forgiveness of national debts of the world's poorest countries; and the spurring of military intervention to Kosovo and East Timor.

While those are no doubt widely-supported causes, they have one element in common: in UN Secretary-General Kofe Annan's words, "they step in where governments are unwilling or unable to act." This is ominous without some understood source of NGO/CSO legitimacy and an agreed-upon definition of responsible government. It is clear that it is vital to identify a mechanism whereby NGOs, which purport to speak for humanity, speak for the people they claim to represent. The WTO in contrast has an explicit formula for settling disputes and for making them enforceable. Civil society groups need to be similarly explicit about how NGOs legitimacy can be assessed, and about how dispute settlement rules can be established within them.

This step is crucial if there is to be any settled understanding between NGOs, the WTO, and future global organizations. The UN Millennium Forum's declared purpose is to draft an agenda for the UN and (according to many delegates at the Montreal "warm-up" meeting in January 2000) to lay groundwork for a third legislative house at the UN, a sort of Parliament of Humankind and for the World Social Forum, February 2001 at Porto Alegre, Brazil.

As for national governments that are the signatories to the WTO, no one can deny there is some legitimacy behind national governments that have at least periodic elections and proper enumerations of who is entitled to vote. Democracy is not perfect, but there is a definite legitimacy afforded to elected governments working by agreed-upon rules. Similarly with WTO dispute settlement and compliance, as we shall see in chapter 3. If a group presumes to speak for humanity at global conferences, it too should contemplate the source of its legitimacy.

Frustrated Cooperative NGOs and Inarticulate Governments

Some civil society groups are willing to do more than carp and dream. Kiml Naidos of CIVICUS, a major civil society promoter based in Washington D.C., and Felix Dodds, cochair of the UN's commission on sustainable development, explain that they wish action not so much at some "third body for humankind" at the UN but in what they call multilateral stakeholders groups "where business, environment groups, government bureaucrats, NGOs and women's groups all sit down together at national and multinational levels to discuss common approaches."[18] There can be no doubt that "business" or "corporate" interests are outnumbered in this scenario, but at least the process is fairly transparent in terms of its process and its members.

In most of the G7, governments are far from being captured by "corporate interests." All sorts of environmental, academic, cultural, agricultural and labor groups have recognized status. Most are government funded. The media regularly quotes them carefully, giving them classic "intervenor" status in terms of public debate. There is an evident dialogue daily between those opinions and corporate opinions, except for one reality, the inarticulateness of business groups in the marketplace of public debate or public policy in the political world. Here the noncorporate interests appear far more visible and attention-getting.

Charlene Barsheysky, U.S. special trade representative for President Clinton, admitted: "the single greatest threat to the multilateral trade system is the absence of public support." Witness this verdict on the effect of "anticorporate" activists by Marie-Josée Kravis, a fellow of the Hudson Institute, who notes that: "Environmentalists, human rights activists and labor union representatives smashed windows, vandalized and looted shops, overturned vehicles and lit fires in the name of a more caring, gentler version of economy and social order and . . . to fight globalization. This armada of special interests from rich countries determined as well to keep out the poor." She asks, "How did they get away with such self-servicing dilettantism?"[19] The *Economist* wrote after Seattle, "governments" far from being captured by corporate interests, let these protesters "get away with this dilettantism." They got away with this because of the "failure of political leaders of major industrial countries to make the case for more open vibrant markets."[20]

Perhaps the least effective, yet damaging, way to build support for free trade is to parade the spectacle of corporate CEOs joining with heads of government on a "trade mission." The only message delivered with this to the average domestic voter back home is that "trade is good for CEOs" and it is not clear who else it is good for.

Political leaders, riding the crest of unprecedented economic growth for over twenty-five years, seldom bother to defend one of the conditions that propelled this precedented growth of rules-based global trade. President Clinton said little. Al Gore promised trade unions that he will review NAFTA. A similar silence emits from "third way" heads of government in Europe, ranging from Tony Blair to Gerhard Schroeder to Lionel Jospin.

> Bill Clinton wants to invite protesters indoors. France's Trade Minister says this is proof that economics and politics cannot be kept apart: Statism lives! Briton's Trade Minister doubtfully insists that "free trade can be fair trade" as if to concur that it quite often it isn't, but fear not, he is on the look-out for any sign of unfairness. God help us. [21]

This pandering to nonbusiness voices is powerful everywhere in the workings of the government in the G7 countries. Robert Putnam identified these voices decades ago in his *New Society*.

To placate elements of this new society *The Economist* suggests:

> Governments have pandered to their (unappeasable) critics, moved half-way to meet their demands and lent credence to their bogus fears. "Corporate interests" who want to slow down the effect of globalization on them in their domestic market are listened to, not the so-called "unfettered free traders." The consumer is nowhere to be considered. . . . Ever mindful of producer lobbies, governments downplay or deny the fact that trade increases incomes, that is why they must be on hand to ensure that trade is fair. [22]

We see the final capitulation as "third way" European, American and Canadian governments call for a "new WTO group" to develop a new agenda on environmental and labor standards (not for a sovereignty-respecting approach like the one represented by the NAFTA side accords).

For those who focus on the WTO's so-called capture by "corporate interests," the Seattle meeting proved to be the opposite. The Seattle debacle not only failed in its role in helping governments sell freer trade to their electorates, it actually assisted those opposed to freer trade by helping those protesting groups to form alliances whose only common goal is to restrict trade. In other words, it strengthened the opposition, it did not undermine it.

The image of the WTO as an independent colossus barreling ahead with little or no member-government influence is untenable, especially in the sphere of negotiations to expand the WTO agreement itself. (Thankfully, even if the new round is stalled, the organization still has some independent effect on settling disputes and enforcing agreed-upon WTO rules). As for WTO's tarnished image:

> Governments are to blame for this, not the WTO or its officials. It is rich-country governments especially America that has argued that trade liberalization was a cost for which countries had to be compensated . . . This tells protesters and the public at large they are right to oppose reform. [23]

However, a potentially fatal blow to the WTO's freer trade agenda lies coiled in the way labor/environmental standards are to be grafted on to the remit and arena of the WTO. If there are trade sanctions for a government that fails to meet some new international environmental or labor code, this can equip protectionists to seek out new environmental and labor arguments under which they can raise barriers by way of sanctions.

That was this writer's complaint with the NAFTA side accords on environment and labor as proposed by the Clinton administration. Canada's delegation was able to ensure Canada would not be vulnerable to trade sanctions but Mexico and the United States are vulnerable under the agreement of 1993. The Clinton administration's enthusiasm for bringing worker protection and ecology into the WTO concedes the argument that trade, unless properly regulated, really does militate against the greens and labor. The "U.S. Administration has conceded much of the ground to its stone-throwing critics and undermined broader support for freedom to trade" wrote *The Economist* after Seattle.[24] So much for the argument that the WTO is an "independent" force propelled by corporate free trade interests.

Privileged, protected producer groups and countless Seattle protesters argued that low wages and insensitivity to environmental and working conditions give developing countries unfair competitive advantage. This is a reprise of the since-disproved Ross Perot argument that NAFTA would cause a great "sucking sound" as jobs left the United States for Mexico. (Six years later the United States enjoyed the lowest unemployment percentage in North America or Europe). If Perot's worry was accurate, sub-Saharan Africa and Haiti would be the most competitive regions in the world. The image propagated by these protesters of wholesale migration of industries to the "Dickensian squalor of the Third World" is a persistent one. It is a lurid picture of a "race to the bottom," i.e., the country with the poorest wages, environmental protections and the weakest child labor laws will do the most exporting. Governments and business should be reminded that as trade barriers have come down under GATT in the last fifty years, living standards have risen, social spending has increased and environmental laws have not only been born, but are more strongly enforced. Environmental clean-up is a cost, but it is moderate compared to a trained, stable knowledge-based labor force. From this, real competitive advantage arises.

True, wages do matter in contexts like labor-intensive assembling industries. "Third World" countries have a clear competitive advantage in assembling electrical goods, clothes, shoes and the like. It is clearly cruel, however, for protesters in developed countries to demand that WTO rules be bent to prevent imports from countries whose wages and labor standards do not match those in the developed world. If these countries can't compete on the basis of lower wages, what can they compete on?

Unrecognized by the protestors in Seattle is the WTO's present protection of the environment. For example, we seldom hear in the political arena that laws of *general* application designed to safeguard human, animal and plant life are now in fact protected under WTO arrangements. Environmentalists who want to sustain environmental policies in a jurisdiction that discriminates for no good reason on behalf of domestic producers over imports are not advancing laws of general application. The WTO rightly adjudicates these and finds against any such discrimination.[25]

The Public and Corporate Agoras

This ideological divide in views is aided by two solitudes. The "public agora" is a phrase one can use to join the Greek word meaning "gathering place" to the political and public debate of policy issues. The word "agora" denotes more than buying and selling. It is a gathering place for discussion, persuasion, reporting, commenting and consumer activity – such as buying and selling. It is the ancient Greek equivalent of where American or other countries media, political actors and opinion groups gather. This agora can be distinguished from the corporate agora, which is an amalgam of business interests doing deals, signing contracts, setting up research facilities and dealing with the business media. This latter agora is about selling and developing things before taking them to the consumer goods corner of the public agora.

The "currency" in each agora is different. Crudely put, the public agora's currency is the supporting or undermining of the elite's economic, political and socio-cultural preconditions for its ascendancy. A topic that interested everyone in the ancient Greek public agora was Greece itself: its families, its politics and its defense against the Spartans, Romans or whoever else might threaten the agora as a whole. If you come with a contribution in this currency you were talking "public agora language." In American terms, this is the world of all sections of your local newspaper or newscast *except* perhaps the business pages or the business programs on TV and radio.

The currency of the corporate agora has always been different and is often indecipherable to those in the public agora: supply and demand, technology, cash flow, depreciation, corporate tax and so on. The one topic that interests everyone here is business. Talk business language, and you are talking the corporate agora's language. For one having been immersed in both at different stages in one's life, one is struck by how little the two communicate with each other. An academic in the humanities or social sciences seldom converses with practical people in business. Mutual comprehension, even mistrust, takes root.

The truth is that those in the corporate agora who carefully sense what is happening in the public agora and know how to deal with it, and speak to it, at the right time and place, can be welcome and can succeed. Another truth is that those in the corporate agora that can move the necessary forces in the public agora to support them will be successful. A moderate amount of intercourse of the corporate with the public agora might help. It might not.

Harvard's political philosophy professor, Carl J. Frederich, once said that most examples of eighteenth and nineteenth century types of political philosophy were already articulated in Plato's *Dialogues*. "Marx, Burke, J. S. Mill, Montesquieu, even Rousseau could be found in Plato's public agora," he said. The public agora was a place teeming with opinions. Occasionally a corporate agora opinion would appear in the public agora in Plato's *Dialogues*, but not often.

Today, we see how these two solitudes seldom still speak to each other, though the vocabulary of the public agora may occasionally enter the corporate. One finds that the corporate agora is abandoning the public articulation of its views to those in government who are dependent on other forces and groups who helped to get them elected. The legitimacy of these "other forces" as uncontested representatives of "the citizenry" remains a mystery. Since political and governmental actions have played a decisive part in bringing them into being, both need each other.

In Seattle, we saw a complete failure of the corporate agora in mobilizing, articulating and persuading the public that it produces the wealth that makes the public agora prosper. It was mute in that Seattle agora. The politicians can't depend on corporate forces to mobilize, articulate or persuade. The corporate agora is good at doing its work in its own agora, but it seems it seldom tries a similar effort in the public agora.

Corporate forces must find political voices that can persuade in the public agora. If Seattle is any example, the "corporate forces" effect is failing miserably. Who among us would discount the possibility that the Greeks' corporate agora long ago eventually suffered because of this solitude.

A fine example of the misinformation inculcating the public discourse on the WTO is captured by the myths refuted by Marcus Gee, a Toronto *Globe & Mail* columnist. Here is a prime example not only of demystification but of the ideas that the political and corporate leaders seldom articulate:

> Now that the din of battle has subsided, let's take a closer look at a few of the myths propagated in Seattle.
>
> *The WTO and expanding world trade are impoverishing the Third World.*
>
> Nonsense. The developing societies that have done best – Hong Kong, South Korea, Taiwan, and now China – are the ones that have joined the world trading system. Japan became the world's second-biggest economy mainly through trade. Countries that have huddled behind high trade barriers – India – have done poorly . . . .That is why China has agreed to make major reforms to its economic practices in exchange for membership in the WTO. And that is why 30 other countries are lining up to join.

Trade ruins the environment.

Nonsense. Countries that have stayed aloof from the world trading system – India again, or the Soviet Union – have managed to do plenty of harm to the environment. Trade leads to economic growth, and economic growth leads to a healthier environment. As countries grow richer through trade, prosperous citizens start demanding tougher conservation laws and governments have the money to clean up the water, land and air.

Trade pollutes local culture.

If you consider [silly movies] to be cultural pollution, then, yes. Western (mainly American) cultural exports are flooding the world. But with the spread of satellite television, videocassette players and the Internet, Disney would conquer the world even without the WTO and freer trade. The interesting thing is that culture is flooding the other way, too – from non-Western countries to Western ones. . . .

The WTO is a secretive, undemocratic organization that is trying to usurp the powers of national governments.

Not so. The WTO is a voluntary organization. Its 135 members, the majority run by elected governments, joined by choice. . . .

If a WTO panel rules against a member in a trade dispute, the member still does not have to go along. It can keep its domestic laws or practices, as long as it's willing to face unilateral trade sanctions from the complaining nation.[26]

Defenders of the WTO would be well-advised to stop being mute. The organization is at risk of becoming the very beast the Seattle protestors fear, One editorial put it clearly:

What some governments are trying to create in spite of critics who see governments as captured by "free trade corporations" is a "package deal" that would load the WTO and associated international agencies with powers they should not have. Trade unions seem to want a trade-discouraging international agreement that would subject trade to a labor code. The same for the environment. "Green protectionism" would become widespread if trade sanctions become the sanction for trade in food, energy, biotech and scores of other products. The WTO environmental agenda could include the Rio *Convention on Biological Diversity* and the UN Environment Program for Sustainable Development for a code to open the way for trade sanctions. They did not get any multilateral new code in the NAFTA, but want one in this round of WTO agreements. This of course could lead to many "labor code protectionist" abuses. [27]

The vision of some Seattle protestors was hugely intrusive on national sovereignty, and would turn trade into a side issue or second priority to labor standards. Moving labor issues to the International Labor Organization to come up with a worldwide standard could greatly stall Third World economic development if this standard was then to be enforced by the WTO through sanctions. Similarly with the Intergovernmental Panel on Climate Change, the biosafety protocol negotiations or the United Nations Environment Program. The WTO will look like a very limited agreement compared to these labor and environmental agreements if the latter are enforced through trade sanctions. If attached to fines or some other sanction other than through trade, they will be sufficiently intrusive on national sovereignty without attaching trade sanctions as well.

A Reprise? From 2001 back to 1986

Expansion of trade through the millennium round will not be propitious in the first few years of the new millennium. This writer remembers how wide the impasse was in Uruguay in 1986. The divide was deep between the Europeans and the Japanese on one side, and the North Americans and the Cairns group (Australia, New Zealand, Argentina, Uruguay, etc.) on the other, over the elimination of agricultural subsidies and tariff peaks and in drafting more precise rules around the use of antidumping as a protectionist devise. Thirteen years later progress on these issues was again deferred in Seattle. At least in Uruguay some progress on subsidies was made.

The fragile construct that is the WTO could dissolve in acrimony with developing nations accusing the developed world, with justification, of using links to the environment and labor as a smokescreen for protectionism. Who wouldn't want to see political prisoners released or child labor abolished, but piling these obligations on the back of the new world-trading system would sink the system. This is the danger of President Clinton's suggestion that a WTO study group "should develop those core labor standards and they ought to be a part of every trade agreement to ultimately favor a system in which sanctions would come for violating any provision of a trade agreement."

The business community maintained a low profile with respect to the (Seattle) negotiations. Perhaps it is because business can negotiate directly with host governments so why bother with lengthy tedious WTO negotiations? Clearly this has in part worked in qualifying China for admission. (See chapter 7). It is true that the Uruguay Round did become more intrusive on domestic regimes as a result of its key reform which was the compulsory nature of the dispute settlement mechanism.

How well is it working? We will explore this in the next chapters in this book. The round also shifted from not simply lowering border barriers, but to moving inside jurisdictions subjecting domestic regulation to conform to GATT. This includes economic regulation such as on telecommunications and financial services, and social regulation such as over food, product safety and the environment. One doubts, however, if that explains the Seattle protesters' core concerns.

Of course trade and the environment and labor are linked to some degree. Some would say "not very much." Still there is a link. However, since there is nowhere else for environmental protests, for example, to fix on, they fix on the WTO. Ostry suggests that something else be created for environmental needs so that the WTO will not be asked to shoulder all of the angst around this topic. A new WEO with a clearly defined mandate will reduce the demand for second-best substitutes such as trade sanctions. Negotiations between WTO and WEO ministers could then define the rules to govern the linkage between both agreements. Similarly the ILO's monitoring and enforcement mechanisms could be strengthened. This would encourage coordination between trade and labor ministers.

The Protestors' Nemesis: Is The So-Called Washington Consensus An Accepted Dogma Anywhere?

Just as this chapter questions the unidimensional ideological arguments of some groups protesting the WTO, we should question too the rigid orthodoxy of some free trade purists and their unidimensional view of appropriate domestic economic arrangements.

If the WTO becomes powered by an insensitive rigid orthodoxy it could face the fate of Phillip II of Spain. He created what was perhaps the first truly global hegemony with his conquest of the Philippines in 1565. He faced the intractable problems of an extensive and detached empire. His greatest challenge was keeping together regions that were distinct from Spain and one another. Parts of the kingdom's sense of attachment to their king were tenuous. Every empire had been built up piece-by-piece but it had to be held together as a whole. This proved to be difficult because the Protestant Reformation divided Europe in two, unleashing religious or ideological wars that lasted well after Phillip's death. The king had to constantly shift attention from one front to another.

By insisting on detailed and orthodox allegiance, Phillip II could not, in the end, maintain his grand strategy. Deep divisions split Europe for two centuries. A middle way eventually emerged for a time through a type of balance of power run by Britain.

The fact that Phillip was able to build a global hegemony at all was a tribute to his detailed micromanagement and grand strategy. It was an impressive individual achievement but it was unlikely to stay in place after he disappeared from the scene. According to royal biographer Geoffrey Parker (as summarized in a review by Anthony Payden) this history:

> Insists that human actions are the outcome not, as so many historians have insisted, of long-term economic or social forces, but of acts of will. Philip was as constrained as any ruler by economics (which he barely understood), by the social world into which he had been born, by climate and geography, and perhaps most of all, by his religious beliefs.[28]

This historical precedent is worth remembering. Some 450 years later, one wonders whether American presidents and legislators have a coherent grand strategy for world trade policy, since it is the United States that so many turn for some leadership, and even if they did could it prosper after various presidents' terms in office?

There are parallels between the religious drive behind the ideology of what has loosely been called the kingdom building of Phillip II and the "Washington Consensus" that seems to propel the IMF, the World Bank and some corporate views of the World Trade Organization. That consensus sees open markets with so-called "free and unfettered pricing competition" and market access as the ultimate goals for the world economy. This may be convenient to some select American business interests, but it is not accurate to describe it as an "American grand strategy" let alone a Republican or Democratic grand strategy. This "Washington Consensus" has adherents and critics in almost every nation. It has critics in the U.S. Congress, the media and in academia. We saw in this chapter its protest manifestation in the streets of Seattle in December 1999. This economic vision's uncompromising contours remind one, if not of Phillip's religious orthodoxy, at least of the king's incapacity to deal with the reformation. Above all, it is not particularly accommodating to differences in political, individual and economic development after the year 2000.

The "Washington Consensus" has been put in place "piece-by-piece" during the Cold War and since (along with some pragmatic exceptions in each piece, as later chapters will show). As we saw in the diverse forces behind the Protestant Reformation, there are multiple resisters to this consensus. Their emanations are legion and not only confined to protesters. Socialist nations, developing nations, culturally protective nations and American anti-free traders resist the modern application of the Washington Consensus. What Peter Hall[29] calls "coordinated capitalist" economies like Germany, France, Austria, Italy and Belgium have dissented as well. Billionaire capitalists such as George Soros and James Goldsmith have written popular best sellers on the same theme.

The world of trade policy politics is not an isolated silo from other global financial goings-on. It is not unlinked to other Bretton Woods institutions such as the World Bank and the International Monetary Fund.

Serving as deputy (or was it "alternate"?) governor at World Bank meetings in Washington some years ago, this writer was struck by how remote the international banking and monetary agendas seemed from the rough and tumble of local domestic politics and trade policies. As a mere minister, one feels a bit déclassé in this well-heeled world of bankers and pension fund managers with their impeccable suits, chauffeured automobiles, and, for entertaining, rented Washington mansions. The agendas are earnest and sensitive to Third World problems, but one felt these agendas and programs were somehow too anodyne, too general to allow any politician to express any pithy or parochial impediments to the smooth flow of macroeconomic-speak and calculations of exchange-rate imbalances. At another level, one saw the World Bank as insulated. It was profoundly regrettable that the Uruguay Round's initiation in 1986-93 of a Functioning of the GATT system (FOGs) working group was nowhere acknowledged at these meetings. FOGs was meant to improve the coherence of international policies by establishing better linkages between the GATT, the IMF and the World Bank. Fifteen years after the Uruguay Round was launched, we see an even more compelling need for this linkage.

None of these elegant speeches or receptions at the World Bank need be dismissed as harmful. On the whole, the World Bank, the IMF and finance ministers have worthy agendas in their too insulated silos. But something has happened in the last fifteen years that flows from these meetings and international institutions that is starting to trouble many people, especially since the collapse of many Asian and other currencies and their economies. Those who are troubled may ask the following: What is the WTO but a superordinate power to bring to bear Washington Consensus standards for expanding trade and for settling disputes? To be fair, the WTO itself is being unfairly burdened with this allegation. The IMF and World Bank may be more protégés to the Washington Consensus than the WTO. The WTO is built on standards infinitely more complex than the orthodoxy of the Washington Consensus.

One of America's more highly respected economists, Joseph Stiglitz, has served as chairman of President Clinton's Council of Economic Advisers. He served as chief economist of the World Bank. Stiglitz has taken it upon himself to challenge what he calls the "Washington Consensus" which he describes as the prevailing orthodoxy of the International Monetary Fund and the Organization for Economic Co-operation and Development. Stiglitz questioned the underlying economic ideology of the past decade. He suggests the economic, social and political chaos in much of East Asia today was a direct consequence of rigid adherence to the "Washington Consensus." The "Washington Consensus," as Stiglitz describes it, posits that good economic performance depends on liberalized trade, macroeconomic stability, unfettered market access and getting prices right.

> Once the government dealt with these issues – essentially, once the government "got out of the way" – private markets would allocate resources efficiently and generate robust economic growth.[30]

But as Stiglitz likes to point out, this familiar political ideology preaches an almost religious belief in the power of free markets to unfailingly yield optimal outcomes for society:

> There was never a presumption that markets yielded an optimal societal or generational distribution of income, and now there does not seem to be any basis for the presumption that markets yield efficient outcomes.[31]

Stiglitz argues that the "Washington Consensus" totally ignores the importance of human capital development and technology transfer and development as key factors in economic growth. He insists the free market alone will never make adequate investments in either, which is why even rich countries such as Canada, France, Australia, the United Kingdom and the United States, invest heavily in both through government. Nick Stern, Stiglitz's successor is more inclusive. He emphasizes the unfairly high tariff and nontariff barriers still in place by the Quad countries (United States, Canada, Japan and the European Community) against LDC exports especially on agriculture, manufacturing and textiles. He targets as well LDC tariffs against other LDCs. [32]

A key source of possible institutional incompatibility with pure market liberalization is in the field of financial services and the "Washington Consensus." Coincidentally, with the opening of the Uruguay Round, this writer was part of the Canadian government's process of reforming financial institutions. As a department, Canada's finance department had responsibility for customs – dating back to Canada's *British North America Act of 1867* when customs was the Ministry of Finance's major source of revenue. In Uruguay in 1986, tariff reductions, especially in agriculture, and the search for clear definitions of what constituted dumping and subsidies were our preoccupation. Minister of finance, Michael Wilson, was still deep into perhaps the most comprehensive reevaluation of Canada's financial institutional framework since Canada's Confederation in 1867 as we prepared for the dicennial review of the *Bank Act*. The review this time examined basic questions such as: Should federal financial institutions be widely held? Should they have commercial nonfinancial owners if they are not widely held? Should federal financial institutions have major downstream nonfinancial holdings? Should banks be allowed to sell property and casualty insurance or lease cars in their branches? Should federal financial institutions have independent directors? How should their regulators be constituted? How should they relate to industry contingency funds and so on? Many of these questions spoke to the danger of contagion of bank depositors or insurance policyholders seeing their savings being wiped out beyond deposit insurance limits or policy insurance limits because of the collapse of their financial institution caused by overexposure to a commercial interest or to the financial institutions parent or to its subsidiary.

These are all questions of architecture or of the appropriate infrastructure and regulatory frameworks. One could not be somewhat aware of the huge diversity of financial institutional frameworks that existed around the globe, or in many cases, of the weakness of many domestic financial frameworks around the globe. Temperamentally and philosophically one believed that these architectural problems had to be faced responsibly prior to easy-sounding 'improved market access' arguments that propelled the liberalization impulse into financial services. China's reticence about total market access in, for example, financial services could be defended. The liberalization impulse succeeds better politically if the architectural context is in place first.

Liberalization of market access to capital flows and to foreign financial institutions should follow the prior installations of appropriate and adequately staffed supervision of banks, securities firms, insurance companies and investment fund companies. Liberalization of market access should follow an architecture that can help minimize contagion and system collapse. It is an understandable belief from observing the world "hedge fund" phenomenon that large surges of capital flows into a system of weak supervision in a rudimentary financial system have been disastrous. The contagion effect of its negative impact in Asia, for example, could also be contagious to the world-trading system not just the financial system. Therefore, it was not difficult to understand why others were enthusiasts for the U.S. push for ever freer and freer financial markets and flows of capital while the basics of the architecture were still not in place in most Asian countries. Indeed the S & L crisis in the United States and the Barings and Long Term Capital debacles show that even mature financial systems are not flawless.

Since then the IMF and World Bank have established a Financial Stability Forum which examines vulnerabilities of various financial systems on matters such as leverage, reinsurance, surveillance and deposit insurance. The G20 Financial Ministers Group which includes not only the G7 industralized nations but developing nations as well, is examining exchange rate mechanisms, debt management and other standards in the 180 IMF member nations. What might appear to be a huge imposition of "Washington Consensus" thinking on developing nations because of the sixty codes the IMF has elaborated for its "financial section assessment system" has been modified somewhat by the IMF's agreement to focus on twelve key standards.

It seems clear that "micromanagement" of all these tensions through the World Trade Organization, though admirable, will be impossible if too much is laid at its doorstep. Similarly, micromanagement of the "Washington Consensus" itself through the U.S. trade representative, the U.S. secretary of the treasury and the chair of the Federal Reserve Bank may clash with the WTO's micromanagers. In addition, the U.S.

Congress, deferential to presidential trade initiatives during the Cold War, is now neither deferential on trade matters nor silent.

Before turning to the functioning of the WTO and NAFTA, especially its dispute settlement arrangements and scorecard, we will look in the next chapter at dimensions of inquiry protesters did *not seem to bring* to Seattle, and see if it can help prepare a wider perspective as we examine working parts, especially the dispute settlement part.

As we turn to this task we are reminded that the two agoras (the two solitudes) that seem not to talk to each other, and may even distrust each other, are reminiscent of the great "science and religion" divide. Both fields of inquiry and reasoning seem to have little to link them. In his *Rocks of Ages: Science and Religion in the Fullness of Life* Stephen Jay Gould [33] advances the argument that one of the great figures in the movement to treat science and religion as something he designates as NOMA – non-overlapping magisteria, or clearly separate spheres of inquiry – is Charles Darwin, father of evolution and modern biology. Darwin began his education as a clergyman, but wound up as a scientist. His life was fraught with misery, specifically the death of his children, but still he never lost his respect for the role of religious morality in society – despite the best efforts of fundamentalists to depict him as an atheist. In extrapolating on Darwin's theory of NOMA, Gould might as well be describing the traditional "left" and "right" of the Euro-Western political divide. "Many folks and movements hold narrow and aggressively partisan positions, usually linked to an active political agenda, and based on exalting one side while bashing the other," he notes.[34] In a recent tantalizing collection of essays The Representation of Business in English Literature, the editor introducing the essays summarizes novelists prevailing mental model as "making money is a dirty game." The essays apply mostly to literary fiction. General fiction and mass-market fiction have been more sympathetic to business.

Translating this notion of a science/religion NOMA to the "dialectic" of corporatism and social-activism can be a risky business politically, as this book reminds us. Darwin's NOMA teaches us then, that the issues of social justice advocated by the Seattle protesters need to be dealt with separately from the trade issues, but with mutual dialogue and respect showing through the process. Human geopolitical interaction, as noted political economist Harold Innis once put it, is a necessary conversation, not a search for dogma.

As we have seen earlier in this chapter, the respect for the "civil society" positioning would be enhanced if its legitimacy to speak for whom it purports to speak was also established on a firmer foundation.

This is a huge challenge for both sides. The tendency on the corporate side is silence or inarticulateness on issues of social justice. At their worst, corporate leaders quote statistics that misrepresent the damage being done to Third World economies and ecologies by their business. By the same token, activist groups often have very little idea of the sort of pressures and responsibilities that face trade ministers, and very little appreciation for businesses as engines of economic growth. Protesters are wrongheaded to suggest that the WTO should set an agenda of ecofeminism or poverty elimination. This is not the WTO's mandate. Instead, a forum with a name (and corresponding purpose) like the World Environmental Organization should be established to deal with ecological concerns and a stronger ILO for labor. Institutions like these can have a say over environmental and labor policy the way the WTO has over trade issues, if they have domestic support.

Let us turn now to some additional dimensions of international relations that might help point the way to some mutual understanding instead of mutual mistrust on these issues.

Notes

1. See *Globe and Mail* (Feb. 19, 2001).
2. John Whalley and Colleen Hamilton, *The Trading System After the Uruguay Round* (Institute for International Economics, New York, 1997).
3. Steven Shrybman, *A Citizen's Guide to the World Trade Organization* (Lorimer, Toronto 1999).
4. See Thomas L. Friedman in *New York Times*, 23 January 2000, editorial section 4.
5. *Now Magazine* (Toronto, 3 December 1999):7.
6. Ibid.
7. For example, the Society's Showcase venue is something called "Action Camp" in over a dozen rural locations in North America. Through these trainings people learn the skills they need to practice civil disobedience safely and effectively. These trainings contained cerebral, as well as physical elements. There are "classroom style" instruction for action planning, communicating with the media and nonviolent philosophy and practice. Safety and nonviolence are integral themes of each subject. Among the courses taught at the camps are basic ropework, belongings, rappelling, knots, harness and hardware. Anchors, hammocks and platforms, JV Marings equipment care and repair, protest situations such as tree sits, bridge blockades, building climbs and stack climbs are also illustrated, discussed and practiced. Some examples that may or may not have been used in Seattle: Declaration of indictment and intention; sky writing and earth writing; mock awards; protest disrobing; destruction of our property; symbolic sounds; rude gestures; "Haunting" officials; humorous skits and pranks; silence; refusing honors; turning one's back; stalling and obstruction; self exposure to the elements; sit-in; wade-in; speak-in.
8. Op. cit.
9. Op. cit.
10. Op. cit.

11. Op. cit.

12. Krugman, Sachs and Bhagwati clearly distinguish between the financial elite's interests and the interests of landed and corporate elites.

13. *Government in Canada* (W.W. Norton & Company, Toronto 1979). In passim. Or "third way" governments such as liberal regimes in Italy, Germany, the United States, UK and Canada do today.

14. *New York Times*, 21 August 1999, 7(M).

15. Op. cit.

16. Op. cit.

17. *National Post*, 8 December 1999, 11(A).

18. *Edmonton Journal*, 10 December 1999, 7(A).

19. *National Post*, 7 December 1999, 17(A).

20. *The Economist*, 9 December 1999, 17.

21. Ibid.

22. Ibid.

23. Ibid.

24. Ibid.

25. One example cited by the *Globe and Mail* (3 December 1999) might be a U.S. law requiring the use of recycled fiber in newsprint. This may appear to be of general application but it favors those with a ready supply of waste paper over those that need timber. The former tends to be American and the latter Canadian.

26. *Globe and Mail*, 8 December 1999, 21(A).

27. *National Post,* 8 December 1999.

28. *New York Times Book Review,* 31 January, 1999, 18.

29. See his chapter in H. Kitschelt et al., *Continuity and Change in Contemporary Capitalism* (Cambridge: UK, 1997).

30. David Crane, *Toronto Star* 21 June, 1994, (D)2. For some robust examples of "Washington Consensus"-thinking in the mid-1990s Lowell Bryan and Diana Farrell, et al., *Market Unbound: Unleashing Global Capitalism* (John Wiley and Sons N.Y.) 1996 and some of the essays in Brad Roberts ed., *New Forces in the World Economy* (Center for Strategic and International Studies and MIT Press) 1996.

31. Op. cit.

32. The *Economist* (January 15, 2001), 94

33. Gould, *Rock of Ages,* 68.

34. A. Pollard ed. The *Representation of Business in English Literature* (Institute of Economic Affairs London 2000).

Chapter Two

Three Ways to Look at the Politics of Trade Policy

Since no purely ideological approach can ensure orderly liberalized trade how do we sort out all these contesting national defenses and ambitions when it comes to trade? The trade policy of nations and international attempts to discipline it do not add up to a tidy business. This untidiness is regrettable. However mundane its workings, failure to discipline trade politics in its essentials will be fatal for the future of the world economy and for the prevention of major political conflict between and among nations. Every day the Internet gives new voice to international associations, which do not subscribe to the rigors of the "Washington Consensus." The financial cost of entry to the debate for such associations has dramatically declined. The Seattle and Quebec protesters' communications and coordination were masterfully done, thanks to the Internet.

The next few pages will introduce some academic categories to help order and elucidate some practical problems around the politics of trade policy.

To understand conceptually the forces that both propel and frustrate the new World Trade Organization, we will try mostly to use a different vocabulary than the standard vernacular of "protectionism" and "free trade." We will speak to the elemental forces and moods which dictate politics. Since this writer's academic days, insight has been drawn from *Man, the State and War*, a book by Kenneth N. Waltz. In this work, the author investigates classical political theory and its contributions to understanding not only the causes of war but to understanding international politics, including trade.[1] He identifies three sets of eyeglasses, or prisms, which he describes as "images," in classical political thinkers' analysis of all this. They reflect what the modern observer or policymaker uses. In academic, political or business life, it is vital to keep these three in mind, not only as explanatory tools but also as keys to solutions. His images are a powerful guide through the political moods and energies behind attempts to grow and regulate a world-trading system.

Waltz's "first image" locates the causes of international conflict in the *natural* behavior of man. This is the basic idea that "bad leaders" are the problem or "good leaders" are the answer. It follows that the first image can be either pessimistic or touchingly optimistic. Pessimists say: "The evilness of men, or their imperfect behavior, leads to war." Optimists say, on the other hand: "Individual goodness, if it could be universalized, would mean peace."[2] This implies, in a rather pessimistic reading of politics everywhere (as aptly stated by George Kennan), that the conduct of government is a "sorry chore . . . devolving upon civilized society . . . as a result of man's irrational nature, his selfishness, his obstinacy, his tendency to violence."[3] This image leads the pessimists to not depend on the nature of man, but to turn to political remedies to circumscribe human nature. "Personal deceit or ambition of Princes leads to international anarchy," wrote Spinoza, St. Augustine and countless others. Bad people make bad leaders who disrupt the international system (witness Hitler or Saddam Hussein).

This easily digested view is much popularized by the media. This "first image" does not exclude the possibility of a "good superman," president or prime minister to lead us through the abyss. Some philosophers view man as essentially good (the perception of Gandhi or Mandela or Havel, in the modern media?) and if their goodness were somehow universalized, world peace would follow. Did not Jean Jacques Rousseau, Karl Marx, Robert Owen and T. H. Green posit their advocacy on this theme? Is this image not akin to many religious fundamentalist views of the appropriate way through to international concord? However naïve it may appear to the Kissingers and Von Clausawitzs of the world, might it not sometimes have some validity? The individual leader's (or his small group's) power of rhetoric or inherited primacy or basic humanity can, in fact, move nations. (Winston Churchill's rhetoric was said to be worth several armored divisions and the Pope's "soft power" magnetism is ignored at one's peril). In spite of this, we do not have to simply concur that this image explains everything about international conflict. Let us instead recognize its validity in some contexts, as well as its universal appeal as an explanatory tool for what bedevils omnibus world trade agreements.

Some attentive observers and social scientists that study international negotiations among states seem to insist on ascribing all major moves not to individual leaders but to disembodied macro forces. In fact, the Canada-U.S. Free Trade Agreement (FTA) in 1987, at the end was saved by a closed group of negotiators, and primarily by the U.S. president and Canadian prime minister. This reality is not unlike Graham Allison's[4] findings about other international crises. In a crisis the "decision group" is often quite small. As former Secretary of the Treasury James Baker put it in the context of the FTA negotiations: "The imperative of political will cannot be overlooked. Only the President and the Prime Minister could commit their bureaucracies, sway public opinion and broker the tough decisions."[5] This commitment President Ronald Reagan clearly made when he agreed to a "deal that is as close as possible to the hoped-for deal" said Baker. This commitment Canada's Prime Minister Brian Mulroney made when he told his chief of staff and key negotiators to get an agreement "that can be clearly seen to be better" for settling disputes than the status quo but "no deal for the sake of a deal." So individual leaders do make a difference in international conflict, for good or for ill.

Let us look to the "second-image" for explaining conflict or for dealing with conflicts.

This "second-image" can be characterized as heavily political, in the domestic sense. It moves from the human content to the container. To quote Waltz, "Water running out of a faucet is chemically the same as water in a container, but once water is in a container it can be made to behave in different ways. . . It can be turned into steam or ice. The proposition of second image thinking is that through the reform of states, war and conflict can be reduced or eliminated."[6] It follows then that not good leaders but a "good" state is the key to this paradigm. This is key to many of the Seattle protesters and to the "Washington Consensus" way of thinking. "Good states' economic systems" are the answer to international conflict. Of course, the definition of "good" and its relationship to international trade is multitudinous. Marx had one view, Woodrow Wilson another. Thomas Hobbes argued for the state, not its leaders when he wrote that authoritarian states are inevitable "since finding life in a state of nature is impossible, men turn to the state to find the security collectively that they are incapable of finding individually."[7] In contrast, T. H. Green, a liberal idealist, could see no reason why, as various states became more generally representative of their people, they "should not arrive at a passionless impartiality in dealing with each other."[8]

Therefore, modern second-image thinkers insist that conflict can only be minimized if all states are improved, for example, from communist to capitalist or from fascist to democratic, or in an extreme Muslim view, from "Godless capitalist" to "Islamic fundamentalist." These second-image arguments are based on the notion that it is the nature of the domestic political regime (its constitution or its elected government) that causes conflict. This view is not idiosyncratic; Immanuel Kant, Adam Smith, John Stuart Mill, Karl Marx, Jean Jacques Rousseau and Thomas

Paine all hearken to this type of explanation. Prescriptive constitutional lawyers also are locked firmly into this tradition of thinking? Prescriptive inquiries into "comparative government and politics" as an academic discipline carry this promise as well.

A contemporary illustration of this model is the current Western view that the structure of China's economic and legal system must change before China can be admitted as a full WTO member. Or to take an American centric view, those scholars who write that American "standards of review" in trade matters in NAFTA or the WTO must be deferential to *domestic* standards of review reflect this second-image bias as well. Senator Strom Thurman's remarks to the UN Security Council is a clear example. He insisted that it is the "quality of states" that is more important than any international organization when he articulated in a touchingly clear fashion in January 2000 that "The UN must be an institution that is needed by the *great democratic powers* and not venture beyond its co-ordination, dialogue and service roles."[9]

Finally, there is the favorite of most Scandinavians, Canadians and moderately wealthy middle powers: the "third image" of theory and observation. What is this image? It does not so much blame 'bad leaders' or "faulty domestic regimes" for international conflict. Instead, it looks to the international relations "system" itself for causes and solutions. This image is, at the same time, both modern and ancient. Roman Senator Cicero wrote to his friends, "for what can be done against force without force?"[10] Greek historian Thucydides implied it when he wrote that it was "the growth of the Athenian power, which terrified the Lacedaemonians and forced them into war."[11] From a more modern twentieth-century perspective, it was the communist threat that threw divergent states together in GATT, NATO and other quasi-free market alliances.

Waltz expresses the third image profoundly:

> With many sovereign states, with no system of law enforceable against them, with each state judging its grievances and ambitions according to the dictates of its own reason or desire – conflict sometimes leading to war, is bound to occur. To achieve a favorable outcome, a state has to rely on its own devices.[12]

Montesquieu and Thucydides counter first-image Spinoza with the observation that the sources of international conflict are not so much in the minds of men as they are in the inherent nature of social activity, especially international activity. This is the third image. The threat to peace or trade lies not only in the princes or in the nature of their states, but in the international situation they face. As Waltz puts it, "Since the world cannot be defined in terms of perfection . . . it is a problem that cannot be changed simply by changing men or regimes."[13]

In international trade terms, Waltz is blunt:

> The trouble is once the competition in protectionism starts, the immediate interest of each country causes it to follow along, or as Scitovsky puts it, "to call for the raising of tariffs on these assumptions irrational would be similar to calling competitive behavior irrational."[14]

How does this third image of international conflict find solutions to trade deadlocks? By playing "international chess" cleverly, either through a balance of powers or through internationally legally agreed disciplines are the two answers. This is the world of Thucydides, Henry Kissinger and of WTO directors general. The third image or prism as a perspective does not see conflict as exclusively the product of (i) weak or predatory individuals such as a prince or a president or a prime minister or a foreign or trade minister, or as the product of a (ii) peculiar domestic regime or of a peculiar domestic constitutional arrangement or of a political domestic ideology or culture. The former is to see international trade conflict through the prism of the first image. The latter is to see international trade conflict through the prism of the second image. The third image is what one could call the "chess player" prism. It sees conflict inherent not in bad people or bad states, but more in the inherent fluidity and instability of the international arena. The key way to survive or to prosper, when one looks at the world in the light of this third-image prism, is to use (i) force or alliances as a deterrence or as a defense or (ii) to "lay into the rule book of international chess" rules of conduct and/or dispute settlement all will agree to follow.

What does this philosophy have to do with the world-trading system today? First it is the failure to see the need for some recognition of second-image realities that weakens the case of free trade or civil society purists. Their failure to recognize that their diagnosis is second-image uni-dimensional, i.e., that "pure capitalist" or "anti-capitalist" domestic regimes are the answer. In international trade terms, GATT and the WTO are clearly third-image constructions *with some allowance for second-image differences*. The WTO views the world through the prism of agreed-upon rules, and agreed-upon conflict resolution procedures, standards and expectations (some clearer than others, as we will see in the next chapter). Similarly, and crucially overlooked by soft liberal internationalists, if a nation legitimately uses the threat or reality of trade sanctions against those who refuse to follow the rules of dispute settlement determinations of the WTO, that nation can be seen justifiably as trying to "shore up" the WTO regime and its legitimacy, not the opposite.

Regardless of the Three Images: What Strategy and Tactics are to be Deployed?

In building a tighter and more effective set of global disciplines within the WTO, or the UN or other worldwide bodies, there is what historian Arnold Wolfers [15] described as two different "traditions" or "strategies" for building a more secure and predictable international environment. One is the "voluntarist" tradition, which is based on the belief that voluntary acts of good will, of good intentions and organizational exertion will achieve a worthy goal. The other is more "realist" in that it does not ridicule voluntarist acts but relies more on such tactics as force deterring force, retaliation ensuring future compliance, giving something for something else in return and negotiation based on mutual reward or punishment. Wolfers originally argued that, in the early twentieth century, voluntarism characterized much of Anglo-American foreign policy, especially Woodrow Wilson's call for the rule of law and the League of Nations, whereas realism characterized the European arena of war and balances of power.

The recent exploration of "hard" and "soft" power tactics as outlined by Joseph Nye[16] are further arsenal within either strategy. Nye argues appropriately that "soft power" assets like public opinion and media approbation must sometimes be coordinated with such "hard power" assets as competence and willingness to use hard military or "trade sanction" forces. Similarly, Michael Reisman has distinguished between "hard law" (clear precise rules) and "soft law" (expressions of future aspiration, general directions and with flexible timetables).[17] For example, the Uruguay Round is replete with soft law, especially in the realm of disciplines over intellectual property which are to be phased in over five to ten years.

Voluntarism is not the same as altruism or self-abnegation. One's short-term interest can be both voluntarist and selfish. Canada, for example, specializes in this. Canada's external affairs minister, Lester Pearson, won the Nobel Peace Prize for his leadership in suggesting and installing peacekeepers in the Suez to avert a war there. Did he do so because peacekeepers could separate combatants and decrease hostilities or because it was a convenient way to enable Canada not to have to choose among allies and the U.S.S.R.? Perhaps not even Pearson could distinguish privately which was more important.

Similarly, one could ask whether Canada's support for multilateral institutions such as the WTO is inspired by its third-image appearance or by the potential of this forum to serve as an occasional counterweight to U.S. influence in U.S.-Canada bilateral trade relations? So far the WTO has ruled inconveniently against Canada on a number of disputes. Since few Canadians depart from the voluntarist approach, they are reduced to grumbling that the WTO is not the savior it had expected against the United States or the European Community or Brazil.

Voluntarists often employ (but not always) what Joseph Nye describes as "soft power." Soft power is not "hard power" (e.g., military intimidation or use of "Section 301" or "Super 301" trade reprisal.) Daryl Copeland insightfully summarizes the application:

> Practitioners of soft power seek to occupy cerebral, not territorial, space. They are developing an adapted version of Nye's doctrine, fashioning it to the contours of an entirely different context to serve quite different purposes. In this campaign the real battles are fought using PR ordnance. The highest authority is the court of public opinion, where image is everything. And soft power is being served up as a panacea for many of the post Cold War world's problems.

> Soft power savants view knowledge brokerage, media savvy, strategic alliances, partnerships with non-governmental organizations (NGOs), and coalition-building with like-minded governments and elements of civil society as fundamental. Less emphasis is placed on more conventional instruments such as development assistance, the military, the intelligence apparatus, and the foreign service. Even if one's nation had more "hard power" assets than it does, the argument is that this kind of influence has become difficult to wield and is often unsuited to the circumstances of globalization and the related tasks at hand.[18]

The use of "soft power" is the process of getting others to do what otherwise they wouldn't do through the power of information on public opinion and assaults on media image of the nation under scrutiny. Other soft power means include deploying cultural, legal or moral examples to attract others to follow suit. Following suit, that is, in initiatives like re-structuring the WTO agenda in ways consistent with one's long term vision.

Nye notes, however, to pacifists of all descriptions that voluntarism cannot work without some "hard power" competence or, goodwill or resources. Otherwise it is empty posturing little more than "touchy feely" good intentions with nothing to back it up. Nye argues that effective use of "soft power" must be integrated with deft deployment or signaling of "hard power." Nye finds that a nation cannot promote "soft power" mono-maniacally without a willingness to play with "hard power" as well. Countries such as Canada sometimes "punch above their economic and military weight"[19] he says, when they link their soft power deployment on such matters as land-mine-banning treaties or peacekeeping to an intrinsic competence in effecting compliance and cooperation with allies on "hard-power" matters. They balance themselves so as not to be dismissed by the superpowers as "flaky" or as "preening moralists" or as to be "not worth paying attention to." Witness Canada's military support for NATO in Kosovo, when it also championed voluntarist land mine abolition globally.

These three prisms or images; these two traditions and strategies of voluntarism and realism; and these inventories of soft and hard power are helpful indicators of moods behind international trade conflict. It is often simplistic and unhelpful to differentiate between "internationalist" and "nationalist" or "protectionist" and "free trader," which is the usual way of describing different approaches to international trade. It is more helpful to observe the "realist and voluntarist" deploying "hard and soft power" and "hard and soft law." For example, a communist, Karl Marx, and a nineteenth-century Cambridge free-market capitalist, Alfred Marshall, both have "internationalist" strategies and interim "protectionist" strategies. To respond with trade sanctions when the WTO has found against your opponent can be seen as "internationalist" if it strengthens the predictability of decisions of WTO dispute settlement bodies. To try to build a more viable WTO by negotiating firmly with an applicant for membership (such as China) to alter somewhat its domestic market regime is no more nationalist or protectionist than it is internationalist. This attempt should be more clearly understood as an attempt to insinuate "third-image" terms of debate to dissolve second-image resistance. Former U.S. Secretary of State James Baker recalls that the Reagan and Bush administrations relied on the third image vision of the advantages of "rule-based global and regional free trade to turn the terms of the debate against skeptics in Congress."[20]

Let us put this argument in a "box-like" summary.

To Summarize the Three Images

*POLITICAL PERSPECTIVES ON GLOBAL PROBLEMS AND
THEIR CAUSES AND SOLUTIONS*

"Individuals are Key"   "The Nature of Domestic   "The International
                            Regimes is Key"   Chessboard is Key"

FIRST IMAGE   SECOND IMAGE   THIRD IMAGE

| "Bad people" as government leaders as negotiators or "good people" as government leaders as negotiators deploying opportunistically insecure or, secure domestic opinion or group opinion is the explanation.. | "Bad" domestic, political or economic arrangements such as "capitalist" or "closed socialist" is the problem; a "better" domestic arrangement is the answer. | "The fluidity and insecurity of all nations against all, the international system itself, of international activity itself, of the international chessboard itself is the problem. The solution? Power must checkmate power and/or 'lay into the system rules of play' all nations and players must agree to follow" |

Political strategies to move others within either image.
Voluntarist "acts of goodwill and organization." Realist "checkmate through use of power against power."

Tactics of the Voluntarist or Realist?
Deploy "hard or soft" power, "hard or soft" law.

The agreement on the original U.S.-Canada FTA dispute settlement arrangement, for example, is a hybrid of realist "second-image" thinking and of "third-image" voluntarist legal momentum thinking. As James Baker puts it, "the enemy of the deal was the ideal." "Principled political pragmatism" produced this hybrid which advanced third-image principle but it also recognized, in Baker's words, second-image "political limits."[21]

Baker also deployed a "third-image" vision through the FTA example –

> to "turn the terms of the global debate to forestall protectionism in Congress by speaking of the broad national interest in the FTA and the Uruguay round of the GATT. With a $300 billion trade deficit, protectionist sympathies will always be strong." The way to combat this was with a broader vision.[22]

To secure this advance in third-image disciplines, strategies vary: either voluntarist or realist. In the Uruguay Round negotiations, Canada usually relied on voluntarism in an earnest effort to coordinate and moderate, but Canada's government probably expected the United States to use its realist muscle to help bring the Uruguay Round to a conclusion. The edifices themselves – the WTO and NAFTA – are a mixture of voluntarist steps forward to liberalize trade and to instill obligatory conflict resolution and "realist compromises" on a host of matters. They are replete with what Reisman calls "hard law" (clear precise rules) and "soft law" (expressions of future aspiration, general directions, and flexible timetables to ensure a transitional stage in the internationalization of issues can be found).[23]

Any free trade agenda between major powers is difficult to achieve. This writer's former colleague, John Crosbie, (Canadian trade minister, 1991-93), explains it in political terms

> Thomas Macauley (1 paraphrase) wrote in 1824 that free trade is always unpopular, "The great collectivity doesn't know or understand its benefits." . . . Today the media loves to promote the negative. Truth is complicated . . . . Fears of people dependent on government are easy to arouse. A single lie is easy to follow.
>
> Yet as Macauley put it almost 200 years ago "If all our neighbors are poor how are we going to get rich?" For us the choice was freer trade with the United States or American protectionism.[24]

In the West after 1991, some international and national think tanks, formerly preoccupied with Cold War matters, shifted their vocabulary and "zero-sum" theories, to the international trade arena. The shift essentially was to move to advocating the amelioration of second-image domestic political rigidities, and to improve the transparency and accessibility of domestic markets that were opaque. As this writer observed as trade minister and before all this gathered steam and became the preoccupation from 1991 to 1994. The conclusion of the WTO Uruguay Round ushered in a profound change to the WTO Dispute Settlement Understanding (DSU) by insisting that compliance to WTO dispute settlements discussions be in effect not *voluntary* but *involuntary*. This new DSU injected a third-image discipline that was applauded by voluntarists who cherished the idea of enhanced international discipline. It did not, however, enjoy the explicit backing and support of the other Bretton Woods institutions at that time.

Now we are in a new era that insists on "second-image" economic and legal improvements to China's domestic regime as a prerequisite to its full membership in the WTO. The realists' objective here is to gain clearer and better access to China's market and also to ensure that the presently tenuous "third-image" advance of compulsory adherence to WTO disciplines by WTO members does not unravel once China rejoins.

The First Image Strikes Back

All this global trade liberalization appears salutatory for third-and second-image enthusiasts. Ominously however, "a first-image" threat, in an unprecedented new guise, is beginning to appear. This could undermine everything. The threat, originally directed at NAFTA, was fixed on the WTO in Seattle. This threat, as the previous chapter outlined, is the specter of not only civil society groups, but of groups and opinion-makers in countless nations that complain their state is impotent in the swirl of change wrought by globalization.

One's political sense tells one that nothing is so dangerous in politics as to assume that a new international order has been accepted. Nothing is more dangerous as to be so far ahead of one's domestic public, of a public that does not comprehend, let alone assent, to what your government is trying to do. (In the Canadian context, this writer thinks of the Canadian Progressive Conservative government's salutary but resented tax reform and trade initiatives in the 1980s, to name but two.)[25] Today in the United States, we have Pat Buchanan's fulminations against the "new world order" of the UN and the WTO. We witness President Clinton's failure to gain passage of fast track legislation for a Free Trade Area of the Americas (FTAA), as evidence that the U.S. public is not yet agreeing to all the assumptions underlying the WTO agreement. Opposition to the Multilateral Agreement on Investment (MAI) is another example. Transnational associations on the Internet and elsewhere are joining with nationalist groups to oppose much of these globalization accords.

The tension from all this will flow to other countries, as we have seen earlier in Peter Hall's contrast between open liberal capitalist economies (e.g., the U.S., UK and Taiwan economies) and "coordinated capitalist economies" which allow extra-market coordination by firms but not total coordination through the discipline of market prices.

A similar angst is developing in Europe about globalization. Here is British Prime Minister Tony Blair on the impact of change in people's lives at the May 1998 WTO Summit:

> Technology transforms their workplaces. Globalization alters the structures in which they work. Financial markets that with the push of a button move sums of money beyond contemplation across international frontiers with stunning rapidity can move whole economies. . . . These are powerful impulses of economic change that leave people feeling powerless and insecure about their future. And in the wake of economic change, social change, communities disintegrating, families destabilized, crime and drugs and social exclusion. The possibilities of our new world may be infinite but for many millions of our citizens, it is the dangers that are more real.[26]

Norwegian Prime Minister Kjell Magne Bondevik, in his speech to the 1998 WTO summit, acknowledged that globalization was changing the world and its economic structures "in an unprecedented manner and speed." Some people, he said, see this as a positive development, creating closer ties and cooperation around the world. Others, Bondevik stressed, have "a different and more skeptical perception of globalization." They question the impact of trade and investment liberalization, with the growing power of multinational corporations, and the free capital flows of financial markets:

> They fear that our democratic institutions are losing control of the international economic forces and environmental and social costs will be high. . . [These are] legitimate concerns related to fundamental issues regarding the well-being of mankind. If globalization cannot answer these concerns, many people will not see it as a positive development.[27]

In response to the need for better understanding, Norway organized an international symposium on the effects of globalization to provide a better understanding of the issues. Recent global Davos World Economic Forum Conferences have done the same in 2000 and 2001.

So, countless leaders are asking, what kind of world is globalization and technological change creating? And if these forces are irresistible, what rules and institutions do we need to counter the power of multinationals and to ensure that democracy, accountability, social cohesion and sustainable development prevail? As former South African President Nelson Mandela asked at the 1999 Davos World Economic Forum, "Is globalization only to benefit the powerful and the financier specialists, investors and traders? Does it offer nothing to those ravaged by the violence of poverty?" At the same meeting, U.S. Treasury Secretary Robert Rubin acknowledged that billions of people have been affected by "the most serious financial crisis of the last 50 years."[28] The WTO cannot be blamed for these heavy reservations but supporters of trade and the WTO overlook the mischief first and second-image arguments can cause to the underlying support for the WTO.

Trade Before the Seattle Protests During the "Cold War"

In terms of Kenneth Waltz's three images it is clear that the United States, during the Cold War, was not rigidly run by any "Washington Consensus." It was gentle with its allies' "second-image" impediments to free trade. The United States hesitated to insist on massive internal changes to the domestic economic, political or trade systems in Japan, Korea, France, Brazil or India, for example. In practice, the United States was able to maintain a GATT that was much more "realist" in its Cold War compromises than "voluntarist". Still it extended impressive wide-reaching international disciplines through GATT. This delicate balance started to shift, as major economic powers such as Japan, Europe and others appeared, (to many U.S. congressmen and senators, faced with a huge American trade deficit), to be taking advantage of what these elected officials described as "the most open market in the world,"i.e., the U.S. market, while not concomitantly opening theirs as much. In the late 1980s, the Cold War was ending. As President Clinton came to office in 1992, a number of studies decrying trade unfairness blossomed.

A new post-Cold War era had enveloped world trade, investments and economic relations. Into this new context a slender reed – the WTO – was inserted to attempt (perhaps too much, in the sense that it seemed to be continually stirring the pot) to produce a third-image crust of consensus or coral reef of a tender yet articulate ordering to trade relations. We cannot assume all this is as potent in its beginnings as the empire of Phillip II of Spain in 1565. It may, even with its weaknesses, be able to gather for its global reach, the assent Phillip could not achieve. Let us examine how well equipped this body, especially its arrangements to settle disputes, with no army and no priesthood – really is. Parenthetically we ask does U.S. trade policy in the new millennium have a rooted vision for the future?

Notes

1. Kenneth Waltz, *Man, the State and War* (Columbia University Press, New York 1961), 39.

2   Ibid., 36.

3. Ibid., 37.

4. Graham Allison, *The Essence of Decision* (Pearson Printing, New York 1971).

5. James Baker, speech from June 2, 1999 at Montreal, Quebec.

6. Waltz, 21.

7. Op. cit., 26.

8. Op. cit., 32

9. *National Post*, 20 January 2000, 12 (A).

10. Waltz, 157.

11. Waltz, 158.

12. Waltz, 171.

13. Waltz, 171.

14. Waltz, 160.

15. A. Wolfers, *The Ango-American Tradition in World Affairs* (Greenwood Publishing Group, New York 1951).

16. J. Nye, interview on March 7, 1999.

17. Michael Reisman and Mark Weidman, "Contextual Imperatives of Dispute Resolution Mechanisms," *Journal of World Trade* 29, 3 June 1995: 7-9 (passim).

18. *Toronto Star,* 18 August 1998, 13.

19. Nye, interview on March 7, 1999.

20. James Baker, June 2, 1999.

21. Baker, June 2, 1999.

22. Baker, June 2, 1999.

23. Op. cit., see note 17.

24. John Crosbie, speech to the PCII, February 20, 1999, at Toronto.

25. Even ten years later, only 26 percent of Canadians think the FTA or NAFTA was good for Canada, according to *Maclean's* magazine of January 14, 2000, even though exports to the United States account for much of the growth in Canada's GDP in the last ten years and Canada has won far more panel disputes than it has lost.

26. David Crane, "Globalization Fears Run Deep, Leaders Tell World Forum," *Toronto Star*, 24 May 1998, 2(D).

27. Ibid., 2(D).

28. *Toronto Star*, 31 January 1999, 3(B).

Chapter Three

Beyond Ideological Challenges to the WTO: Varieties of Capitalist Development in the Post-Cold War Age

Beyond ideology there are huge challenges to the WTO caused by its members' different varieties of economic and capitalist development. These differences largely account for much of the weekly WTO agenda.

Walking into the lobby of the World Trade Organization (WTO) headquarters in Geneva, all is hustle and bustle. Computer cables snake across polished floors. Bold signs are slapped over freshly painted walls. Countless officials race through the corridors, making last minute preparations and dashing off to meetings. Despite the frenzied activities, one can not help but be struck by Lac Leman sparkling in the distance through the great bay window. It glistens as a symbol of third-image and voluntarist energy, hope and promise nestled in this beautiful Swiss city. It reminds one of when this city was home, 225 years ago, to Jean Jacques Rousseau, perhaps the Enlightenment's most passionate exponent of how individualism and community can coexist and coalesce.

The agreement establishing the WTO, adopted by 124 countries, is not only the longest international agreement ever concluded (comprising some 26,000 pages) but also the most important worldwide agreement since the UN Charter of 1945. It is filled with "third-image" ambition and it struggles with the restraints of "second-image" disruptions of the international trading system. Fifty years after the Bretton Woods conference, the entry into force of the WTO agreement in 1995 completes the legal structure of the Bretton Woods system based on the International Monetary Fund (IMF), the World Bank Group and the WTO. By replacing the so far separate international regulations of transnational movements of goods, services, persons and investments by a new worldwide "integrated" legal system, the WTO agreement was intended to lay the legal foundation for a new international economic order for the twenty-first century. As we have seen, like the IMF and the World Bank, the WTO aims to serve essential global functions.

Let us not exaggerate, politically the WTO is a necessary but insufficient accomplishment. In Waltz's terms, its membership is built upon "third-image" hope and tenuously "soft" and "hard" legal fabric. It is still vulnerable to disruptions from national entities. For example, it is vulnerable to the "second-image" European or American or Japanese or ultimately Chinese refusal to digest its determinations. It is vulnerable to other political opportunists (such as first-image leaders rhetoric such as American James Buchanan's or Prime Minister Mahatir's of Malaysia). The WTO's strength lies in its scope and integrated nature, as well as in the consent of member nations to its "hard and soft law" and to its dispute settlement mechanisms. From a "third-image" globalist perspective, however uncertain the WTO future, these are impressive gains. Most attentive observers know these gains are far from secure, hence it is a palpable exaggeration to describe the WTO as a new international juggernaut riding roughshod over national sovereignty.

It will be problematic for some time as to whether these gains are permanent in nature. To endure and to be enhanced, the "realist bargain" which underlies the WTO defects (such as lack of clarity on antidumping and other matters) must not abuse the WTO's functioning and evolution. (Further explanation of this point is provided later). We have seen the first brute reality of the political pressures on national governments that are buffeted by those who feel "left behind" or those who would question the legitimacy of the discipline and pain inherent in "globalization" (see Seattle for example). These will have to be managed. It is not enough to quote the Washington Consensus, or Adam Smith, or David Ricardo or their modern-day equivalents who find globalization to be logical. This deference to those who have not heard of Smith or Ricardo, let alone subscribed to them is the lesson taught in the political arena.

What exactly is so comprehensive about the WTO and the agreement that brought it into life, the Uruguay Round? According to Europe's most distinguished trade scholar, Ernst-Ulrich Petersmann, the most radical innovation of the WTO Agreement is its "single undertaking approach" which aims "to develop an integrated, more viable and durable multilateral trading system" encompassing the General Agreement of Tariffs and Trade, (the result of past trade liberalization efforts), all the results of the Uruguay Round of multilateral trade negotiations," and other agreements such as the agreement on Trade-Related Intellectual Property Rights (TRIPs). By integrating the thirty Uruguay Round agreements and about 200 previous GATT agreements into one single legal framework, "the WTO Agreement will reduce the current fragmentation of separate international agreements and organizations for movements of goods, services, persons, capital and payments."[1]

Yet was this a rich nations enterprise? During the Uruguay Round of multilateral trade negotiations in GATT, many developing countries played an active role and engaged in far-reaching programs of trade liberalization and deregulation. The WTO requirements of substantive GATT concessions, and of acceptance of essentially all Uruguay Round results by all WTO member countries (Articles XI, XII and XIV of the WTO agreement), "promotes more freedom, more rule of law and more welfare through a more efficient use of domestic resources in all countries." [2] The gist of these understandings and agreements is to give further precision and strength to the existing general GATT rules, especially with regard to agricultural, textiles and "gray area" trade restrictions (such as voluntary export restraints) which have historically escaped effective legal discipline by GATT.

For agreements on trade in services, the GATT rests on three pillars. The first is a framework agreement involving all WTO member countries whose principles (such as most-favored-nation treatment) apply to any service in any sector, excepting services supplied in excess of government authority neither on a commercial basis nor in competition with other services suppliers. The second consists of national schedules of "market access commitments," "national treatment commitments" and other "additional commitments," as well as the national lists of temporary, "most-favored-nation" exemptions made in accordance with the GATT "Annex on Article II Exceptions." The final third pillar is made up of a number of annexes addressing the special situations of individual services sectors such as financial services, telecommunications, air transport services and maritime transport.

As for intellectual property, there is explicit recognition "that intellectual property rights are private rights." The various competition rules created to prevent intellectual property rights abuse by right-holders, combined with relatively high minimum standards for protecting and enforcing copyrights, trademarks, geographical indications, industrial designs, patents, layout designs, undisclosed information and other related rights, all illustrate that the TRIPs agreement introduces many new legal principles into the multilateral trading system based on GATT. In the view of GATT experts, the formal linkage between multilateral trade rules and relevant intellectual property agreements may serve as a model for similar future agreements, for instance on trade-related environmental measures and trade related anticompetitive practices.

In the long run, we are told, no trading country can afford to stay outside this new world-trading system. It is therefore to be hoped by most "third-image" globalists that the WTO will progressively evolve into a worldwide organization with almost universal membership and that it will prompt member countries to transform the WTO into a specialized UN agency similar to the Bretton Woods institutions.

We have seen that the meeting in Seattle to start a new round suffered a postponement. Still it is clear the WTO will serve as a negotiating forum for future "GATT Rounds" on the multilateral liberalization of trade in goods as well as for future "GATT Rounds" on the progressive liberalization of international services trade through "successive rounds of negotiations . . . .with a view to achieving a progressively higher level of liberalization" (Article XIX GATT). [3]

All voyages begin similarly, launched with hope. It is the arrivals that differ. The League of Nations, set in motion with ambition, never reached its potential. The United Nations, established over fifty-five years ago, was fuelled with high hopes, yet only an incorrigible optimist would claim that the organization has adequately attained its desired objectives. With equal feelings of expectation and doubt surrounding the fate of world trade, the question must be raised: how exactly will the future of liberalized trade and its institutional incarnation, the WTO, emerge?

This book now suggests that the WTO, despite its unprecedented capacity to succeed in liberalizing trade, must be cautious of becoming overloaded with "teeth-rattling" disputes and of the ultimate risk of losing some key members. Can anyone doubt such losses could lead to impotence, paralysis and a likely economic depression, causing a new worldwide financial collapse? These problems would prove especially dire if they occur (probably inevitably) coterminously with severe exchange-rate dis-equilibriums. We have seen it is clear that the WTO must be allowed to be a part of other Bretton Woods institutions' efforts to deal with trade imbalances and exchange rate distortions. We have seen that although WTO-IMF-Word Bank coordination is essential, it cannot be tied to a puritanical "Washington Consensus."

The WTO, however hopeful its launch, runs the risk of crashing if it cannot meet a credible amount of its main challenges on its own agenda. This book now centers on the key test to be faced in delivering the goods and services of expanded world trade, that is the credibility of the WTO's dispute settlement mechanism. We will explore the intricacies of this "motor," noting that "agenda overload" could cause a breakdown of the entire mechanism. Many members are unable to implement what they have negotiated, let alone add to the WTO mandate. The WTO agreement itself is rife with purposeful ambiguity ("hard" and "soft" law). This is clear from the lack of clear definitions of what constitutes subsidies and antidumping, and a lack of clarity among members of how they make and implement trade policy. But should we press for a degree of perfection that cannot be met?

This is why the agreement has "soft law" as much as hard, realist compromises in addition to "soft" ambiguities. These will be outlined later.

Although trade is affected by everything: the environment, labor rights, trade imbalances, exchange rate manipulations (the list is endless): effective dispute settlement must take priority over members' individual interests in expanding those linkages.

Even present commitments are unclear. Years into the WTO mandate, many of its members had yet to notify the organization of its subsidies and safeguards as required under the agreement of entry. Nor should one forget the emotional and political cloud of skepticism about the WTO, not just by Seattle protesters, but by the "regionalists," and "cultural relativists." These forces will be as enduring in relevance as they underwrite causes understandable to everyday citizens. Take the "regionalists," for example. Was not former European Deputy James Goldsmith correct to suggest that "a WTO" resonates poorly with the growing class of European unemployed compared with the idea of a "European Community"? Aren't some in the Democratic and Republican parties of the U.S. Congress correct to be suspicious about how readily any newly jobless will embrace an abstract "world-trade bureaucracy" compared to a more accessible entity? These cavils may trouble those who see the logic, economically, of an uncheckerboarded world trade regime. However, this logic will not help national heads of government through the difficulties of building political support. Consider too, nation states defending their culture or religious foundations or of nation states at different stages of development or of vulnerable sectors of society with their capacity to mobilize resistance through unions, students, academics and so on. These are political realities this writer glimpsed in working for a regional free trade association as a minister. Consider the forces of political resistance orchestrated on a global scale, as in the recent international citizens' movement against the Multilateral Agreement on Investment (MAI), and at Seattle.

Why All Politicians Can Get Nervous Over Freer Trade

In the flow of world and domestic politics, does all this "international trade stuff" really matter? There is no doubt that without a strong center, chaos ensues: "Untune that string, hark what discord follows." The calamity of a GATT and WTO collapse will affect us all with prospects for world-wide economic dislocation following as aftershocks. Few people understand this. Some say that the obscurity of WTO processes presents a classic opportunity for governments, business and academic leaders to control progress without being impeded by those who don't understand, that the abstruse nature of the WTO will allow it to develop without much public notice. This did not happen at Seattle. In fact, trade issues can dominate elections. Pat Buchanan's *Great Betrayal* interprets many American presidential elections as turning on trade issues. Can anyone doubt that "Corn Laws" were not the pivotal issue in much of nineteenth-century UK politics?

A classic example of the profound resonance of the trade issue was the Republican party's 1996 presidential primaries. A candidate, Pat Buchanan described the WTO, the Trilateral Commission, the Council on Foreign Relations and the United Nations as constituting the "new world order." Buchanan objected to what he called "the continued American surrender to the new world order." He opposed both NAFTA and the Uruguay GATT agreements, arguing that they are costing American jobs:

> It is immoral and it is un-American to force American textile workers who make $9 an hour to compete with Chinese workers who make $0.25 an hour. Neither party up there seems to be concerned about the working people.[4]

When accused of taking a stand "left" of President Clinton, Mr. Buchanan scoffed, noting that even his campaign opponents have not been supporting NAFTA or GATT. "If that's their philosophy, why don't they come out and defend it?," he said "When you've got somebody who no longer defends his position or articulates it, the high ground has been conceded and eventually you take it."[5] According to Kevin Phillips in 1995: "We've seen the commitment to free trade unravel. People just don't believe that it's job-creating any more. The party would have moved in that direction. Pat crystallized it."[6] In Waltz's terms, the demands of third image solutions seemed without vocal proponents in the march of the American political arena.

A more extensive view of the dark side of globalization was penned by Thomas L. Friedman in the *New York Times* on the last day of 1995. He recollects seeing a man and his two children in Mexico City that year dressed in clown costumes, entertaining motorists and begging at a stop light. Friedman pondered the degradation: "The man represents for me all the left-behinds, all those who have not shared in the benefits of the market place." The "brutal" global competition for "investment dollars and trade" is forcing companies and workers to tighten their budgets and to constantly upgrade skills:

Those who have the savvy to keep up are thriving, those who don't are panhandling at stop lights. Unfortunately, this same global competition is forcing governments to downsize and they are doing it by shredding their social safety nets and junking their welfare programs so the "left-behinds" are left in free fall.[7]

Other countries also contain critics of the pace of global competition. The director of India's Research Foundation for Science, Technology and National Resource Policy, Vandana Shiva, is concerned about the destruction of India's rural communities as a result of global free trade. She says globalization will bring:

a further destruction of our communities, uprooting of millions of small peasants from the land and their migration into the slums of over crowded cities. GATT destroys the cultural diversity and social stability of our nation. . . GATT for us implies recolonization.[8]

The potential resurgence of former communists in Poland and Russia, the Welfare party in Turkey, and the increased militancy of unions in France indicate that those who are marginalized by global free trade are starting to challenge those who are reaping its benefits. For example, months before he died, the billionaire Sir James Goldsmith noted the European dilemma vis-à-vis the developing economies in his essay *The Trap*:

The number of people employed annually to produce one billion dollars worth of high-tech products in the developed countries could be under a thousand. But the number of people employed in the low-cost areas to manufacture the goods that we import would be in the tens of thousands, because these are not high-tech products but ones produced with traditional levels of employment. So our trade might be in balance in monetary terms but if we look beyond the monetary figures we find that there is a terrible imbalance in terms of employment. That is how we export jobs and import unemployment.[9]

As for economists who counter with their argument that the growth in service industries will compensate for the lost jobs in manufacturing, Goldsmith retorted:

Even service industries will be subjected to substantial transfers of employment to low-cost areas. Today, through satellites, you can remain in constant contact with offices in distant lands. . .

TWA has recently transferred a significant part of its accounts department to India.[10]

Much has exploded and mystastisized in the e-commerce world since Goldsmith's *"cri de coeur."* These global changes will have unprecedented political consequences. The worst-case scenario is a first-image one. We could see an "ambitious prince" or modern head of government of a country of consequence playing on these fears and realities to disrupt the WTO.

As we have seen, the possibility of national governments unable to sustain support for the disciplines of the WTO do not spring from political or union or business actors alone. They flow from intellectual or literary impulses as well. One finds comprehensive examples of this in the perplexity stemming from all this talk of "citizens," "cultures," the "marginalized" and of those "left behind."[11] Free traders point to the "consumer" ultimately benefiting from free trade. In rebuttal, "citizen" groups point to the potential job and national identity losses from global free trade.

The literary and cultural leaders who doubt the market often compare the "consumer" (pejoratively) to the noble "citizen." All of us are both, yet we prefer to think of ourselves as the latter. The word "consumer" suggests a strange disembodied force acting in its own right, independent of the living, breathing people of which it is composed. "Citizen" seems less pejorative and more sympathetic:

> The "consumer" would seem to inhabit a bleak world, the landscape barren of anything save the strip malls and McDonalds he is said to prefer. On his television, there is only sex and violence, in his diary there is but one entry, "went shopping." The "citizen," on the other hand, is a stout fellow, much given to licking envelopes, attending meetings and otherwise combining his efforts with those of like mind in pursuit of worthy causes. [12]

In response one could retort: why precisely should decisions on how society's resources are to be deployed not be guided by the choices of the people who use these resources i.e., the consumers? To assert this is not to endorse "mindless consumerism," but to simply register that coercion by a select group of citizens i.e., some educated media cultural or elected political elite should not always prevail instead. Politics is about coercion. The ideal of markets, conversely, is about voluntary relationships based on mutually beneficial exchange. "Competition," the market's essential feature, is "merely the means of enforcing this voluntary regime," writes Andrew Coyne.[13]

Not long ago a book by John Ralston Saul (a celebrated North American literary figure) makes complaints about consumers and the market. Saul situates his complaint in what he describes as the "Unconscious Civilization" that seems to dominate us all as we enter a new millennium. He writes that today, this unconscious civilization comprised of big business, governments, unions and the media, are comfortable with an international trade agreement so:

> A series of international binding agreements of great complexity have been signed for the consumer against "citizen-type" concerns over the past few years.[14]

Catching the spirit of the "left behinds," or of the "marginalized" or of the activist "citizens," absolutely nothing prevents, he writes hopefully that:

> the negotiation of matching agreements on job equity and social standards. Like regional free trade, this can begin at regional levels. Nor is there any need for such agreements to begin at the all-inclusive international level. Like trade, social policy can first be established on a regional basis. What is described as the impossibility of international social regulation is actually the unwillingness of the corporatist elite to enter into such negotiations.[15]

Saul's advice is quintessentially from the school concerned about globalization and its pace. He envelops his advise in a "citizen" wrapper: His solution calls "therefore, for a pure act of political will." In other words, he is saying the "citizen" should be able to coerce the "consumer" to some degree. We can find this desire to prefer coercion by the political will of a select group of "citizens" (not "consumers") exists in every society. It will always have appeal. It may have started with Plato's *Republic*. Robust challenges to globalization persist in this and it could contribute to the collapse or marginalization of the WTO if not properly understood and spoken to.

These immediate political stresses around liberalizing world trade will not be short-lived. They flow from central causes. They are not evanescent. They testify to the resilience of first-and second-image influences that are with us still. Consider for example, the United States and its possible future in trade with Asia. Not only is there an underlying clash of civilizations between Asia and the West, as Samuel Huntington describes it, but there is the more immediate problem of a conflict of institutional relationships. It cannot be denied that there are fundamental incompatibilities that characterize the economies of the major participants in world trade. It will be tremendously difficult – but not necessarily impossible – for any World Trade Organization to tune this basic disharmony. The United Nations was not able to end the Cold War. Nor could endless arms control and security fora settle strategic military rivalries. Similarly, the WTO will be challenged by underlying incongruities of civilizations and institutions, as explained in the previous chapter in the discussion of domestic financial architecture.

How Fragile Is the World Consensus Underpinning the Uruguay Round's Agreement? A Personal Recollection.

This writer's perspective in attending ministerial rounds leading to the Uruguay Accord, is that the round was a necessary albeit insufficient accomplishment. It would be an overstatement to say that the "Uruguay Round has been a diversion" as Karl Wolferen wrote in the *Washington Post* on June 28, 1994. It is fair to say that the Uruguay Round allowed trade ministers and trade officials to stimulate trade expansion discourse while skirting some of the political differences at the center of the agreement. The Uruguay Round sought to expand what was a fundamentally ineffective and unbalanced discipline over new areas such as services (other than financial), intellectual property and agriculture.

As one of Canada's ministerial negotiators, this writer remembers the first week of negotiations in Uruguay in September 1986. Even though the venue was a beach resort, the weather was cold, rainy and very windy – rather like the negotiating atmosphere. As a country highly reliant on trade, yet equally dependent on major power cooperation, Canada took the only stance it could. Canada fought hard for the removal of subsidies on agriculture and for the removal of tariffs and nontariff barriers on goods and services and the unfair invocation of trade remedies against dumping. Other countries spoke out similarly, but all had exceptions they wished to protect. The early days of the negotiations in that magnificent casino on the beach, reflected the basic incompatibilities that existed among trading partners.

Very little was accomplished during the first five days of the week until Clayton Yeuter, the American trade representative, made it clear that the American delegation was leaving Sunday for the opening of the United States Congress. Under hasty improvisations on all fronts, agreements were hammered out at four and five that Sunday morning. Exhausted negotiators agreed tentatively to give sufficient momentum to claim that a new round had begun. Charles Carlisle, former deputy director general of the GATT from 1987 to 1993 pithily concludes "The Uruguay Round was not about free trade, but freer trade, yet it almost failed."[16] This writer remembers the American delegation proposing that all agricultural support and protection be abolished over ten years. (The Clinton administration fourteen years later increased American subsides to agriculture from $28 billion to $42 billion in the year 2000.) The EU's reaction in Uruguay was negative. So was Japan's. The agriculture stalemate brought those rooms, where negotiations on other subjects such as tariffs on goods, on services and on protecting intellectual property rights to a virtual standstill. Endless cups of coffee in the casino's corridors frequently substituted for negotiation. All waited for a breakthrough on agriculture. Finally, at 4:00 a.m. on the last day, our miracle came. A hastily patched, but not unsubstantial, set of initial understandings, expressions of sentiment and delayed timetables fell into place. The round was launched.

As we know, the American political class, (not the major business voices,) was greatly divided over this round. Launched in 1986 it was finally signed as an agreement in 1994. Perhaps the round had to be agreed to because too many parties focused too much time on it and they had promised its success. At the Quad meetings two days before the Heads of Government Summit of the G7 in Tokyo in July of 1993, so little basic harmony existed that we Quad trade ministers discussed minor issues in excruciating detail sometimes into the wee hours of the morning. To give the reader a taste of what this was like, the Japanese were objecting at one point to any decrease to zero from four percent on brown-colored alcoholic beverages! We were also challenged by the fact that the French government would have great difficulty living with our negotiations. Protection would be demanded by the French farming community for agriculture and for the French cultural sector for the nation's cinema industry. When we did reach a consensus and a new set of lower tariffs, (some new "zero for zero" agreements, and some new understandings on various aspects of trade in services, intellectual property and trade related investment) we were able to unveil these successes only hours before our bosses, our heads of government, landed at Narita airport and headed downtown to participate in the summit. To this day, one wonders what our heads of government would have celebrated if we had not struggled to achieve some sort of agreement, hours before, in the Quad trade ministers meeting.

This writer's prime minister asked this minister to informally reflect on this to the other heads of government in Tokyo's heavily guarded, ornate oddly French-style chateau in which the summit was held. This writer found seven jet-lagged and slightly bored, but visibly relieved heads of government.[17] This writer's argument was that the agreements reached during the previous night's trade minister Quad meeting be adopted if we were to bring the Uruguay Round to any sort of satisfactory conclusion. The prime minister recalled that they were listening to the sole minister present at the summit who had been also present at the launch of the Uruguay Round seven years earlier. The presentation recounted the effort that countless officials, ministers, and heads of government had put into this round over these past seven years. Then this writer offered the view that the global economy would suffer a severe psychological shock if this round was not successfully concluded along the lines of what had been agreed up to the night before the summit meeting. The argument was evident. Compromises had been made; interrelationships had been worked out; complicated nuances of understanding had evolved hard and soft law; transitions had been worked out. All would be painfully difficult, perhaps even more time-consuming to duplicate, if the round failed; it was time for all governments to make some sacrifices politically to bring the round to a successful conclusion. Their meeting at the summit level would risk being described as a failure if they could not back up what we ministers had concluded the day before.

Mere hours later, the agreements hammered out in that trade ministers' Quad meeting were accepted by the G7 heads of government. Vital momentum crucial to concluding the round was secured. Brinkmanship through unilateralism followed a few months later when the United States Congress imposed a deadline for the Clinton administration to reach agreement by the end of 1993. American and EC bilateral negotiations were required to address the demands of the French farmers and moviemakers, unlocking a stalemate left over as an unfinished piece of business from the Tokyo summit from months earlier.

In essence, this minister's argument was that the amount of *effort* that had gone into the round up to then justified its existence. Its failure would cause great psychological shock to world financial and trade markets. Today, many observers have little doubt that these fears are the reasons why the round was finally agreed to and why it was agreed to in member legislatures. The 1994 conclusion of the round is an imperfect document, but it had to be signed for fear of the danger to "free market" economies of not signing it. As Carlisle puts it:

> To be sure, the result of the Round was to stimulate more trade among the United States, Japan, Europe, Canada, Asia, Latin America and emerging countries. It has left a robust "built-in agenda" of further work. [18]

Varieties of Economic and Capitalist Development

If the initiative almost seven years later (early in 2000) by Japan, some European countries and Mike Moore (the WTO director general) to accomplish a zero tariff and quota-free access for developing country exports to developed countries succeeds, then developing countries will find better access to industrial economies and many industrial countries will find better access to each other's markets. However, the 1994 agreement finally signed in Marakesh, and the WTO that it envisions, did not offer automatic solutions on how to deal with the conflicts that will be produced by civil society groups or by institutional incompatibilities, let alone by the basic clashes of the various civilizations that comprise world trade. In practice, the WTO could increase institutional incongruities. It could in fact become a tool for the world's more Machiavellian trade managers to promote their own interests. The WTO, instead of becoming an instrument for reconciliation, may become an instrument for division.

For example, five long years before its 1998 national financial crisis, Japan's Ministry of International Trade and Industry released a report recommending that Tokyo make full use of the WTO's dispute settlement procedures against countries that have barriers against Japanese exports. In fact, the 1994 Japanese report, in evaluating the practices of trading partners in twelve areas, listed the United States as an unfair trader in ten of the twelve areas. Since the American domestic market is more openly visible than Japan's, the former may actually have an unfair disadvantage when the dispute settlement mechanisms of the WTO operate. China's economy is even more opaque than Japan's, and the WTO mechanisms are not designed to deal with an economic system that is defined by informal arrangements and is only lightly supervised by domestic law. (Developments in China will be explored later in this book.)

Japan and other major trading countries could very well take the moral high ground and accuse the United States of violating free trade rules. Later in this book we will examine the Super 301 provision in U.S. trade law. Now it is pertinent to recall that it is obvious Japan and the EC will object to any revival of the various emanations of the U.S. "Super 301" trade law or of any United States antidumping actions. Close examination shows a trend of the Japanese government countering American and European antidumping measures as a first priority. It is difficult not to agree with Karl van Wolferen's suggestion that Japanese officials will:

> Proceed in this manner, not because they are bad and must be
> taught the path of virtue, but because they consider it their task.
> Appeals to shared global common good, may make sense to them

individually, but as members of institutions whose mission it has long been to promote Japan's industrial fortunes, they cannot heed it. [19]

The Japanese challenge to the United States through the WTO is nothing new, yet an increasing number of countries are adopting its tools and tactics for the first time. The powerful new economies of East Asia, the fastest growing region in the world, follow the Japanese example and pose similar problems of institutional incompatibility when compared to the Anglo-American economies. Remember the West's incomprehension over the caning of an American youth for vandalism by Singapore authorities – was this not a clash of civilizations, and moreover, a clash of social institutions? While the western media generally portrayed the punishment as barbaric, Asian culture considered it just. The clash between East and West is also exacerbated, because both are at different stages of economic development and neither has the same capacity to weather exchange-rate crises and failures of major financial institutions.

Harvard scholar Peter Hall and others distinguish between two types of capitalist models. One, typified by the United States is the liberal capitalist model which sees the firm coordinating its relationship with financial sources, unions, vocational institutions and so on, through the market. He contrasts this model to "coordinated capitalist models" like those of Germany, Belgium, Japan and Korea, wherein the firm coordinates such relationships somewhat outside the market. He admits that these differences, even in capitalist economies, pose long run challenges for the WTO because they present different value systems.[20]

Adding further complexity to the ongoing WTO, China's new and fast-growing economic power still is controlled not by an entrepreneurial class, but by a powerful bureaucracy, a kind of "China Inc." wherein the fabric between the state corporate technocrats and the entrepreneurs is tight and difficult to unravel. (This is evolving and will be explained later in this book.) India too will soon be a key player in world trade, especially in computer services. Its more dirigiste economy will present challenges to the WTO. If entrepreneurial behavior and consumer welfare are the guiding principles in the Anglo-American economies, we should not presume all Asian countries, let alone the republics of the former Soviet bloc, to be driven by the same codes. The expectation that the WTO will eventually make open, liberal, market-mediated capitalists of all member countries is touching but naïve and very much in the second-image "solution" mode. Instead, the WTO may simply become a blind watchdog vis-à-vis cultural incompatibilities ineffectively enforcing clause-by-clause implementation of narrow, specific rules. This may or may not advance "third-image" rule-based transformations, or the international trade system.

The brute challenge to the WTO then is political. In the industrialized world, democratic governments will probably resist large pieces of their industrial structure being replaced by imports from foreign economic organizations, entities that are government subsidized and protected however noble the purpose.[21] Even somewhat statist Canada complained of Brazil to the WTO over precisely those reasons on the issue of aircraft manufacturing subsidies in 1999 and 2000. The WTO framework cannot possibly dissolve worldwide institutional and political cultural incompatibility, so the WTO is not to be blamed for all these varieties. Yet these gaps could mean that the WTO will fast become overburdened and little more than an acrimonious arena for countries' disputes (similar to the UN General Assembly), if the WTO cannot help governments effectively resolve disputes, taking into account the institutional differences among countries. Later we will examine bilateral or regional "safety valves" as an accompaniment to the WTO, enhancing its mandate and offering the organization some breathing room along with some measure of WTO potency. Perhaps the voluntarist has to be humbler in his or her ambitions for the WTO and focus too on bilateral and multilateral solutions at the regional level.

Chalmers Johnson and other scholars have isolated yet another stress on world trade, namely the "capitalist development state." In a very broad sense, the degree to which a given country will benefit from the Uruguay Round agreement will depend on the extent to which its economic future is tied to international trade. That is why so many East Asian economies were once seen as being among the biggest "winners." In 1980, this region accounted for about one-seventh of world trade. By the year 2000, the Australia-Japan Research Center predicted the proportion was likely to rise to one-third.

Developing countries can no longer count on industrialization through becoming platforms in *closed* domestic markets. Until a decade or so ago, this type of industrialization was possible because GATT was not only an economic entity, but also a Cold War institution with a higher political purpose, namely the victory of "mixed economies" and of "capitalism" over "communism." Certain concessions were allowed for the sake of that victory (for developing countries, in particular). However, the fruit of these wide latitudes was enjoyed not only by developing nations. Potential trade frictions between the United States and Japan were held in check for many years because of the latter's importance to the former as a Cold War ally. Thus, under the old GATT system, the end of the Cold War increased a number of global trade conflicts, most often with the United States and/or Europe on one side and one or more East Asian nations on the other. The emergence of this new East-West division became a source of concern to many East Asians. There are various explanations for this disparity, these have less to do with any "clash of civilizations" than with gaps between what Chalmers Johnson calls stages in development of capitalism.

Asia was slow to adjust to the new post Cold War world. Many East Asian countries were victims of either foreign armed confrontation or of internal subversion during the Cold War era. These memories seared into the popular conscience. For example, it is an adjustment for many South Koreans to shift their perception of the United States as a protective "big brother" to that of a possible economic competitor.

Most successful economies in East Asia, with the exception of Hong Kong and Singapore, are characterized by a much greater degree of state intervention, a less open domestic market and a lower level of welfare provisions than the advanced Western economies. This is why Chalmers Johnson coined the term "capitalist developmental state" to describe this type of policy. Among Western countries, Germany most closely resembles the East Asian model of development, except in the area of welfare provision.

In fact, most contrasts between Western and East Asian economies are more likely the result of a particular stage of economic development. An example of this disparity is East Asia's reputation for weak protection of intellectual property rights. In the nineteenth century, the United States had a similarly poor reputation, particularly in regard to Britain. English novelists such as Trollope and Dickens complained about American pirating of their books through unauthorized reprints. Patents on industrial machinery were no better protected among Western traders. Later in the century however, when the United States began to overtake Britain in key industrial sectors, intellectual property protection gradually improved. "Capitalist developmental states" will find themselves incapable of maintaining their impervious nature. Although their intricate corporate /government bureaucracies do not adapt to changes quickly, they will have to change or lose competitive advantage. Moreover, their ability to mobilize and channel national resources – raw materials and skills – will no longer be a permanent advantage. When individual factors of production can be accessed by other countries, and brought together almost anywhere, a company's global reach will become far more important to its competitive position than will a strong national base. Under these circumstances, the "capitalist developmental state" will start to adapt in order to follow the changing tides of worldwide competition. The door will be open then for more transparent policy realignment and perhaps more dispute settlement at the bilateral level, as well as at the WTO level.

The question is regularly raised then by Fred Bergsten and his colleagues at the Institute for International Economics in Washington: Why argue at all for bilateral or regional agreements when there is a potentially super ordinate world trade organization in place to manage all trade issues?[22] The answer may lie in the fact that citizens recognize legitimate "regions" more readily than an abstract world organization. One notes that the communiqués from WTO meetings are tentative and cautious about extending the WTO to include agreements regarding labor and the environment. The underlying political consensus at the global level simply has not been present to allow this extension. The potential genius of NAFTA, for example, is that it allows for regional free trade and it can strengthen the social cohesion in the region through side agreements on labor and the environment. "Regions," it is argued, such as those in NAFTA, can then maintain political and social integrity and can be influenced by the disciplines of competition. (However, critics argue there has been little recent effort to expand this region under the auspices of NAFTA until President Fox of Mexico and U.S. President George W. Bush called for more expansion after their elections in 2000.) The European community is cited as a model in this regard, particularly by those who first championed the Treaty of Rome forty years ago. Goldsmith, for example, wrote against global free trade but supported a European Community. He felt that there is social integrity *and* competitiveness in such a community. Moreover, he wrote, this type of model promotes the development of organized social obligations.

Rolf Dahrendorf, in his *A Precarious Balance: Economic Opportunity, Civil Society and Political Liberty*[23] argues that all Western societies are at risk because there is a considerable tension between the competitive demands imposed by globalization and the need to maintain social cohesion for a civil society. Civil society, he stresses, is one in which "the people behave toward each other in a civilized manner" and in which all members enjoy the "status of citizens" with all it entails. In feudal times, for example, this meant that one was a member of the kingdom; after the French Revolution it meant "fraternity" as a member of the new republic; and in old Tory traditions, as traced by Samuel Beer,[24] it meant that each citizen had his or her place as part of what Edmond Burke called an "organic society." Civil society, says Dahrendorf, "describes the associations" and feelings in which we conduct our lives to meet our needs and initiatives rather than to the state.

The problem was perhaps overdramatized in Seattle in December 1999. The problem however persists that in the United States and in other Western societies today, the threat of globalization is basically the fear of social exclusion. This isolation is manifest not only in the growing inequality between those at the "bottom" and those at the "top," but also in the increase in long-term unemployment. Countless people are excluded as the economy grows without them. They in turn become costs as opposed to benefits for societies based on the pure "market model." This results in increased social tension. If people have no sense of belonging or purpose, they have little reason to observe the law or its founding values.

Until the collapse of Asian currencies and the resulting shocks to financial markets in 1998, tensions were further compounded in wealthy Euro-Western societies by those who felt excluded as wealth seeped out of Western states to the Pacific Rim and to other countries. One sensed daily in North American and British political life the resentment felt by those working for low wages toward welfare recipients because of the latter's access to dental and medical care, subsidized housing, etc. Another example of this kind of resentment would be the feelings of employed women who may have postponed the decision to have children for fear of losing their place in the work force toward single welfare mothers. Welfare mothers have been referred to as "queue jumpers who have managed to have it both ways, who can enjoy children without having to worry about financial security."[25]

An equally strong tension in industrialized societies is the tendency of those who do pay taxes to resent "special interests" and loud pressure groups. Theodore Lowi in the United States, and many political scientists in Europe and Canada, have noted how the media in developed economies romanticize strikes, labor "action days," political rallies and other acts of civil disobedience; a tendency that fueled resentment by the silent taxpaying majority against those who are challenging the norms of civil society. All of this adds to the political fever pitch ignited by these issues, even in richer societies. "Globalization" may or may not be the politicians' alleged perpetrator of this stream of implications.

This indignation is heightened by an impatience many feel toward the *victims* of civil society. Robert Hughes resents the "whining" tone that has surfaced in the United States in particular, increasing still more resentment against the victims:

> The range of victims available ten years ago – Blacks, Chicanos, Indians, women, homosexuals – has now expanded to include every permutation of the halt, the blind, the lame and the short – or to put it correctly the differently-abled, the other-visioned and the vertically challenged. Never before in human history were so many acronyms pursuing identity. It's as though all human encounters were one big sore spot, inflamed with opportunities to unwillingly give and ungratefully receive. [26]

What do these waves of resentment occurring even in developed economies have to do with global trade? It reminds us of political forces –

it reminds us of first image forces. It reminds us of the political reality that can be exploited by cynical realists playing on the fears of those who feel marginalized, which, of course, is classic "first-image" strategy. It also reminds us not to neglect sources of social legitimacy before throwing all of our hopes to the WTO before its legitimacy is credibly established. One safety valve might be regional trade agreements. Regional free trade, along with credible settlement of disputes that does not exclude any region from trading with the rest of the world, has a legitimacy at present that globalists might wish to recognize. There is little possibility of every region opening its markets to every product with blatant disregard for the effect that trade will have on a region's economy, employment or its effect on the stability of society. The millennium WTO round will certainly test the limits of this possibility.

The fears of exclusion and inequality both nationally and among nations has not dissipated since the "successful" conclusion of the Uruguay Round. In Uruguay in 1986, in Montreal at the mid-term GATT ministerial meeting in 1990, and at the conclusive Quad meeting at the G7 Summit in July 1993 one saw many examples of deeply engrained restraints against over-hearty globalization. These restraints still exist despite the uneasy truce known as the "successful Uruguay Round." The scaffolding of dispute settlement in the WTO has been working moderately well as chapters 4 and 5 will demonstrate. It can be made to work better but should be overburdened?

When it comes to the impact of the WTO on lesser developed countries (LDCs), it appears that an unwritten consensus exists not to overburden LDCs in the early years of the WTO. It should be acknowledged that the WTO may turn out to be a less harsh enforcer on developing economies than for other countries. Trade policy and trade disciplines should not be viewed as fully regulated in practice by the GATT and the WTO, even for developed economies since national trade agencies can generate multiple and incompatible interpretation readings of GATT/WTO informal and formal GATT settlements.

Most trade scholars conclude therefore that merely identifying some important sovereignty values does not, by itself, provide a persuasive argument justifying panel review deferential to domestic agencies. This essential third-image advance will be explored in a later chapter. Still a balance must be struck between national authorities' interests in protecting their sovereignty on the one side and the broader gains of international coordination on the other. A reasonable, nuanced approach by WTO panels is important for the credibility of the global trade forum's dispute settlement system, and such an approach will lessen the dangers of inappropriate unilateral reactions by governments and citizen constituencies.

Christina Sevilla's research shows that the selection of complaints for litigation, out of a universe of possible complaints, is subject to a complex political process of demand by private producers and supply by governments. The result of this process is that the "rules of multilateral trade agreements are unevenly enforced."[27] She found that, of 295 GATT complaints against all parties from 1948 to 1994, 250 were against the Quad developed nations (EC 127; United States 83; Japan 22; and Canada 18). LDCs accounted for only 24. This means five-sixths of the complaints were brought against the Quad countries who comprise but half of world imports and exports.

Like the illegal parking of poor owners' automobiles in a fairly forgiving or "political" jurisdiction, not all infractions of GATT rules by states become subject to complaint, let alone sanctioned. In fact, despite the specter of a heartless "globalization" phenomenon crushing developing countries, the "largest countries in world trade may be more constrained in a de facto sense by their GATT/WTO obligations across sectors than the smaller, especially the smallest countries, contrary to the expectations of most theories of international relations."[28] Sevilla shows that the industrialized countries refrained from using coercive tactics prior to the dispute settlement stage in a systematic fashion to hold LDCs to the GATT obligations which they did undertake. She finds that large states have accounted for 86 perent of all complaints over the four decades of GATT's operation.

Thus, she assesses the number of underlying treaty violations by poorer countries to be arguably greater than the frequency of formal complaints against them.[29] Perhaps a realist compromise exists – unwritten, unacknowledged – that developing countries are to be spared some of the bite of early WTO experience so as to encourage their eventual buy-in.

In 1986 at Punta del Este, Brazil and India became integral parts of the trading community. This writer remembers how these countries challenged progress on goods and services, trade liberalization and intellectual property protection, presenting themselves almost proudly as culturally protectionist. Today, Brazil has altered course. In 1992, India made an about-face on its previously protectionist posture as exemplified by its "anti-multinational" poster campaigns up to then. The social and political implications of globalization are felt not only there but by all elected officials.

In the U.S.-Canada negotiations leading to the free trade agreement there were many shared interests, cultural affinities and geographical and geopolitical similarities among the two countries. These helped the negotiations to proceed. Still, as mentioned earlier, Canadian (and some American) media, in a period of relative prosperity in North America, (1986-88) obsessed about the "potential job losses" and "threats to sovereignty" rooted in the proposed FTA. An encouraging result from the FTA in Canada for example, such as for the auto-parts industry or the red meat cattle industry or the skilled Canadian high-tech and software industries, were buried as backpage items in the business pages in Canada. Only "threats" and "job losses" received front-page attention. Still, the agreement was signed, the government that supported it was reelected in 1988 and the general efficacy of the agreement is now seldom questioned by the Liberal party that opposed it. Ironically, American protectionists who complained about the agreement are now criticized by the very media that once doubted the FTA. The lesson to be learned here is that a strong regional base can bring credibility to the international base. It is vital to bring some regional and bilateral sustenance to the project if the worldwide trade movement is to help the majority of Earth's people. The FTA and NAFTA chapters will explore this. First, let us move to mechanics and examine how robust is the WTO's dispute settlement mandate and experience.

Notes

1. Ernst-Ulrich Petersmann, "The Dispute Settlement System of the World Trade Organization and the Evolution of the GATT Dispute Settlement System Since 1945," *Common Market Law Review* 31 (1994): 1161.

2. Op. cit., 1160.

3. Op. cit., 1160.

4. Patrick James Buchanan, *The Great Betrayal* (Blake Pub., New York 1997), 23.

5. *New York Times*, 31 December 1995, 10.

6. Ibid., 10

7. Ibid., 10

8. James Goldsmith, *The Trap* (Center for the Study of Democratic Institutions, London: 1995), 45.

9. Ibid., 40.

10. Ibid., 30.

11. See John Ralston Saul, *The Unconscious Civilization* (Free Press, Toronto 1995), Part III.

12. Andrew Coyne, *Globe and Mail,* 7 November 1995, 14(A).

13. Ibid.

14. Saul, Op. cit., 152.

15. Ibid., 151.

16. Charles R. Carlisle, "Is the World Ready for Free Trade?" *Foreign Affairs* (November-December 1996): 115.

17. Including newly elected President Clinton, Prime Minister John Major and Kim Campbell and veterans President Mitterand and Chancellor Kohl.

18. Carlisle, Op. cit., 116.

19. *Washington Post*, 30 December 1994, 18.

20. Peter Hall, in Kitschelt et al., 137.

21. Regardless of John R. Saul's argument in Part III, see note 11.

22. C. Fred Bergsten, "Globalization and Free Trade," *Foreign Affairs* (May-June 1996): 105-20.

23. Rolf Dahrendorf, *A Precarious Balance: Economic Opportunity, Civil Society and Political Liberty* (Central European University Press, New York 1992).

24. Samuel Beer, *British Politics in the Collectivist Age* (W.W. Norton & Company, New York 1968).

25. *Toronto Star*, 30 September 1995, 4(B).

26. Robert Hughes, *The Politics of Resentment* (Oxford University Press 1993), 33.

27. See Christina Sevilla of Harvard University Monograph on this in 1998.

28. Ibid.

29. Ibid.

Part II

The Mechanics

Chapter Four

How WTO Disputes Get Settled and the U.S. Scorecard

Third Image Advances with Second Image Compromises

In the waning months of 2000, it was reported (*Herald Tribune* Oct. 23, 2000) that the WTO's dispute-settlement mechanism had received since its inception in 1994, two hundred and eight complaints stemming from one hundred and sixty-five cases. By the end of 2000 most of them were in various stages of consultation, review or appeal. Only sixteen had been resolved and another twenty-six were being implemented.

The American nightmare is this: Has member failure to settle and comply damaged the dispute-settlement system and is it suggesting to existing members and future members such as China, that the dispute-settlement system is either not working or is not producing "the final word on trade spats" as the *Herald Tribune* report put it? In this study we ask the same question about NAFTA. The news about both the WTO and NAFTA is not yet nightmarish as we shall see but there is valid cause for concern.

The mechanism that makes trade agreements work day-to-day is the process called "dispute settlement." Perhaps one of the reasons the WTO has not yet been overwhelmed with disputes is that there are still lots of opportunities for political compromise outside of formal panels. The notion that the WTO solves everything like a juggernaut is an outlandish exaggeration. In cabinet dealings with some trade issues, one remembers asking oneself: "Why won't our public servants framing recommendations recommend pushing this issue to a formal FTA or NAFTA or GATT dispute settlement panel? Why not be vindicated by international panels? We, as a government of an industrialized nation need not worry too much about the legal costs. Let's vindicate ourselves in the multilateral forum."

Then, one remembers one's international relations reading and recalls that regardless of how strong the legal case of a middle power's, or super power's influence, it is not always wise – in the context of an internally accepted international system – to press every issue to a formally adjudicated conclusion. Achieving a multinational system that is both cohesive and united necessitates a thorough attempt at presettlement of differences before dispute settlement systems are brought out as a last resort. We will see in chapter 7 this is quintessentially a Chinese tradition.

The writings of Henry Kissinger and Stanley Hoffman do not share the popular American penchant for pushing all disputes to a litigated conclusion. They see that national interests depend on keeping an accepted international system. It is neither neighborly nor helpful to seek litigation over each and every event that one might consider to be offensive in some way. This same logic applies to a local neighborhood or a community of nations.

To be sure, it can be tempting to draw the litigious sword when suffused with a sense of the righteousness of one's case. However, if the legal processes are overused, the formal dispute resolution apparatus may crumble through overuse, regardless of your power against the offender. Let us examine the WTO with this in mind, recalling, of course, that to many cultures, as the relevant chapter on China will show, formal arbitration to achieve resolution is viewed as an embarrassment rather than a vindication.

The severest test to the WTO will not, in this writer's view, be its expansion through another millennium round, but the credibility of its mechanisms for settling disputes. Since the Dispute Settlement Understanding (DSU) was established to ensure fairness, consistency and compliance with "the process," member states do not vote to use it. There is no vote. Unilateral sanctions against a WTO contracting party are permitted when that party refuses to change trading action after the WTO panel has delivered a verdict against it. That said, a complaining party must first attempt to find a solution through consultation, conciliation or moderation before requesting a panel.

Section 301 allows the U.S. administration to unilaterally impose trade sanctions if it believes WTO determinations are being ignored by a WTO member. In spite of occasional unilateralism in its trade policy by its use of Section 301 trade threats, the United States generally has favored the WTO course for trade complaints over the imposition of unilateral trade sanctions. In its drive to increase auto exports to Japan in 1995, it threatened to file a WTO case. The United States also filed a WTO complaint against Japan's tightly controlled film industry, trying to pry open the Japanese market for American filmmakers in 1996. In 1997, the United States won a WTO case against Canada over a Canadian law demanding split-run magazines with Canadian content.

Clearly, it would be bogus to argue that the United States is not benefiting from GATT/WTO disciplines and panels. United States former trade negotiator Rufus Yerxa and Demetrios Marantis found in early 1998 that of the eight U.S.-backed cases to the beginning of 1997 which reached the stage of final panel decisions, the United States. had won seven.[1] The United States lost three decisions as a defendant, none of which led to the diminution of health, safety or environmental laws.

The new WTO dispute settlement process is less effective than the United States had hoped in attacking the more subtle forms of trade discrimination characteristic of Japan and other Asian markets. (One panel decision on Japanese measures regarding photographic film and paper represented a real setback for the United States.) Despite extensive evidence in the photography decision that Japanese government measures were intended to counteract the effects of trade liberalization, creating an environment in which domestic and imported film traveled through completely separate – and potentially inefficient – distribution channels, the panel found the evidence insufficient to support a claim of either *nonviolation* or denial of national treatment. In large part, the age of the measures in question became the pivotal issue. The panel found that, for most of the measures in place since the 1960s and 1970s, the United States could not claim a nullification and impairment of tariff concessions because it should have "reasonably anticipated" such measures by the time of the Tokyo and Uruguay Rounds. The panel was also clearly reluctant to draw conclusions about the real purpose and effect of many of the measures in question. It established a very high burden of proof for those wishing to show that government measures create "less favorable conditions of competition."

Notwithstanding that case, we have seen that when the United States was on the attack, WTO results were generally favorable for the United States. On the basis of the national treatment principle (GATT Article III), the United States was joined by the EU and Canada in challenging Japan's liquor tax regime, a system which levied a substantially lower tax (one-fourth to one-sixth) on Japanese shochu than on imports of whisky, cognac and spirits. The United States had obtained a GATT ruling against Japan's liquor taxes in 1987. At the time, however, the United States had little ability to enforce it.

Canada's measures applied to importation and sale of periodical magazines were deemed to be inconsistent with GATT rules on national treatment (Article III) and quantitative restrictions (Article XI). This was a significant victory for the United States (particularly for its "cultural industries") which had been unable to negotiate away these restrictions in both the U.S.-Canada Free Trade Agreement of 1988 and the NAFTA of

1994.

With regard to Argentine customs duties, the panel report upheld U.S. claims that certain duties on textile and apparel imports were in excess of Argentina's bound rate, contrary to GATT Article II, and that a statistical tax of 3 percent *ad valorem* violated GATT Article VIII.

On computer networking equipment, the United States brought a case after European Community customs authorities reclassified local area network (LAN) goods into a higher tariff category, nearly doubling the tariff on over $1 billion in U.S. exports. The panel found that the reclassification of goods in such a manner was inconsistent with the EC's GATT tariff commitments, as set forth in their schedules, in violation of GATT Article II.

The decision on the European Community banana regime upheld allegations by the United States, Ecuador, Honduras, Guatemala and Mexico that the EC's banana export regime violated a host of WTO obligations. In the India Mailbox case, the right of patent applicants in the pharmaceuticals and agriculture sectors to preserve exclusive marketing rights was upheld. The ruling also held that India had violated the TRIPs agreement by failing to establish a "mailbox" mechanism to receive and date patent applications and a system through which to grant exclusive marketing rights.

Another ruling assured that non-science based restrictions on agricultural products will be found to be contrary to the WTO Sanitary and Phyto-Sanitary (SPS) agreement. Although it seems to defy any sense of proportionality, two cases have brought the United States and the European community to the brink of a trade war (the first was over bananas, the second involved American and Canadian dispute settlement proceedings against EU measures which prohibit imports of meat and meat products treated with growth hormones). The United States, although not itself a banana exporting nation, claims the European Community regime favors fruit from former British and French colonies in Africa, the Caribbean and the Pacific, discriminating against American distributors of cheaper Latin American fruit (such as Chiquita Brands, headquartered in Cincinnati, Ohio). After two judgments against the regime before the new GATT/WTO was in place (both ignored), a WTO disputes panel found against the arrangement in late 1997. This finding must be enforced. The EC made some changes but the United States said they were insufficient. The United States promised to retaliate with sanctions later. As *Financial Times* columnist Guy de Jonquieres wrote in 1999:

> Even liberal internationally-minded Congress members say that unless the US prevails, already shaky popular and political support for the WTO will crumble further . . . Furthermore, the

dispute looks like a warm-up for a battle over the EU's ban on hormone-treated beef, against which the WTO has also ruled …Japan, long a target of aggressive US trade onslaughts, recently over steel, sided with the EU (in January, 1999) by leading 10 WTO members in a challenge to Washington's sanctions plans.[2]

This issue continued well into the new millennium and will be revisited later in chapter 5.

When the United States was a defendant, there were modest losses by the end of 1997. The three rulings against the United States found only slight problems and required only modest changes to adapt to WTO disciplines. Critics' Cassandra-like predictions that the dispute process would result in the wholesale invalidation of American sovereignty and the shredding of health, safety and consumer protection have not come true. Let us consider these.

The "gasoline" case, brought against the United States by Venezuela and Brazil, found certain aspects of the way the Environmental Protection Agency (EPA) calculated the baseline for foreign refined petroleum products to be a denial of national treatment. The case tested the U.S. commitment to live by the rules its own foreign policymakers had created. The U.S. administration modified the WTO-incompatible Gasoline Rule at the same time that it successfully portrayed the (negative) decision as upholding its freedom to protect the U.S. environment. To conform to the WTO ruling, the EPA changed its methodology to be trade neutral without any real diminution of environmental protection.

Two cases brought to the panel by Costa Rica and India, involving U.S. safeguard measures on textiles and apparel, led to the overruling of restrictions as violations of the WTO Agreement on Textiles and Clothing (ATC). For developing countries, these cases serve to reaffirm the utility of the WTO in challenging the trade practices of the big traders while providing much-needed evidence of the value of universal trading rules, particularly at a time when skeptical domestic audiences and critics in other countries believe that the WTO favors the United States. Neither case significantly impacted upon U.S. trade.

Two areas stand out as major sources of future disputes: antidumping policy and sanctions policy. Exporting countries are likely to be active in challenging U.S. determinations of trade law. However, officials of the U.S. Department of Commerce and the International Trade Commission are well aware of the new antidumping rules and have extensively considered how to conform their rulings with WTO obligations. Further, many other countries, developed and developing nations alike, are now beginning to use antidumping measures. Any decisions limiting U.S. flexibility will also limit theirs.

The use of trade sanctions for non-trade objectives raises significant WTO problems. National security exceptions will not be effectively controlled by the WTO system. In the end, these matters will rest more on diplomatic relations than trade rules. GATT Article XX recognizes an exception for measures relating to the conservation of exhaustible natural resources. However, decisions interpreting Article XX strongly indicate that application of such measures, on the grounds that a country is protecting natural resources outside its own territory, will not qualify for the exception.

Yerxa and Marantis conclude the following:

1. The United States has used both the treatment of disputes and the filing of cases in an effective manner to obtain some important results for exporters and to create valuable precedents.

2. The film decision demonstrates the limited utility of WTO rules in attacking certain kinds of nontariff barriers which are deeply imbedded in some Asian economies.

3. The predictions that U.S. health, safety and environmental laws would be shredded by the new WTO agreements have proven to be untrue, and even the cases the United States has lost suggest that it can maintain such safeguards in the absence of unnecessary trade discrimination.

The Uruguay Rounds' Integrated Legal System and Its Implications

The determination of which side wins a formally resolved dispute between parties is crucial to the parties involved, but only incidental to the trading system as a whole – unless, of course, major parties to the world-wide agreement are seen back home to be losing too many battles on too many key issues. It is vital to the furtherance of international comity that a plurality of opportunities exist to resolve disputes outside the formal dispute resolution process. How does the WTO system work exactly? Is there room for not only resolutions that are perceived to be fair but also for preformal settlement?

The agreement in Marrakech is where the WTO was launched. It outlines the dispute settlement understanding of the Uruguay Round which established the WTO in 1994.[3] This agreement does not topple, it enshrines the regional models for dispute settlement (e.g., NAFTA), as well as WTO-supervised consultation stages, expedited negotiation stages and other settlements reached in conjunction with one of the WTO's facilitation mechanisms. It also explicitly permits settlement opportunities under non-WTO mechanisms – such as NAFTA or bilateral discussions (i.e., U.S. -China, U.S.-Japan).[4]

By replacing the separate international regulations of transnational movements of goods, services, persons and investments by a new worldwide "integrated" legal system, the WTO agreement lays the legal foundation for a new international economic order for the twenty-first century. As noted earlier, the most radical innovation of the WTO agreement is its "single undertaking approach" which aims to develop an integrated, more viable and durable multilateral trading system encompassing the General Agreement of Tariffs and Trade, the result of past trade liberalization efforts, all the results of the Uruguay Round of multilateral trade negotiations," and the Agreement on Trade-Related Intellectual Property Rights (TRIPs). By integrating the thirty Uruguay Round agreements and about 200 previous GATT agreements into one single legal framework, the WTO agreement reduces the current fragmentation of separate international agreements and organizations for movements of goods, services, persons, capital and payments. GATT itself was not recognized as an institution under international law, and now no longer exists. The WTO, on the other hand, is most definitely recognized, and has essentially replaced the GATT system.

In a move initiated by Japan, some European countries and Mike Moore, director general of the WTO, a package was put together in March 2000 for 48 of the least developed countries giving them tariff-free and quota-free access to developed countries. This package is seen as an attempt to convince LDCs to support the millennium round.

During the Uruguay Round of multilateral trade negotiations in GATT (1986-1994), many developing countries played a very active role and engaged in far-reaching programs of trade deregulation. In the words of Europe's most prominent and prolific trade scholar Ernst Petersmann, the WTO requirements of substantive GATT concessions, and of acceptance of essentially all Uruguay Round results by all WTO member countries (Articles XI, XII and XIV of the WTO agreement), "promotes more freedom, more rule of law and more welfare through a more efficient use of domestic resources in all countries."[5] The gist of these understandings and agreements is to give further precision to and strengthen the previous existing general GATT rules, especially with regard to agricultural, textiles and "grey area" trade restrictions (e.g., voluntary export restraints) which have escaped effective GATT legal disciplines for a long time.

The Uruguay Round Agreement contains a new accord on dispute settlement which is formally called: "The Understanding on Rules and Procedures Governing the Settlement of Disputes," known as the "Integrated

Dispute Settlement Procedure." The agreement comprises improvements of the GATT dispute settlement procedure, as well as a substantial number of new reforms intended to make the old GATT dispute settlement much more effective.

In the past, the dispute settlement procedure could proceed only if all GATT members were in agreement, meaning that the defending government had the power to stop the dispute settlement procedure at any time. Under the Uruguay Round Agreement, the procedure moves forward automatically at the request of the complaining government. Panels are created, the panel's ruling are legally binding, and if the ruling is not obeyed, the right to retaliate is automatic. How did this revolution of automaticity come about? Clearly, the hard-nosed American "realist" application of Section 301 drove other key nations to accept this revolution. This format appealed to GATT members because Section 301 requires the president of the United States to take action unilaterally against other GATT countries who are deemed to be impairing U.S. legal rights. Even if the legal complaints of the United States were justified, the unilateral procedures followed by the United States appeared to violate GATT law by the use of section 301 trade sanctions. When the United States broadened and strengthened this law significantly in 1988 by adopting a new "Super 301," "Special 301" and "Telecom 301," other GATT governments concluded that stronger action was needed to curb this new surge of American unilateralism. One might justify this United States use of realist muscle because it brought about a "third-image" international benefit.

The United States justified its unilateral actions on the grounds that the pre-1994 GATT dispute settlement procedure was neither strong nor rapid enough to provide satisfactory remedies. Like links in a chain reaction, the other GATT governments proposed a bargain under which the GATT would make its dispute settlement system strong and rapid enough to satisfy the criteria of Section 301 and cause the United States to promise, quid pro quo, that the GATT would adjudicate all its appropriate legal complaints, rather than try to resolve them unilaterally. To quote the understanding:

> When members seek the redress of a violation of obligation . . .
> (or of related legal claims), they shall have recourse to, and abide
> by, the rules and procedures of this Understanding.[6]

Any government may submit a legal complaint against another government or governments, and no limitations are stated in the agreement.

In the past, the defendant government often sought to delay adjudication of the legal complaint through a long process of consultation. Now, under the WTO, if the consultations do not yield a resolution of the dispute within sixty days, the complaining government can hasten the process by requesting the appointment of a panel. The WTO membership must authorize the creation of a panel within about two months, and the members of the panel must be appointed within twenty days. The panel must then decide the case within six months, or nine at the most.

The Uruguay Round Agreement also provides that, if both governments agree, the conflict may be submitted to alternative forms of dispute resolution such as mediation, conciliation or "good offices." These alternative procedures are entirely voluntary and may be stopped whenever either party wishes. If these procedures fail, the complaining country may still seek a legal ruling from a panel.

A GATT panel consists of three individuals drawn from the GATT delegations of governments with no immediate interest in the dispute. Although panel members are government officials, they are instructed to serve in their "individual capacity." which means that they must give their own expert opinion; and they are not allowed to accept instruction from their governments. One or more of the panel members can be a private citizen who is an expert in GATT law.

Panels are assisted by officials of the secretariat. The secretariat advisors usually include one officer from the Legal Affairs Office of the secretariat and one other officer from the division of the secretariat responsible for the substantive areas for example, the Agriculture Division if the complaint involves an agricultural product. The secretariat advisors are expected to provide research, historical information, assistance on legal issues and help with drafting. In practice, secretariat advisors can exert a substantial influence on panel decisions.

Panels receive written legal briefs from the parties. Oral hearings are conducted where the parties argue their positions and the panel questions the parties. Panel rulings are then submitted privately to the involved government parties who are given an opportunity to comment. The panel then has an opportunity to revise the ruling in consideration of the comments. The final ruling is then released to the full WTO membership.

The revision of Article 16 (4) provides that the losing party no longer has the right to block the adoption of legal rulings, however, the winning party now has the right to block a decision rejecting the ruling. In effect, the panel's ruling were meant to be automatically binding. The agreement further provides that a panel's legal ruling can be appealed to an "appellate body," which will hear and rule upon any claim of legal error within sixty days. The ruling of this body is immediately adopted within thirty days unless the GATT membership unanimously decides against it. However, the devil appears in the smoke of post-ruling details. The ruling can be appealed, and the losing party's response after an appeal can appear so weak that the winning party feels thoroughly shortchanged. Trade sanction threats are thus brought out to force a more adequate response, as seen in the banana dispute.

The appellate body consists of seven individuals who serve for four years and can be reappointed once. The seven members must be private citizens, and not affiliated with any government, and possess recognized authority in the subject matter of the GATT agreements while being "broadly representative of the membership of GATT." The appellate body must have a staff independent of the staff of ordinary panels.

Before 1994, most GATT legal rulings were respected. Yet in a small, significant number of cases, the losing party was able to delay compliance indefinitely. To satisfy the requirements of the Section 301 law in the United States, the WTO dispute settlement procedure had to contain an automatic procedure for dealing effectively with noncompliance.

The agreement established a sequence of enforcement steps all of them tested to the limit in the EC-U.S. dispute over bananas, which will be recounted later.

The first step is to define the amount of time allowed for the losing party to comply. This should not exceed fifteen months from the date the legal ruling becomes final. If compliance does not occur within that time the losing party is given another twenty days to negotiate compensation acceptable to the winning party. If compensation negotiations fail, the winning party is free to retaliate. The agreement established a binding arbitration procedure for resolving issues that may arise over the correctness of the retaliatory measures proposed. If these procedures work as designed, the winning party cannot be prevented from retaliating if compliance does not occur within a reasonable time.

This issue was particularly important to developing countries who did not want cross retaliation. The Uruguay Round Agreement established a preference for retaliation to say a non-goods agreement, if the complainant can demonstrate that same-sector requital is "not practicable." It appears that in the new WTO, the few instances of insufficient compliance (pre-1994) still exist if both winning and losing parties fundamentally disagree about the adequacy of the losing parties' response to a WTO ruling. As a result, Section 301-type retaliation is still a part of the international trade landscape.

Scope of the Integrated Procedure

The new dispute settlement procedure defined in the Uruguay Round agreement applies to all the mutual understandings contained in the Final Act, including the agreement establishing the World Trade Organization. (See Appendix B of this book for authoritative sources on all WTO panels).

One of the most important provisions strengthening the new dispute settlement procedure is Article 26, which allows the GATT to extend the scope of its law beyond the specific legal obligations created by GATT agreements. It allows the WTO to provide a remedy in cases where a perfectly legal action nonetheless impairs the "reasonable expectations" of another government. Decisions about reasonable expectations can involve subjective judgements. The Uruguay Round Agreement applies its rigorous new procedures to these nonviolation complaints as well. Panel judgements about "reasonable expectations" are automatically binding.

The most troublesome complaints under Section 301 law have been those from the United States against measures that were GATT-legal, but were unreasonable and unacceptable from the American point of view. In order to obtain U.S. agreement to submit these claims of unreasonable behavior to GATT dispute settlement, GATT governments promised a third-image discipline in the Uruguay Round that there would be effect automatic remedies in these nonviolation cases as well.

The complete Uruguay Round contains two "third-image" parts that purport to address the original concerns that prompted the establishment of Section 301 retaliations. The first issue applies to each U.S. claim of an allegation of legal violation or an allegation of nonviolation nullification and impairment all covered by GATT Article XXIII. In respect to such complaints, the United States has undertaken an unqualified obligation to pursue the complaint through the GATT dispute settlement procedure and to abide by the ensuing results, including the provisions of governments of when and how retaliation may be used. The only way to escape this commitment is to confess that a complaint has no GATT legal basis at all. Pre-war international trade was bedeviled when tariff reductions, even if reciprocal, were effectively nullified or impaired by other dramatically engineered schemes such as governments subsidizing production or putting nontariff barriers in place. These are now known as "violation complaints" because they impede attainment of the trade agreement objectives or nullify or impair benefits that can be expected from the agreement. These comprised a significant proportion of complaints.

If a country decided to pursue a complaint without going to WTO dispute settlement, it suffers one of two legal consequences. First, if its complaint rests on a GATT claim, it will be committing a direct violation of the dispute settlement agreement, which is itself a binding obligation. Second, if it seeks to avoid GATT dispute settlement by stipulating that there is no GATT legal basis to its complaint, it will be confessing that any trade retaliation it is planning to take has no GATT justification. This confesses that any such trade action is GATT-illegal.

Has the "third-image" legal-momentum school won a solid and

permanent victory? There will be challenges from political opportunists (first image) and national political elites (second image). It could be, however, that, just as the agreement is partly the result of realist "second-image" maneuvering the new system's stability will likely need, for domestic political reasons, some room for these maneuvers. Indeed, it is dangerous to think that all political contexts require WTO dispute settlement. These "contexts of noncompliance" can sometimes be managed in other ways – but not always.

Member parties now have the opportunity to resolve disputes among themselves, while still operating under the guidance and supervision of the larger agreement. Through these provisions, member nations have garnered far more control over their own international trading systems than was even permitted under the abortive provisions of the 1947 General Agreement on Tariffs and Trade. The distinction between the provisions for party-oriented dispute resolution in GATT 1947 and the 1994 DSU will be evaluated. Finally, there will be a brief examination of how WTO members may employ party-driven dispute resolution under the auspices of non-WTO trade agreements while still operating under WTO rules. This will be demonstrated by showing how regional deregulated trade agreements (like NAFTA) can work in tandem with the WTO to help parties find reasonable trade solutions.

The original conceptualization of the GATT in 1947 is far from the final manner in which it eventually emerged in 1994. Historically, the GATT was supposed to be part of a larger trade body, the International Trade Organization (ITO). As John Jackson succinctly observes:

> The original intention was for GATT to be placed in the institutional setting of the ITO, and the draft ITO charter called for a rigorous dispute settlement procedure which contemplated effective use of arbitration (not always mandatory, however), and even appeal to the World Court, in some circumstances.[7]

Since the ITO never emanated, the GATT parties were left only the rules laid out in the GATT document of 1947 so far as dispute resolution was concerned.

Dispute settlement in GATT 1947 was limited to Articles XXII and XXIII. It is the first of these, Article XXII, that provides for some ability by individual parties to control disputes autonomously within the agreement. In Article XXII.1, the parties are obligated to "afford adequate opportunity for consultation" to other parties in the accord, regarding matters affecting the GATT. Article XXIII.2 gives parties the ability to consult other contracting parties of the GATT regarding issues unresolved under XXII.1. These provisions contrast with the modern provisions found in the 1994 WTO Dispute Settlement Understanding (DSU). The GATT 1947 provisions are extremely open-ended obligations, and they have been definitively revised in the intent of a more practical application, under the 1994 DSU.

In fact, the 1994 agreement built upon the 1947 foundation by creating a far more integrated dispute resolution mechanism. The DSU incorporates Articles XXII and XXIII of GATT 1947, except as modified by the new accord: the alterations are more than cosmetic. The DSU possesses a specificity lacking in the GATT 1947, both in the terms of resolution tools and the time limits in which to exercise them, that is available to the parties. The following is an explanation of the DSU provisions, primarily applying to party-oriented dispute resolution, with a brief explanation of the panel system used by parties that are either unsuccessful, or unwilling to pursue dispute solutions agreeable to all players involved.

Governing over the dispute resolutions process of GATT 1994 is the Dispute Settlement Body (DSB). The panel system employed in the GATT 1947 continues to be used in a modified format. Member parties are guided toward panel evaluations if efforts at resolution among the parties fail to meet deadlines. This new panel system seeks quick determination of results, as opposed to the GATT 1947 procedure:

> [T]ime limits for forming a panel, conducting a panel review, and issuing findings are reduced to ensure that disputes do not languish and that WTO violations are remedied more quickly. [8]

It is worthwhile to note that the total time for delivery of an award, including appeal, has been changed from "indefinite" to fifteen to twenty months, including the consultation period.

Trade disputes among nations are increasing, While this may be in spite of multilateral accords, it seems that just as many disputes arise among trade treaty partners. United States membership in both the WTO and the NAFTA has not prevented Canada and the United States from bitter trade disputes over products such as cold-rolled steel, wheat and softwood lumber. While the GATT 1947 did provide some limited opportunities for contracting parties to resolve disputes themselves, GATT 1994 has expanded on these opportunities for "realist informal calculation of advantage" outside of formal dispute settlement panels.

Consultation, Conciliation Arrangements in the WTO

The WTO of 1994 encourages more harmonious trade relationships by attempting to end a dispute among the parties at the early stages of conflict, through a consultation process. While the DSU's new regimented panel decision system will provide greater certainty to the contracting parties, it still fails to guarantee that the disputants will be able to return to a positive trade relationship. The entire rationale behind dispute resolution mechanisms in trade agreements is the preservance of positive trade relationships. WTO member parties now have the opportunity to resolve a problem among themselves first, before moving to a full panel enquiry. While nothing guarantees this process will result in a successful settlement, the DSU recognizes the benefits of "prompt settlement of situation . . . to the effective functioning of the WTO and the maintenance of a proper balance between the rights and obligations of Members."[9]Though the new rules do make for faster panel decisions, the resolution of disputes by parties acting independent of the panel scheme is intended to ensure faster and more agreeable results for all concerned. What matters is ongoing positive trade relations between disputants, not who wins or loses in any particular dispute.

Among the powers in the jurisdictional scope of the DSB is the administration of the consultation as well as the formal panel dispute resolution processes. By joining both the formal and informal aspects of dispute resolution found in GATT 1994 under one supervisory body, the WTO writers ensured that one method of resolution would not take precedence over another. To ensure the success of the informal negotiations, the parties are free to find the most appropriate solution. The DSU helps centralize the process by demanding that members who come to a "mutually agreed solution" within the confines of the consultation process report their outcome to the DSB. This step will notify the other WTO members of the resolution of the dispute, and help shed light on the methodology used to achieve a jointly amenable solution. The panels composed under the GATT 1947 have developed a repertoire of decisions over the years, and it is likely that a similar corpus of negotiated solutions will become part of the WTO information base. In light of this knowledge, it is realistic to expect that the process will yield better access to members to the successful resolution of disputes while still in their embryonic stages, before they have an opportunity to grow.

The DSU makes it clear, in the text of Marrakesh, that "a solution mutually acceptable to the parties to a dispute...is clearly to be preferred." This reminds members that awards given to one party in favor of another will receive as much support as an agreement where both sides have made some concessions. Further, the general provisions of the DSU mandates a "good faith" approach to be taken by all members in respect to disputes, specifically demanding that "requests for conciliation . . . should not be intended or considered as [a] contentious act." This understanding should act as a reminder that negotiated settlements are viewed as promoting trading relationships in the long run as much as formal panel decisions. With these imperatives fixed as priorities in the minds of national delegates, the DSU lists various methods by which a consensual resolution may take place. All of these invite a realistic assessment of advantages and disadvantages, i.e., realist analysis and negotiation, as opposed to blind adherence to a code or standard.

For consultations to provide multilaterally agreed solutions to WTO disputes, the members must sincerely undertake an attempt to resolve contentious topics between themselves. The DSU has created a regimen with clear deadlines and obligations to ensure that parties embarking on consultations understand their limits, fostering a proscribed process instead of a "realist" jungle. In this manner, one party in the consultations cannot tie up the other indefinitely, thereby avoiding WTO supervision at the "discussion stage" between the parties. Article 4.3 outlines an expedited schedule that must be followed. A member receiving a request to consult must either begin consultation within ten days or refuse the petition. If there is no response within the ten-day period, or no consultations within thirty days, the requesting party may proceed to the DSU panel system. In the context of international trade dispute resolution and expedience, this time frame is unprecedented.

The maximum duration of a consultation is just as important as the time taken to open said discussion. As noted earlier, while the parties may mutually agree to extend the process, either party may request the formation of a panel after sixty days of consultation without a settlement. Alternately, both may do so at any time during the process if efforts seem futile. This "time trigger" will most likely only be used when there is little hope of a negotiated settlement. With this rule, parties cannot be bound to the process interminably by one side, and are unlikely to request a full panel if measurable progress is being made. Instead of the months and years that occurred in the past to resolve a dispute, the new consultative process could conceivably end a dispute before one would even begin under the old GATT 1947 system.[10]

To help the DSB track the progress of the consultation, and to help point members in the proper direction, the DSU demands that members who consult under this process notify both the "DSB and the relevant Councils and Committees" of both the dispute itself and the issues at stake. This notification scheme is useful for the consulting parties as it allows them to utilize outside help of the DSB and other relevant committee, while maintaining a positive working relationship with the opposing party.

While exhorting the consultation process to the candidates, the DSU does not make the process mandatory. DSU Article 4.5 makes this a clear exhortation stating that while consulting a disputed matter, members "should attempt to obtain satisfactory adjustment of the matter" and that confidentiality of the consultations should be respected.[11] Additionally, it forbids further use of any information gleaned during these negotiation sessions. By barring the use of consultations in subsequent proceedings, the DSB gives positive encouragement to parties who wish to settle the matter amongst themselves first. If the product of consultations is available to be used as information in a later panel investigation, for example, the parties could choose not to divulge sensitive information to each other, markedly impeding the process as it is precisely this kind of knowledge that can resolve disputes.

Independent verification critically depends on some types of data in panel hearings. When parties discover facts presented in consultation through independent means, it seems reasonable to allow this knowledge to be utilized. Considering that the source of the information presented in consultation holds less relevance than the independently supplied data, it should not pose a threat to the divulging side. Members utilizing the consultation process should keep in mind the potential to move to a panel hearing if the negotiations prove unsuccessful.

Using the models of international dispute resolution, the new DSU provides a further expedited consultation service to members. This process of consultation follows the process as described above, with stricter time limes. If the matter in issue is one of "urgency, including those which concern perishable goods," the parties have ten days to begin consultations, and a panel may be arranged by the complaining party if no result appears within twenty days of the consultation notice's receipt.[12] By creating a swift system of consulting on trade differences, the DSU is more applicable to modern international commercial realities. If trading partners recognize that conflicts which require immediate attention will receive it, they are more likely to employ that mechanism. This expedited consultation provision will allow GATT to function in the future as it has in the past, as an effective mechanism for resolving trade conflicts. Enforcing the provision also allows for realist compromise if the disputants prefer it for whatever political reasons. This path may in fact provide a better context for major power and trade conflicts in the future – alas, third-image momentum cannot cover everything.

Finally, the consultation process shows concern for developing countries, echoing traditional GATT support for this section of membership. The DSU states in Article 4.10 that the "particular" problems and interest of developing country members should be given special attention during the consultation process. What this fails to clarify, however, is exactly how increased sensitivity to poorer nations should affect the negotiations. It is evident that developing countries come to the negotiating table with obvious concerns for topics such as transactional costs and the perceived advantages of more developed nations. What is not so obvious, is the rationale for placing such a reminder in the agreement. Considering the consultation process cannot succeed without mutual agreement on an issue, lesser developed nations have the right of moving to a panel evaluation to determine rights and liabilities as insurance against bullying by developed nations. Placing such a reminder in the DSU smacks of paternalism, equating the paucity of certain resources in a nation with an inability to adequately negotiate with a more developed nation. Since the lesser developed nations were among the parties who negotiated the understanding, however, it can be considered a reminder of the framework used to advance consultation with poorer countries.

The DSU consultation process offers member nations a unique (and potentially last-chance) opportunity to resolve international trade disputes among themselves while maintaining access to a world body able to step in and settle the matter as a last resort. Explicitly expanding the role of prior consultation within the GATT has enabled the member nations to extol the virtue of resolution without adjudication, while concurrently protecting the right to an impartial investigation of their claims.

Consultation is not the only method available to members who wish to resolve disputes among themselves under the WTO system. Along with mutual consultations overseen by the DSB, members can approach Good Offices, Conciliation and Mediation: referred to collectively as Facilitators. These capabilities of the DSU allow for the involvement of impartial parties in a dispute, while the ultimate resolution of the matter remains with the parties themselves. As such, the DSU enables the potential disputants to reach a solution that will protect their continuing trade relationships by allowing both parties to benefit from the process.

In some situations, members may be wise to voluntarily agree to facilitation. As with consultation, the information presented during the facilitation process carries a protection of confidentiality between the parties, meaning that the rules defining the admission of facilitated information parallels those derived from consultation. Before the implementation of a panel, the parties may first attempt the facilitation process, beginning at any agreed time. According to DSU Article 5.4, the parties may request the simultaneity of the facilitation and consultation processes, likely indicating an inability of the parties to resolve the dispute on their own. If the parties enter into facilitation within sixty days of the consultation request's receipt, the original complaining party must wait for the expiration of this time before requesting a panel. This approach affords the parties the greatest latitude possible outside of the panel system to resolve a dispute autonomously, offering supervision and intervention while leaving the decision in the hands of the parties.

The DSU offers two other facilitation opportunities during the dispute resolution process. First, the parties may mutually agree for the facilitation to continue while a panel investigation proceeds, potentially providing several benefits to the members in opposition. In reaching an agreement among themselves, the parties avoid an outright loss based on the merits of the issue, a large problem with the panel system. This is significant to parties who discover during the panel process that their opponent's case may be more credible than they originally thought. This presents the difficulty in bringing a member to the facilitation process when panel hearings are distinctly leaning in one member's favor. Also, resolving a dispute rather than awaiting an award will likely help protect continuing trade relationships among the parties, an advantage not offered by the traditional winner-take-all panel award.

Finally, there is an opportunity for the director general of the WTO, in an ex-officio capacity (Article 5.6) to facilitate an equitable resolution of a dispute among members. This provision can prove to be a useful mechanism for settling impasses that may arise during either a party-driven resolution process, or a panel hearing. While the provision lies in the facilitation section of the DSU rules, there is no express direction as to when the director general may involve himself or herself in such a role, lending the assumption that the capacity lies at the director general's discretion. If this is indeed a correct interpretation of the section, the director general's discretion becomes a more powerful tool than if it functioned simply at the prepanel stage.

The potential prestige and resources of the director general's office could lend strong political resolve to the quest for a middle ground on an issue. This quasi-Herculean force will obviously be reserved for special matters affecting the entire WTO community. Nevertheless, it seems reasonable to assume that the impartiality and influence of the office may help lead otherwise doomed negotiations to a successful conclusion.

We have seen that two or more WTO members are able to resolve a matter without going through the DSU system. First, GATT 1994 specifically notes that it is embodied in the text of the GATT 1947 in s.1 (a); therefore the GATT 1947 agreement applies to GATT 1994 parties. Second, GATT Article XXIV.5 specifically allows for parties to enter into agreements creating "a customs union or free trade area." Further, nothing in this provision prevents the parties from creating individual side agreements for rules regarding dispute resolution. Logically, then, GATT 1994 allows for alternative trade dispute resolution mechanisms, at least with reference to parties with custom unions or free trade agreements. With this in mind, GATT 1994 members such as Canada or Mexico may uphold their WTO obligations while resolving disputes with other WTO members such as the United States, in NAFTA or elsewhere.

In summary, there exists within the WTO framework, lots of opportunity for non-panel as well as panel settlement of disputes.[13] This can allow for realist calculation of political advantage instead of rigid rules-based panel settlement. The WTO is a third-image construct, no question, but it is interlaced with room for second-image compromise as well.

Notes

1. Paper presented by Rufus H. Yerxa and Demetrios J. Marantis, "Assessing the New WTO Dispute System: A US Perspective" (January 1998).

2. *National Post,* 28 January 1999, 16(C).

3. The Marrakesh Agreement Establishing the World Trade Organization, ("Marrakesh Agreement") including all annexes and declarations (to be noted where applicable), signed at Marrakesh on April 15, 1994. *The Results of the Uruguay Round of Multilateral Trade Negotiations: The Legal Texts* (Geneva: GATT Secretariat, 1994).

4. Rather than denote this as "bilateral" dispute resolution, the paper shall refer simply to party-driven resolution, so as to also encompass situations which may involve more than two trading partners. The emphasis, however, will still revolve around a party-based solution.

5. Petersmann, *supra,* 1134.

6. Robert Hudec has written extensively on this subject.

7. J. H. Jackson, *Restructuring the GATT System* (UK: RIIA, 1990), 60.

8. Ibid., 61.

9. See note 3 above.

10. See Article 4.4.

11. See Article 4.5.

12. See Article 4.5.

13. J. Schott, *The Uruguay Round: An Assessment* (Washington: Institute for International Economics, 1994), 129.

Chapter Five

The WTO in Practice: Systematically Offending National Sovereignty?

"Very Seldom" or "Too Early To Tell"

As we have seen, the ultimate goal of dispute settlement mechanisms in the Uruguay Round agreements of 1994 and the NAFTA was not to delineate winners and losers, but to implement detailed provisions to help ensure that differences are resolved before they impede the expansion of worldwide trade. They are designed to protect and foster continuing trade relationships. The power to finally settle an issue between parties is an incidental objective. It is necessarily used on occasion to protect continuing trade relationships. By giving the parties as many opportunities as is practical to resolve an issue on their own, goodwill and positive impressions about trading relationships may be fostered. It is hoped that further harmonization of these relationships will lead to increased trade, thereby bringing the dispute resolution system in sync with the ultimate goal of the WTO.

As American frustration with the EC over inadequate responses in the years 1999 and 2000 on the banana and beef hormone cases reveal, a lingering contradiction is at the heart of the new WTO. The ambiguity is this: if a WTO member fails, in the judgment of the complaining party, to adequately respond to a judgment against it, what can it do to effect a more adequate response to the?

A particularly slippery example is bananas. In 1993 the European Community introduced rules to discriminate in favor of Caribbean suppliers. Washington first complained to the WTO about this in 1995 as being contrary to GATT. By 1997 the EU had lost twice before dispute resolution panels and had been told to open up its banana trade and to change its rules. The EC modified the rules slightly. Some observers thought the new rules were even more restrictive against non-Caribbean suppliers than the ones they replaced. Stalling for time, the EC called for the WTO to rule again on whether its new EC rules were sufficient as a response to the WTO ruling.

The EC called a general WTO council meeting when the United States announced the list of products it would countervail under its Section 301, complaining in the words of European trade commissioner, Sir Leon Brittan about the United States "flagrantly, blatantly, breaching world trade rules."[1]

This dilatory EC behavior frustrated and angered most American trade observers to say nothing for (American owned) Latin American banana exporting companies, such as Chiquita Brands. In effect in the interim the United States asked the EC 'to post a bond' on Section 301 by scaring U.S. importers from buying these Section 301 targeted products.

The WTO ruled against the EC on its favoring of imports of bananas from Africa, Caribbean and Pacific producers over imports from Latin American banana growers and their U.S. distributors. The dilatory and insufficient EC response prompted Washington to suspend liquidation on a EC import list on March 3, 1999 worth $520 million annually based on its own assessment of the so-called trade damage from the EC's discriminatory banana import regime.

Seven weeks later, the WTO did authorize sanctions of $191.4 million. The United States reduced its product list to match this authorization but applied the 100 percent penal tariffs from the March date. Washington justified this by saying it was justified by the dispute rules of the WTO. In an interim ruling on March 15, 2000 the WTO said the United States was wrong to act unilaterally before an arbitrator had decided on the issues outstanding on the trade losses involved. The WTO earlier in January 2000 had said the U.S. Section 301 trade law which allows Washington to take unilateral sanctions in certain instances was permissible as long as it agreed to abide by WTO rules and determinations in trade disputes.

A disputes panel for the World Trade Organization had ruled explicitly that U.S. legislation that allows for the imposition of sanctions in trade disputes doesn't violate world-trade regulations, but the panel warned that the United States mustn't use the legislation in a manner inconsistent with the system by which the WTO resolves disputes. The case was instigated by the European Union, and both the EC and the United States claimed that the ruling supported their positions. U.S. Trade Representative Charlene Barshefsky said the disputes panel had ruled that the United States when invoking the legislation, has always proceeded in accordance with its agreement with the WTO.

Tightening the relevance of dilatory and inadequate EC responses to the WTO rulings on beef hormones and bananas was the WTO appellate body's upholding on February 24, 2000 of an October 1999 panel ruling that tax breaks granted to U.S. companies on income from exports channeled through offshore foreign sales corporations constitute illegal export subsidies. The United States, which was also found in breach of the WTO's agriculture agreement limiting subsidy payments on farm exports, was given until the start of the new fiscal year in October 2000 to bring its FSC measure "into conformity" with international trade rules. According to the EC, FSC subsidies assist U.S. exports worth around $250 billion annually, at a cost to the U.S. budget of tax foregone of an estimated $3.5 billion in fiscal 1999. This dwarfs U.S. retaliation of just over $300 million annually that the WTO authorized for the EC's failure to comply with WTO rulings in disputes over bananas and hormone-treated beef.

Awkwardly, the ruling required the U.S. Congress to change important tax legislation in a presidential election year, a tall order if not impossible. Charlene Barshefsky, U.S. trade representative, said after the ruling that the United States respected its WTO obligations and would "seek a solution that ensures the U.S. firms and workers are not at a competitive disadvantage with their European counterparts."[2] Too much pressure from Brussels could be counterproductive, jeopardizing the delicate transatlantic trade relationship in general and further compromising U.S. congressional support for the multilateral trading system. The WTO ruling takes the world-trade body firmly into the realm of domestic tax policy where EC members too have sensitivities. "Both sides recognize that this is something we have to manage," a senior U.S. official said.[3]

The United States maintains that FSCs were consistent with WTO rules, they merely grant U.S. companies the same tax benefits as European companies receive through value added tax (VAT) rebates on exports. This justification was nevertheless rejected by the panel and appellate body. In its ruling the appellate body said it was not making a judgment on the relative merits of the "territorial" and "worldwide" systems of taxation used by the EC and United States respectively. But countries were not entitled to use the tax system to provide subsidies contingent on export performance, which are outlawed by the WTOs subsidies accord. The appellate body also rejected a U.S. defense that FSCs were covered by a footnote to the subsidies agreement which it claimed reflected a 1981 "understanding" in the General Agreement on Tariffs and Trade (GATT), the WTO's predecessor, that exports could be exempted from tax.[4]

Even with these definitive "third-image" rulings both sides, apparently for third-image reasons, are jockeying and trying to lower the political temperature. The EC sensibly avoided public gloating, despite being pilloried by the United States for failing to comply with WTO rulings against it on bananas and hormones. Urged on by business and congressional leaders, Washington meanwhile signaled that it wanted an amicable settlement with Brussels. Provided Washington is genuinely committed to finding a solution, Brussels should, or will be flexible on timing and will realize that this case makes it more – not less – important to comply rapidly and in full with the banana and beef rulings. Continuing failure to do so would not only deprives the EC of any claim to the moral high ground; it can only undermine United States readiness to accept WTO disciplines. Both sides must also avoid trying to trade away their mutual trade grievances in a package deal. Such an agreement, even if it were practicable, could easily become a pretext for excusing each other from their WTO obligations and would be a dangerously high price for the WTO even if it ended transatlantic hostilities.

As the *Financial Times* wrote on February 25, 2000;

> The latest U.S.-EU dispute poses a serious test of their capacity to manage a bilateral relationship increasingly threatened by trade conflicts. It is economically vital to the rest of the world that that relationship be sound. But it is at least as important that the two biggest trading powers accept the responsibilities imposed on them by multinational rules.[5]

Supporters of the WTO say the organization can withstand all challenges, seeing as how a party refusing to respond appropriately after a panel ruling against it can be governed by invocation of trade remedies, or, in the U.S. case, by the use of Section 301 (or "Super 301"). Still, excessive use of these remedies or repeated failures in responding fully to panel rulings will trivialize the WTO and its mandate. Paradoxically, the WTO, as the bananas, hormone beef and FSC issues show when handled politically, is a "voluntarist-legal momentum third-image" edifice filled with safety valves and "realist" compromises to assuage pressures arising from its members' domestic political needs. In other words, examples not just of "soft law" and ambiguous clauses but of outright "realist" compromise still live on in the WTO bargain.

Let us recall a few of these "realist" exceptions from overly tight third-image disciplines. Cleverly contrived countervail and antidumping legislation and administration are still WTO-consistent resources a nation can employ to slow or even stop some imports despite WTO membership. Until recently, countervail and anti dumping legislation was used extensively in the United States, the European Union, Canada and Australia. Yet now more and more countries, including Japan, are moving to use countervail and antidumping laws for the purpose of moderating the influx of imports. Korea, Mexico, Finland, New Zealand,

Sweden, Taiwan and India have all increasingly favored antidumping provisions to deal with import problems:

> Between 1969 and 1993, the United States initiated anti-dumping investigation in 813 cases, the European Union in 403 cases, Australia in 746 cases, Canada in 473 cases, Korea in 14 cases, India in 8 cases, Taiwan in 3 cases and Japan in 3 cases.[6]

In a well-known Japanese example, a controversial decision was made to impose an antidumping duty in early 1993 on the import of ferro-silicon manganese from the People's Republic of China. This was followed by Japanese antidumping petitions against cotton imports from Pakistan and Egypt.

Another safety valve is the clever use of the "safeguard" clause. It should be noted that the WTO permits member countries to provide relief to domestic industries suffering from the pressures of foreign competition in the form of safeguards further to Article XIX, as well as some other less frequently utilized measures. The safeguard measures are a way to give relief to a domestic industry seriously injured by increased imports (considered "fair trade"), whereas the antidumping rules serve as a countermeasure to increased imports (otherwise known as "unfair trade"). In practice, of course, the distinction between fair trade and unfair trade is not always clear; domestic industries and governments of importing countries have been known to interchange the remedies. We have seen, however, that antidumping actions are used more often than safeguard measures when dealing with import problems.

Another clever safety valve was the use of voluntary export restraints (VERs), or voluntary restraint arrangements (VRAs), whereby the government of exporting and importing countries agree that the government and industry of the exporting country should restrain the export of a commodity to the importing country. In the Uruguay Round of multilateral trade negotiations, conducted under the direction of the GATT, a new international agreement on safeguard measures was incorporated. As a result, VRAs involving governments are to be prohibited, and industry-to-industry VRA situations are to be discouraged under the agreement. Now that VRAs are less acceptable, antidumping laws will likely be employed to ward off the pressures of some imports. A large portion of the expected disputes to be settled by the WTO will center on antidumping allegations. Let us take a look at the way the WTO is organized to deal with this.

The seemingly easy task of defining "dumping" was a major challenge for all ministers negotiating the Uruguay Round and the mid-term ministerial round in Montreal, which occurred later. A group of negotiators from the United States and the European Union claimed that provisions for countering the circumvention of antidumping laws should be incorporated. Conversely, another group of negotiators from nations including Japan, Korea and Hong Kong argued for more stringent disciplines on the enforcement of member countries' antidumping laws.

One remembers many late-night meetings of the ministers in Montreal not leading to anything close to agreement on a definition. To save the round from faltering, the director general of the GATT, Arthur Dunkel, filled in the gaps of the draft final act with compromises. Member countries accepted the "Dunkel Draft," but the U.S. administration stressed, among other things, that the provisions regarding anticircumvention measures were too narrow. The draft was altered to preserve the status quo and the final act contains no provision for anticircumvention measures. Realist muscle prevailed over the voluntarists.

Let us look now at the "antidump" measures of protection as a clever safety valve, almost certainly the biggest definitional trade challenge facing the WTO. In the Kennedy Round negotiations of 1964-67, an antidumping code was fashioned. The code contained a number of requirements to regulate the enforcement of antidumping laws in the signatory countries, including the rule that dumping must be demonstrated to be the major cause of injury to the complaining domestic industry. Criticized as being too idealistic, the Tokyo Round of 1973-79 code was superseded with less rigorous requirements in the enforcement of antidumping laws by signatory countries. For example, Tokyo required that injury to a domestic industry caused by factors *other* than dumping should not be attributed *to* dumping.

The greatest complaint in this whole affair is that "dumping" is so ill defined that it enters into general usage as a "tool to prevent imports." In Japan, a subcommittee of the Industrial Structure Council published an analysis of the issues behind antidumping enforcement. The report maintained that antidumping legislation in the United States and elsewhere has been used in a manner that creates dumping even where it did not exist:

> It analyzes eleven categories of practices in the enforcement of anti-dumping law and states how they deviate from the reasonable scope of anti-dumping law. The last include such points as (I) a lack of symmetrical price adjustments, (II) unfair use of average prices for comparisons, (III) disregard of normal commercial practices when assessing sales below cost, (IV) arbitrary minimum rates for calculating 'constructed

value', (V) a lack of appropriate adjustment for exchange-rate fluctuations, (VI) an arbitrary determination of 'standing', (VII) the initiation of proceedings on the basis of insufficient evidence, (VIII) an unjust expansion of the scope of products subject to anti-dumping duties, (IX) the delay of administrative review, (X) the lack of a 'sunset clause' and (XI) problems involved in applying anti-circumvention measures. [7]

With regard to the European Union's antidumping law, nine categories of practices and their enforcement were analyzed and found to be beyond the reasonable scope of an antidumping law:

They cover such points as (I) a lack of symmetrical price adjustments, (II) unfair use of average price for comparisons, (III) a disregard of normal commercial practices when assessing sales below cost, (IV) arbitrary rates of profit for calculating 'constructed value,' (V) problems involved in injury determination, (VI) the initiation of proceedings on the basis of insufficient evidence, (VII) the imposition of maximum duties on companies not subject to investigation, (VIII) the deduction of anti-dumping duty as costs and (IX) problems involved in applying anti-circumvention measures. [8]

The Japanese are particularly sensitive to the fact that the mere appearance of any antidumping investigation works as a disincentive to importers handling the products in question. Investigations catalyze a fear of marketing the products (after all the "fear whispers," an antidumping duty could be imposed later). In this sense, the *mere initiation* of an anti-dumping investigation can stifle imports, even before a final determination is decided. In the United States and the European Union, over 70 percent of the cases in which an inquiry is commenced ultimately result in the discovery of dumping and therefore the imposition of an antidumping duty. It has also been estimated that about one million American dollars a year are necessary for a foreign respondent to defend an antidumping case. Another trend emerged: the rate of antidumping duty is increasing. Between July 1991 and June 1993, the average antidumping duty was 26 percent and close to 10 percent of U.S. imports are affected by such duties. [9] Realist school negotiators have both (second image) domestic support and likely international confirmation to buoy them through the process as they press antidump accusations against respondents. Without clear definitions of dumping, this category of trade improvement will continue to weaken domestic political support for the World Trade Organization.

An Achilles' heel in the WTO lies in the problem of the circumvention of some WTO disciplines through cleverly deploying countervailing duties raised by governments against so-called "subsidized exports." (A later chapter will describe just such a case – softwood lumber – in the CUSTA and NAFTA context.) While substantial, the 1994 Uruguay Round Agreement and subsequent clarifications are still insufficient. In 1990, John J. Jackson, one of the leading academic observers of these retaliations, characterized the problem as follows:

> The subsidy rules of the GATT system could substantially undermine the post-World War II Bretton Woods system as it applies to trade, unless these rules are refined and disciplined by current or future international trade negotiations. An expansive interpretation of subsidies and countervailing duty rules could result in the application of countervailing duties to almost any imported product. If this were to occur, the forty-year effort to liberalized border trade barriers could be largely nullified.[10]

Yet refining the trade rules for subsidies presents political, legal and economic challenges. Robert Hudec describes the hypocrisy in his many writings. "Most politicians and businesses want to countervail but can they afford to punish all the things they do themselves? As a result, the only accurate legal definition of subsidies in most countries is something your government does for you that my government does not do for me."[11] The policy balance reflected in the 1994 GATT Subsidies Agreement shows an intentionally strict discipline imposed on the use of subsidies, including those employed by developing countries, as well as universally greater limitations on the unilateral application of countervailing duties.

All members of the WTO are subject to the following: the GATT (1994); the thirteen agreements pertaining to trade in goods concluded in the Uruguay Round; the General Agreement on Trade in Services; the Agreement on Trade-Related Aspects of Intellectual Property Rights; the understanding on Rules and Procedures Governing the Settlement of Disputes; and the Trade Policy Review Mechanism. The WTO, including all the annexed agreements, is to be applied definitively, and there are no "grandfather rights" as there were under the GATT (1947).

Of course, the WTO's Subsidies Agreement itself is still subject to the integrated dispute settlement rules that govern the DSU. The WTO dispute settlement mechanism builds on the reforms of the GATT dispute settlement method, adopted after the Montreal Ministerial in 1990. As mentioned, countries are not empowered to block the adoption of panel reports. Losing countries' only recourse is to appeal to the Appellate Body, which presents a binding decision to the WTO. Although the Subsidies Agreement is subject to the understanding on dispute settlement, there are a number of special dispute settlement procedures for the Subsidies Agreement under various provisions.

All debates about subsidies involve definitions. The Subsidies Agreement opens with the definition of a subsidy. Article 1 states:

> 1.1 For the purpose of this Agreement, a subsidy shall be deemed to exist if:
>
> a) (1) there is a financial contribution by a government or any public body within the territory of a Member referred to in this Agreement as "government", i.e., where:
>
> (i) government practice involves a direct transfer of funds (e.g., grants, loan guarantees);
>
> (ii) government revenue that is otherwise due is foregone or not collected (e.g., fiscal incentives such as tax credits);
>
> (iii) a government provides goods or services other than general infrastructure, or purchases;
>
> (iv) a government makes payments to a funding mechanism, or
>
> entrusts or directs a private body to carry out one or more of the type of functions illustrated in (i) to (iii) above which would normally be vested in the government and the practice, in no real sense, differs from practices normally followed by governments;
>
> or
>
> a) (2) there is any form of income or price support in the sense of Article XVI of GATT 1994;
>
> and

b)   a benefit is thereby conferred.

1.2 A subsidy as defined in paragraph 1 shall be subject
to the provisions of Part III or V only if such a
subsidy is specific in accordance with the provisions
of Article 2.

This definition of subsidy is obviously derived from U.S. legislation
and administrative practice. The Subsidies Agreement follows this
approach, with the lone exception that export subsidies or domestic
sourcing subsidies are deemed to be specific.

Expanding on this issue of interpreting "specificity" or "general
availability," a 1994 Report of the U.S. House Ways and Means
Committee report states:

> The court in Cabot provided a sound interpretative rule to be
> applied in those cases where broadly available benefits are at
> issue. The test for such programs is whether there is a
> sufficient degree of competitive advantage in international
> commerce being bestowed upon a discrete class of
> beneficiaries that would not exist but for government action.
> This necessarily involves subjective, case-by-case decisions to
> determine whether there is such a discrete class of
> beneficiaries.[12]

The Dunkel Text (the Draft Final Act of December 1991) not only
imposed a specificity test on the definition of actionable subsidies (which
in itself imposes a stricter standard on subnational governments) but also
defines all subsidies by subnational governments as actionable (Article
2.2). The new final Subsidies Agreement modified this provision by
identifying specificity within the jurisdiction.

The Subsidies Agreement specifically prohibits subsidy tied to export
performance or domestic sourcing. This is clearly a third-image,
voluntarist victory.

3.1 Except as provided in the Agreement on Agriculture,
the following subsidies, within the meaning of
Article 1 above, shall be prohibited:

a) subsidies contingent, in law or in fact, whether
solely or as one of several other conditions, upon
export performance, including those illustrated in
Annex 1,

b) subsidies contingent, whether solely or as one of
several other conditions, upon the use of domestic
over imported goods.

It must be remembered, however that weakening the agreement's
third-image discipline in the interest of "realist" compromise are
provisions of 3.1 (a) or "export subsidies." They no longer apply to
countries listed in Annex VII to the agreement of subsidies, or to other
developing countries, for a period of up to 2003. There are special
provisions for eliminating export subsidies when a developing country
member has achieved export competitiveness in a particular product, as
measured by tallying exports in excess of 3.25 percent share of world
trade in that market.

An enormous challenge is presented then for developed economies. A
1991 United Nations study reported that:

> European governments offer cash grants up to 60 per cent of
> the cost of the entire investment; state governments in the
> United States have given as much as $325 million per project
> (or $108,000 per job) to foreign firms. While no explicit
> domestic content or export-performance regulations are
> involved, it would be disingenuous to argue that such efforts
> were not trade-related investment measures. The Federal
> Reserve Bank of St. Louis found a positive statistical
> correlation between the expenditures of individual states in the
> United States on investment promotion, on the one hand, and
> exports from those states, on the other. No less real is the
> import-substitution dimension of such policies among the
> developed nations. The trend, moreover, is worrisome.
> Average state expenditures in the United Sates to induce
> inward investment and to promote exports have grown over
> the past decade by more than 60 per cent. [13]

The mandate of the WTO Agreement on Subsidies and
Countervailing Measures is to discipline, but not eliminate, the use of
domestic subsidies.

Clearly, this new process may create a fresh mechanism for
multilateral discipline on the use of export subsides. Some of these new
provisions limiting the use of subsidies also apply to developing
countries with significant caveats. [14] There must be "positive evidence" of
adverse trade effects and tariff-bindings on the relevant products before
these provisions can be enforced on developing countries. Furthermore,
there are special provisions, which forgive debts and other liabilities for
privatization programs in these poorer nations. While some subsidies that

are also not specific, they meet criteria for regional development and environmental protection.

In the final negotiations of the Uruguay Round, the Clinton administration shifted its position away from that taken by its predecessor with respect to government assistance for research and development. The established thresholds permitting government assistance now exists for up to 75 percent of industrial research and 50 percent of pre-competitive development activity.

Part V of the Subsidies Agreement contains detailed rules and procedures governing the administration by national authorities of injury investigations and the application of countervailing duties. Thanks to the Uruguay Round, countervailing duties must be reviewed after five years and a minimum level of 1 percent is set before duties are imposed. In addition, the requirements for "standing" in a domestic industry are more stringent. At a minimum, firms accounting for 25 percent of domestic production of similar products must support the petition.

Since a number of developing countries have instituted countervailing duty laws, they will become subject to these procedural obligations, these new responsibilities include submitting propositions for independent, judicial or arbitral review. The complex internal arrangements of Brazil, Canada, the European Union, India and the United States, all of which have federal structures, will all be examined.

The Subsidy Agreement imposes multilateral discipline upon the use of subsidies, but offers only limited discipline upon the uses of unilateral countervailing measures. The details of the U.S. legislative implementation further tilt the balance toward greater use of countervailing duties on imports.

This underlines the challenges faced by the WTO, not only in establishing credibility against circumvention techniques through antidumping measures, but also by countervailance. Both have been memorably challenged in the bananas and beef hormone cases well into 2000.

There are parameters around how the complainant can respond under GATT if remedies are not explicit. The authorization of countermeasures is optional and admissible only "if . . . the circumstances are serious enough to justify such action" and the suspension of concessions or other obligations are "appropriate in the circumstances" (Article XXIII:2). The power to "give a ruling" includes the power to decide on whether a disputed trade measure is consistent with GATT, and, in this context, to decide on the interpretation and application of the GATT provisions that are relevant to the particular dispute to be settled. This also includes the authority to determine the legal responsibilities and "secondary obligations" of a contracting party that has violated GATT law.

In the field of antidumping and countervailing duty, at least five panel reports up to 2000 have recommended not only the revocation of illegal antidumping or countervailing duties, but also their reimbursement. Clearly, the specific legal context of antidumping and countervailing duty law and the particular rights granted to traders subject to "unfair trade investigations" prompted GATT panels to establish explicit remedies in this area.

In the field of antidumping law, for example, GATT dispute settlement panels seem to have been more willing in the past to scrutinize national antidumping determinations than have certain domestic courts or the EC Court of Justice. The international GATT dispute settlement procedures appear less "protection biased" than domestic court proceedings when considering discretionary trade remedies for third-image voluntarists, though promoting deregulated trade is still the consistent mandate of the WTO. Until the beginning of the Uruguay Round negotiations in 1986, almost all panel reports submitted to the GATT Council under Article XXIII:2 had been adopted and, in most cases, implemented. The acceptance of panel reports continues to be strong. Significantly, there had been no instance in which a panel report was neither adopted nor implemented merely because the complaining party refused to accept the panel's recommendations. With the system boasting an overall success rate of 88 percent in the 1990s, up from the still respectable rate of 81 percent a decade earlier, it comes as little surprise that at least four of five valid complaints are being dealt with successfully. The accomplishments to this point, if not unique, are at least rare in the history of international legal institutions. Still there is a limit to this good news for the third-image voluntarists. Since the 1990s, the political pressures in the Uruguay Round negotiations have led to the "blockage" of an increasing number of panel reports submitted under Article XXIII to the GATT Council, or under the special antidumping code dispute settlement procedures to the antidumping committee. Still, Petersmann sees problems ahead starting with environmental excuses for stopping some imports:

> The GATT dispute settlement proceedings demonstrated not only that unilateral "green protectionism" and "green imperialism" are real threats to the multilateral trading system . . . . But the increasing number of "competition rules" in the Uruguay Round Agreements and the new US policy of extra territorial application of US antitrust laws to anti competitive conduct in foreign markets even if only US exports rather that US consumers are harmed, make it likely that undermining of the competitive opportunities deriving form the liberalization of tariffs and non-tariff trade barriers by private anti

competitive practices will give rise to more complaints under
the GATT-WTO dispute settlement system and will prompt
more systematic negotiations on competition rules in the
future WTO.[15]

This writer witnessed, as a member involved in the final years of the
Uruguay Round negotiations, that there was increasing evidence of
second-image, realist style friction. Conflict was obvious in concerns
over such issues as delays in the establishment of panels, and "forum
shopping" by disputants among the eight different dispute settlement
procedures offered under the GATT and the Tokyo Round agreements.
These delays were also closely linked to attempts at "norm shopping,"
that is, the selection of preferred legal provisions under which trade
conflict was to be decided.

Another problem existed in the stalling of a panel report (e.g., the
outstanding requests for the adoption of panel reports in 1993/94). There
was a "dramatic increase in non-compliance" with dispute settlement
rulings during the 1980s (notably by the United States, the European
Community and Canada), working in tandem with incomplete or
conditional implementation of dispute settlement findings. Petersmann
has expressed concern regarding the "high percentage of legal failures in
antidumping/countervailing duty [AD/CVD] cases, their low rate of
settlement, their increase in volume during the 1980s . . . the typical
arbitrariness of AD/CVD criteria and the legal rigidity of the measures
once taken."[16] Equally perplexing was the impediment to the adoption of
a large number of panel reports under the Antidumping and Subsidies
Codes and political interference by the United States into the dispute
settlement process in antidumping and countervailing duty cases. This is
illustrated by the limited participation of the GATT legal division in
disputes over antidumping and countervailing duties. The world
community was also witness to many U.S. attempts to limit the "standard
of review," a provision which explicitly legalized the protectionist cases
of antidumping laws. (See the chapter in this book on how such cases are
bedeviled by "standard of review" questions.)

Despite the wonderful increase in clarity for third-image disciplines
and scope for second-image dispute settlements, clouds of confusion still
obscure issues of compensation for pirated intellectual property. When
benefits relate to intellectual property owners' rights and the prevention
of rights being used without authorization, what happens to the owners'
rights of remuneration? Take, for example, the case of compulsory
licensing: What will happen to the rights (e.g., under Article 20) to
trademarks in the course of trade? Even if dispute settlement practices
should reveal a practical need for protecting benefits under the TRIPs

agreement, a slippery question remains as to what the appropriate remedy would be for nonviolation complaints if there is neither an obligation to terminate the problematic measure nor a right of the affected country to withdraw voluntary TRIPs concessions. It appears that intellectual property disputes (like the ones that will surely arise between the United States and China when the latter accedes to the WTO) may have to be settled bilaterally – that is, by good old-fashioned negotiation.

U.S. Trade Representative Charlene Barshefsky pointed out in December 1997 that "U.S. copyright industries exported more than $50 billion in software, video, CD, printed matter and film products."[17] Clearly, intellectual property rights are vital to American prosperity. To protect its rights abroad, the USTR has resorted to unilateral acts such as the "Special 301" provisions created in the Omnibus Trade and Competitiveness Act of 1988. The United States also, of course, pursues these rights under the GATT TRIPs agreement (Trade-Related Aspects of International Property Rights) and NAFTA.

Section 301 (of which Special 301 is a part) was created over a quarter of a century ago as a way to enforce U.S. rights against "unquantifiable, unreasonable, or discriminatory" foreign trade practices restricting U.S. commerce by authorizing Washington to threaten and act against "unfriendly traders" up to the year 1998. Since first enacted, by 1997 the USTR had initiated 116 investigations pursuant to Section 301.[18] Corporations make detailed representations to the USTR every year regarding their market access and intellectual property concerns, generating substantial political pressures on the USTR to take action. This pressure is built up under the prescribed "consultation" and "identification" phase of Section 301. Also, under the Section 301 statutory provisions, the USTR lists "priority" foreign countries and a "watch list."

Significantly, a Special 301 investigation does not necessarily proceed as a unilateral U.S. action if the GATT TRIPs and NAFTA are involved. As James McIlroy points out:

> This dovetailing of the Special 301 with international agreements like TRIPs is an intriguing example of Washington's attempts to reconcile conflicting domestic forces, which favor unilateralism, with American rights and obligations under international treaties. [19]

Or in words to match the framework of this book: a nice dovetailing of realist and voluntarist styles.

Similarly, what happens if a state or a private party claims it does not have a comprehensive national procedure to deal with complaints? Simple: only "if final action has been taken by the administering authorities of the importing member to levy antidumping duties or to accept price undertakings" (Article 17:4) can recourse to the DSB be taken. The law also allows the submission of disputes to the DSB "when a provisional measure has a significant impact and the member that requested consultations considers that the measure was taken contrary to the provisions of paragraph 1 of Article 7" (Article 17:4). Also, although private rights of action are still guaranteed (e.g., in Section 301) in the case of foreign WTO rule violations, these rights are explicitly excluded as a means of ensuring U.S. compliance with the Uruguay Round agreements.

It can be argued that a nation's trade laws, governments and courts do not effectively protect the "general interest" of its citizens in strict compliance with the GATT-WTO guarantees. If so, what then happens to freedom, nondiscrimination, transparent policymaking and rule of law over international trade in the relevant country? If there was a requirement of prior exhaustion of local administrative and judicial remedies before one could go to the WTO with a dispute, this would simply weaken GATT-WTO law and counter the "public interest" of the citizens involved in issues of unregulated trade and rule of law. This leads one to ask: Does the strengthening of judicial remedies at the national level require changes to current GATT-WTO – especially considering that national court proceedings can be "bypassed" by WTO dispute proceedings? Should a requirement of "prior exhaustion" of administrative and/or judicial remedies be introduced in traditional fields such as the GATT antidumping law? This remains a question of debate as we go into the future.

Further structural flaws in the GATT dispute settlement procedures were exemplified by increasing instances of unilateral trade sanctions engaged after requests to authorize the suspension of concessions pursuant to Article XXIII:2 has been opposed. Consequently, it can be argued that the "consensus practice" led to a blockage in the GATT Council. Not surprisingly, criticism over the lack of transparency of the GATT dispute settlement proceedings grew and grew. In turn, a U.S. district court has ordered the office of the U.S. trade representative to release copies of defendant submissions to dispute resolution panels that were established pursuant to GATT.

Deference to Domestic Administration of Trade Law and the New WTO

Another profound realist cleverly used "safety valve" that arises from the new WTO is the lack of certitude about whether WTO panels should defer at all to domestic trade agency reasoning and evidence. A torturous conflict between "second-image" national standards and "third-image" world-trading system standards haunts American observers. The best example is explored by Steven P. Croley and John H. Jackson in "WTO Dispute Procedures, Standard of Review, and a Deference to National Governments."[20] It deserves extensive summary.

Croley and Jackson ask to what extent an international WTO dispute settlement procedure should second-guess a decision made by any national government agency that proves inconsistent with an international rule. Should the international body approach the issues involved (including factual determinations) *de novo*, without any deference to the national government?

Article XVI:1 of the WTO Agreement mandates that GATT jurisprudence will "guide" the jurisprudence and practice of the WTO. In a 1985 case brought by Finland against New Zealand's application of antidumping duties to imports of transformers, the panel ruled that New Zealand authorities had not sufficiently established the validity of a "material injury" determination. It rejected New Zealand's contention that neither contracting parties nor a GATT panel could challenge or scrutinize that determination. The panel said that to refuse such scrutiny "would lead to an unacceptable situation under the aspect of law and order in international trade relations as governed by the GATT." The 1985 panel shared the view expressed by a 1955 predecessor, that "it was clear from the wording of Article VI that no anti-dumping duties should be levied until certain facts had been established . . . . As this represented an obligation on the part of the contracting party imposing such duties, it would be reasonable to expect that that contracting party should establish the existence of these facts when its action is challenged."

Nevertheless, some later cases have suggested that the panel's authority may not be all encompassing. For example, in the 1994 case of U.S. restrictions on tuna imports, the panel noted that "the reasonableness inherent in the interpretation of 'necessary' was not a test of what was reasonable for a government to do, but of what a reasonable government would or could do. . . The test of reasonableness was very close to the good faith criterion in international law. . . It was a standard of review of government actions which did not lead to a wholesale second guessing of such actions." Similarly, in twin 1992 complaints (by Norway against the U.S. antidumping and countervailing duties on imports of Atlantic salmon), the panel responded to a Norwegian letter criticizing its restrained approach by pronouncing: The panel found it "inappropriate to make its own judgment as to the relative weight to be accorded to the facts before the USITC."

The Uruguay Round texts contain several different explicit or implied references to the standard-of-review question. The most prominent of these applies only to antidumping measures, is found in the Anti-Dumping Agreement at Article 17.6:

> (i)   in its assessment of the facts of the matter, the panel shall determine whether the authorities' establishment of the facts was proper and whether their evaluation of those facts was unbiased and objective. If the establishment of the facts was proper and the evaluation was unbiased and objective, even though the panel might have reached a different conclusion, the evaluation shall not be overturned;

> (ii) the panel shall interpret the relevant provisions of the Agreement in accordance with customary rules of interpretation of public international law. Where the panel finds that a relevant provision of the Agreement admits of more than one permissible interpretation, the panel shall find the authorities' measure to be in conformity with the Agreement if it rests upon one of those permissible interpretations.

Subsection (ii) appears to establish a two-step process for panel review of interpretive questions. First, the panel must consider whether the provision of the agreement is open to more than one interpretation. If this is not the case, the panel must vindicate the provision's only permissible interpretation. If, on the other hand, the panel determines that the provision indeed admits of more than one interpretation, the panel shall proceed to the second step of the analysis and consider whether the national interpretation is within the set of "permissible" interpretations. If so, the panel must defer to the interpretation given the provision by the national government.

In terms of the general approach to resolution tactics for the panels (outside the antidumping area), there are no provisions in the DSU explicitly concerning the "standard of review" as such, but some language may be construed as relevant. The most interesting, perhaps, is found in DSU Article 3.2: "Recommendations and rulings of the DSB cannot add to or diminish the rights and obligations provided in the covered agreements." This language could be interpreted as a constraint on the standard of review, but possibly not to the extent of Article 17.6 of the Anti-Dumping Agreement.

A key turning point in the international debate on the amount of deference agencies' determinations should be paid came in 1984: the U.S. Supreme Court rendered its *Chevron* decision. Until this case, reviewing courts exercised considerable deference with respect to agencies' factual determinations, while at the same time according less deference to agencies' legal decisions. Now, courts applying the *Chevron* doctrine face two sequential questions. First, has Congress "directly spoken to the question at issue," or is the statute interpreted by the agency "silent or ambiguous?" To answer this question, the reviewing court applies the "traditional tools of statutory construction." *Chevron* provides sufficient leeway for lower courts to find ambiguities, or not, as they will. Accordingly, lower court decisions vary widely with respect to what constitutes sufficient ambiguity to trigger step two of the legal doctrine.

If the court concludes that Congress has effectively spoken to the issue in question, then "that is the end of the matter." If, however, the court concludes that the statute is "silent or ambiguous," a second amusing question emerges: is the agency's interpretation of the statute "reasonable" or "permissible"? If not, the court will supply an interpretation that is adequate in the context of the situation. In the event that the court determines that the agency's interpretation to be reasonable, it will defer to the agency's interpretation, even if the agency's interpretation is not one the court itself would have adopted had it considered the question on its own. Overall, agencies now have significant authority to determine what exactly Congress "meant." Unless agencies exercise that authority unreasonably, courts theoretically have to choice but to be led along.

In practice, however, *Chevron* ties courts' hands only requiring judicial bodies to defer to interpretations they would have otherwise invalidated. *Chevron* shifts power to the courts, however, insofar as step one allows a court to defer to what it considers a preferred interpretation of a statute that would have been insupportable under the pre-*Chevron* regime. Courts are permitted to vindicate welcome interpretations that, before *Chevron*, they would have been required to invalidate. The U.S. Congress must now speak with greater specificity, or else run the risk that an agency will interpret a statute, with judicial blessing, in a manner that pre-*Chevron* courts would have said Congress did not intend. This re-focuses Congress' place in the picture even more sharply with respect to trade policy.

Like *Chevron*, Article 17.6 requires a GATT/WTO panel to defer to a party's interpretation of an ambiguous agreement provision so long as that interpretation is "permissible." As Jackson and Croley make clear, "both *Chevron* and the standard-of-review issue in Article 17.6 have important implications for the distribution of legal and political authority." American beneficiaries of antidumping duty orders probably sought a *Chevron*-like standard of review so that panels would be less powerful. But considering the diversity of what panels like *Chevron*-observant courts rule to be ambiguous, the standard could result in a shift of power to panels.

Jackson and Croley remind us that at least two important differences distinguish the standard of review embodied in Article 17.6 from *Chevron*'s historic deference. First, Article 17.6(ii) uses the word "permissible," which may not be identical to the meaning of either "reasonable" or "permissible" as construed in U.S. law. In U.S. law, the essential test for step two of the *Chevron* analysis is whether the agency's interpretation is "rational and consistent with the statute," a test that agencies can quite easily pass. Second, the "customary rules of interpretation of public international law" referred to in Article 17.6 certainly are by no means identical to the "traditional tools of statutory construction" in U.S. domestic law. Articles 31 and 32 of the Vienna Convention aim to resolve any facial ambiguities in treaty text. By way of contrast, application of the traditional tools of statutory construction in the United States can exacerbate statutory ambiguities instead of eliminating them.

Should GATT/WTO panels exercise *Chevron*-like deference? Or should they instead interpret the word "permissible" rather narrowly, applying the Vienna Convention's rules on treaty interpretation in a manner little conducive to the conclusion that an agreement provision "admits of more than one interpretation"?

Three main arguments can be employed to justify *Chevron*-type deference by courts: agency expertise, democratic accountability of agencies and national coordination. Each of these justifications is subject to serious objection when applied to international review.

Even U.S. industries seeking antidumping duty orders on foreign imports will have greater difficulty proving injury in the wake of a recent court decision, this one less deferential to agencies. In December 1997, the Court of Appeals for the Federal Circuit (CAFC) ruled in *Gerald Metals* v. *United States* that the antidumping statute requires adequate evidence to prove that harm (to a domestic industry) has been inflicted "by reason of" unfairly traded imports. In addition, the CAFC ruled that mere contribution to material harm caused by dumped imports is insufficient for an affirmative injury determination. The decision appears to overturn two decades of established practice at the U.S. International Trade Commission (ITC), the body responsible for determining injury in antidumping investigations.

Jackson has asked: what is the legal effect of a final ruling of the dispute settlement process in the WTO?[21] Another key consideration has to do with legal options: Does the international law obligation deriving from such a report give the option either (a) to compensate with trade or other measures, or (b) to fulfill the recommendations of the report mandating that the member reform its practices or law? Or, (c) does the report establish an international law obligation, with compensation or retaliation existing only as fallbacks in the event of noncompliance?

Judith H. Bello argued in the same article that "WTO rules are simply not 'binding' in the traditional sense," and emphasized voluntary compliance as the cornerstone of the regime.[22] However, according to Jackson, Bello overlooks the essential real effects of international law. In some legal systems, the legal obligations arising from a report have a self-executing effect. Even in the United States, courts are bound to take into account international law obligations when interpreting national law. In addition, noncompliance by a state with some "pesky" international legal obligation can result in ominous diplomatic ripples. Various responses are permitted under international law, not to mention the arsenal of more informal pressures that can be applied. For example, a U.S. refusal to respect the results of a GATT case on domestic international sales corporations (DISCs) in the 1970s prompted other countries to decline serious discussion of their own subsidy programs while the United States. neglected its obligations. Realism responded to realism.

Eventually, this power "checkmate" regime seemed to be giving way to incipient legal momentum. By the last two decades of the GATT's history, the agreement contracting parties were essentially treating the results of adopted panel reports as legally binding. As we have noted earlier, the basic problem with business under the old GATT procedure was the ease with which nations could block consensus votes on adoption and thereby keep a panel report in legal limbo. It was generally agreed that an unadopted report was essentially toothless – that is, without legally binding effect. In contrast, the new WTO procedures ban blocking. Adoption is thus virtually automatic. This is clearly a victory for the third-image voluntarist legal momentum school even though its acceptance flowed (mostly) from realist epiphany on the part of the United States and others: If trade distortions like dumping and international subsidies were to be minimized, legal limbo had to give way to legal certainty. Sometimes, however, second-image realism prevails, as a member nation will implement a panel decision with a bare minimum of responsibility.

According to Jackson, the language of the WTO Dispute Settlement Understanding (DSU) strongly suggests that the legal effect of an adopted panel report is the international law obligation to perform the recommendation of the panel report.[23] Article 3.7 of the DSU provides that "the first objective of the dispute settlement mechanism is usually to secure the withdrawal of the measures concerned . . . . compensation should be resorted to only if the immediate withdrawal . . . . is impracticable." Article 21:1 adds that "[p]rompt compliance with recommendations or rulings of the DSB is essential in order to ensure effective resolution of disputes to the benefit of all Members." Article 22:1 states it most clearly: "[N]either compensation nor the suspension of concessions or other obligations is preferred to full implementation of a recommendation to bring a measure into conformity with the covered agreements." The DSU establishes a preference for the performance of a recommendation by an obligation. It also notes that the matter shall be kept under surveillance until performance has occurred, suggesting that compensation shall be resorted to if the immediate withdrawal of the measure is impracticable. Perhaps most strikingly, the DSU stipulates there is no obligation to withdraw offending measures in nonviolation cases, implying there is indeed an obligation to perform some compensation in these situations. Hence, in Jackson's view, WTO rules are binding in the traditional sense of international law. The bananas and beef hormone cases tested Article 22:1 to the near-breaking point from 1999 on.

Are We Witnessing Some Third-Image Rules Based Progress?

As we have seen, the 1994 Uruguay Round Agreement trumped these "realist style" "second-image" frictions by instituting an agreement to the effect that "consensus" is no longer needed for a panel's interpretation to be adopted. As we have noted in chapter 2, authoritative interpretations originate from a majority decision (Article IX:2 of the WTO Agreement). This leads to the "quasi-automatic adoption" of most panel reports and of appellate body reports by the DSB. So now there is clearly a mechanism for specifying to what extent the legal interpretations underlying dispute settlement ruling shall become applicable. Article 23 on "Strengthening of the Multilateral System" is clear: it emphasizes the legal primacy and exclusive character of the WTO dispute settlement system vis-à-vis alternative dispute settlement systems outside the WTO.

The article requires:

> When members seek the redress of violation of obligations or other nullification or impairment of benefits under the covered agreements or an impediment to the attainment of any objective of the covered agreements, they shall have recourse to, and abide by, the rules and procedures of the Understanding.

GATT law makes some insightful references to the dispute settlement procedures enshrined in other international agreements, such as arbitration clauses in international air transport agreements. These illustrate how the WTO dispute settlement system is closely related to the dispute settlement procedures of other international organizations. However, one must keep in mind the limits to enforcement at the international level. For example, among the five permanent members of the UN Security Council, only the United Kingdom currently accepts the mandatory jurisdiction of the International Court of Justice in the Hague. In fact, for international organizations other than the EC and the Council of Europe, mandatory court and arbitration procedures continue to be the exception rather than the rule.

The effectiveness of any dispute settlement understanding is largely a function of the underlying rule system: dispute settlement decisions based on vague or "result-oriented" rules are more likely to generate controversy than those based on general, liberal trade rules. The mutually consistent legal and economic rationality of liberal trade rules have enhanced the growth of a highly developed case law on a worldwide, regional and national level (e.g., in GATT, in the EC and in federal states). Conversely, in international financial organizations such as the World Bank and MIGA, international arbitration procedures are instituted solely for the protection of the property rights of private lenders and foreign investors. They are not international trade rules per se.

The good news for third-image, legal momentum "voluntarists" vis-à-vis trade remedies at the global level is that coherence and consensus on rules may well be developing. This is very important to those who wish third-image disciplines on first-and second-image disruptions to the international trading system. Providing another key boost for growth is the connection between regional trade agreements and GATT rules for DSUs. Is there some evidence of crystallization of international norms for trade? Schoenbaum and Arnold have concluded that:

> In international trade organizations – such as GATT, NAFTA and the Andean Common Market – there is a continuing trend towards "legalization" and "judicialization" of dispute settlement procedures. As international relations are

increasingly determined by economic relations, this change
from power-oriented "diplomatic" to rule-oriented "legal"
methods of dispute settlement can be seen as a new stage in
the development of international law.[24]

In addition, the regional law of free trade areas (such as NAFTA) and
customs unions (such as the EC) are influenced by the worldwide GATT
rules (e.g., Article XXIV). Worldwide and regional dispute settlement
practices reveal many parallels.

Tariffs and nontariff trade barriers can be reviewed by domestic
courts in most GATT contracting countries. In turn, decisions such as
U.S. court rulings in the field of antidumping law as well as the EC court
decisions relating to the customs union law of the EC may influence
GATT proceedings. These rulings in domestic courts have encouraged
international GATT dispute settlement proceedings to focus on the
consistency of such judgements. There have been enough cases under
Article XXIII to see an evolution of rule consistency and promptness.

Still, the extent to which WTO panel decisions act as precedents is
never clear. In some ways, it is natural for a WTO appellate body to
recognize the value of its rulings as precedent-setters. If one appellate
body report after another relies on past opinions, perhaps some clarity is
afforded to WTO members involved in a single case involving the issue
of the reports, otherwise disputants cannot be sure precedents are "out
there" to be followed. Political disputants cannot know for sure if the
game is suddenly governed by new rules as if precedents are taken as
binding.

Even though the DSU continues to offer both political and legal
methods for the settlement of disputes under the WTO without complete
panel recommendations, the reality is that the judicialization of panel
procedures with the possible recourse to national court and international
arbitration procedures has been further strengthened.

As we saw in the previous chapter, the way is clearly open for
informal settlement of disputes. Mutually agreed solutions to matters
formally raised under the consultation and dispute settlement provisions
of covered agreements must be notified to the dispute settlement board
and the relevant councils and committees. Therefore, dispute settlements
through bilateral arbitration and mutually agreed arrangements must be
transparent and consistent with WTO law. Article 3:9 further confirms
and extends some of the existing GATT dispute settlement principles,
such as the obligation to withdraw illegal measures and the prima facie
assumption of "nullification or impairment" in case of an infringement of
obligations under the covered agreements. [25]

As for "speedy" (or at least predictable) time periods to conclude panels and get their decisions adopted, the new Article 15 follows the precedent of the dispute settlement mechanism under the Canada-U.S. Free Trade Agreement. Basically, it requires each panel to issue procedures within an allotted time frame:

> An interim report to the parties, including both the descriptive sections and the panel's findings and conclusions. Within a period of time set by the panel, a party may submit a written request for the panel to review precise aspects of the interim report prior to circulation of the final report to the members. At the request of a party, the panel shall hold a further meeting with the parties on the issues identified in the written comments. If no comments are received from any party within the comment period, the interim report shall be considered the final report and circulated promptly to the members. (Article 15:2)

Since panel reports and appellate body reports are deemed "adopted" without an appeal not to adopt the proceedings, a significant legalization and clarified time periods are both implied. Therefore, in view of the independence of panel members and the appellate body, one may predict that this will deliver over time a "quasi-judicialization" of the WTO's dispute settlement process. The insertion of appellate review should help discourage losing parties from using "noncompliance" as an argument to show a dispute settlement ruling to be unfair, erroneous or incomplete because certain arguments were not addressed.

> Unlike the WTO dispute settlement procedures for consultations, good offices, conciliation, mediation and panel procedures (which are to a large extent codifications of time-tested GATT dispute settlement practices) the appellate review is a novel procedure for the settlement of international trade dispute among governments. [26]

As Canadian minister of international trade in 1993, this writer returned from the G7 Heads of Government summit and read, within hours, information that the U.S. trade representative and other executive branch officials gave to the media and Congress about how the new agreement would not effect Section 301 (which allows the United States unilateral action against trade responses it deems insufficient). One understands that all governments try to minimize the restraining effect of any new international legal obligation where regulations are more broad than the norm. All ministers are hard-pressed to downplay any erosion of national sovereignty. The USTR's. explanation promised continued freedom of action for the United States in a wide range of GATT-illegal actions. Could there, in fact, be a gap between what the GATT governments wanted to achieve in restraining American unilateralism and what was in fact accomplished?

The answer is many faceted. In part, the United States executive branch's explanation carefully avoided any description of the full degree of restrictions that the new Uruguay Round Agreement imposes on unilateral action. For example, in Section 301, with respect to trade action on claims with no "GATT legal" basis, the code strictly outlines that certain unilateral actions will result in a virtually automatic finding of GATT violation. To be sure, Hudec writes, "unilateral actions have always been a violation of GATT law but that did not stop the United States before."[28] Therefore, no country, including the United States will be able to hide behind vague claims of GATT justification. Moreover, the entire dispute settlement reform represents serious political commitment of the GATT membership to stop tolerating unilateral behavior. In these circumstances, the costs of unilateral trade action will be high. Now a country runs a greater risk of prompt retaliation. Perhaps more important, if it does this more than a few times, it will forfeit its ability to bring legal complaint against others.

Patrick Buchanan emotionally reminds his readers that the United States may have a more open market than do fellow member of the GATT. Of course, the United States imposes significant market restrictions in areas such as agriculture, textiles and steel, but these limitations are no more severe than those of many other nations. Still, the new dispute settlement portion of the Uruguay Agreement promises WTO enforcement of new market access agreements. Moreover, let us not forget that the United States made some market access commitments of its own when it agreed to the new dispute settlement rules.

Unfortunately, there are more issues left unresolved. As we ministers moved to the 1993 Tokyo Summit negotiations over the Uruguay Round, we moved *ipso facto* toward meeting more U.S. demands. This list of demands grew at the same pace in the early days of the Clinton administration, thanks to both the new presidential regime and the influence of many members of Congress. The United States vigorously argued that additional trade imbalances had arisen due to U.S. compliance with environmental and labor regulations while other countries failed to even come close to approaching such standards. In the view of many Americans, these imbalances justified other reservations about the Uruguay Round deal. This informed the "Section 301 worldview," which seemingly had a "remarkable capacity to etch out new elements of imbalance, justifying unilateral action,"[29] writes Hudec.

U.S. realists, operating out of second-image domestic political pressure, can still identify a safety valve: Section 301.

Patrick Low in *Trading Free: The GATT and U.S. Trade Policy*[30] delineates the dilemma and the realist/voluntarist dichotomy when he writes that the absence of fairness in trade relations bespeaks the need for greater intervention and planning in the domestic economy to avoid the privations that will follow from foreign foul play. Examples of hard-line realist confrontational tactics abound in U.S.-Japan trade. This writer witnessed this on public sector procurement practices in Japan in the 1993 summit. This was followed by U.S. complaints of Japan's spare automobile parts market, which it described as favoring domestic firms in 1995. Then followed the big showdown on steel imports from Japan in 1999 with a bill in the U.S. House of Representatives establishing quotas on steel imports. Clearly realist confrontalism is still a viable tactic. However, unilateral measures when the case is in the midst of the WTO process is particularly upsetting. An example is the use of Super 301 sanctions over the banana dispute with Europe when the WTO appellate panel had not done its work. Sir Leon Brittan, EU trade commissioner, called such sanctions "Unilateralism at its worse." [31] It is not just the retaliatory regime that comes with violations or impairments of trade benefits, as this can be seen to be consistent with GATT; it's the spirit of unilateralism in multilateral and regional bargaining arenas that trouble other countries, especially in recent FTAA negotiations with Mercosur and APEC. This strategy can undermine the purpose of the GATT and the WTO, pushing countries into defensive, market-sharing pacts with the United States and regional trading blocs in which the United States. is a member. Still it is difficult not to recognize that when the realist turns to unilateral sanctions this is not prima facie contrary to the international trade rules on dispute resolution. On the right occasion it can strengthen the latter. On the wrong occasion it can be deeply damaging.

Unilateralism in bilateral or regional *negotiations* on lowering tariff and nontariff barriers is not solely an American specialty. From this writer's experience it was Canadian unilateralism not American that led to the FTA and in part to a key change in the side accords to the NAFTA on questions of sanctions for environmental or labor violations of the accords. In the FTA negotiations it was the Canadian delegation that decided to leave Washington when James Baker and the United States negotiating team would not consider a binational panel system to reconsider agency determinations. It was the Canadian delegation that was confrontational and threatened unilaterally to end the negotiations and to go home. Hours later, the United States relented as James Baker persuaded President Reagan to accept. As outlined in a later chapter, during the negotiations on the Environmental and Labor Side Accords to NAFTA in 1993, Canada would not consider under any circumstances the possibility of using trade sanctions against Canada in the event of a nonperforming monetary assessment against Canada under the agreement. Non-performances could never occur because Canada's federal court would confirm and direct our payment if properly authorized by NAFTA. This writer threatened to pull Canada out of the negotiations by returning to Ottawa. Eventually Mickey Kantor, the U.S. trade representative, and his Mexican counterpart backed down as far as Canada was concerned.

In reality a multinational third-image result is not always denied, but in fact can be assisted through well-timed unilateralism. The coming-together to launch a new GATT round in Uruguay in 1986 was pushed by a unilateral decision by the United States to leave the negotiations at the end of the week regardless. Hastily cobbled together pieces of progress on a range of issues then fell into place after midnight on the final day before the U.S. delegation was to leave is mentioned in an earlier chapter. The same thing happened in Tokyo in July 1993 in a 3:00 a.m. meeting before our heads of government were to deplane. Within hours the United States. and the EC more or less summoned Prime Minister Miyazawa to the 3:00 a.m. meeting to reconsider Tokyo's stand on a few technical matters. Otherwise, they argued the messaging around the summit would be negative instead of positive and our Japanese hosts badly wanted the messages to be positive. Japan relented on these matters by 4:00 a.m.

In Petersmann's view, gradual transformation of traditionally "power-oriented" trade and other international strategies, into "rule-oriented" policies constitutes one of the most important achievements of international law since World War II. In spite of the very sketchy legal and institutional underpinnings of GATT's dispute settlement procedures in Article XXIII, the contracting parties of the GATT have increasingly "legalized" and "codified" GATT dispute settlement practice. He expands on this third-image disciplining of trade in a voluntarist, legal momentum style:

> Rules, and their "rule-oriented" rather than "power-oriented" interpretation and application, enhance predictability and legal security, limit the risks of abuse of power, reduce transaction costs of traders and producers, increase the scope for decentralized decision-making and thereby promote liberty and economic welfare. It is an every day experience that traders, investors and consumers prefer to do business where rules are observed and enforceable.

Panel reports, dispute settlement rulings, arbitration awards and court decisions can build up consistent case law and evolve into time tested precedents, generally accepted interpretations and new rules which may fill "gaps" in existing treaty law and progressively transform multilateral treaties into more consistent legal systems[32]

Where Are We Now?

We have seen real improvements in the Dispute Settlement Understanding under the WTO. They are obligatory. We have noted the beginning of a coral reef of assents to panel findings and to continual refinements in codes and definitions, enough to give hope for third-image internationalization of key concepts and fundamental assent behind dispute settlement.

All this is worth preserving and enhancing. However, can the DSU at present handle huge political trade controversies and masses of references? Beneath the tender membrane of improvement boils forces and tumults already visible. Intellectual property rewards based on settlements still must be negotiated bilaterally. The antidumping code still lacks clarity. The antisubsidy provisions are better defined, but ambiguity remains. Nor are disciplines on countervailing measures much advanced by the Uruguay Round.

By the closing months of 2000, with six years of experience under its belt, two conclusions about the Dispute Settlement Body's performance are clear. First and perhaps foremost, the facility is being heavily used, but is not yet overwhelmed. On November 9, 1998, Ely Karan of Reuters reported:

The number of disputes brought before the World Trade Organization has topped 150 since it was created nearly four years ago. Compared with 300 handled by its predecessor's 47 years. The United States . . . has filed a third of the cases. Other nations have brought 25 against Washington. The European Union has filed 38 complaints and been accused by other member states of breaking the trade rules 23 times. Developing countries were complainants in 38 cases and respondents in 52.[33]

This can be seen as an expression of member nations' confidence in the DSU, in that it is being well employed. On the other hand, its bite and teeth, its ability to anger the loser has not been greatly tested. Of the 150 total disputes, 127 were withdrawn after consultations, 74 remained under consultation, 19 were being examined by panels, 5 were the subject of panel reports, 15 were at the implementation stage, 3 were fully implemented and 6 closed without reaching implementation. Since less than one-fifth has reached the enforcement stage, it is too early to tell if realist first- or second-image frustrations with the discipline of losing and implementing have really been put to the test.

Notes

1. *Financial Times,* 25 February 2000, 1
2. Op. cit.
3. Op. cit.
4. Estimates of the number of companies using FSCs range from 3,000 to 7,000. Users include all the big U.S. corporations such as GE, Monsanto, Microsoft, Ford, Exxon/Mobile, Boeing and Procter & Gamble. See note 1.
5. Op. cit., see endnote #1.
6. *Analysis of Administrations Anti-dumping and Countervailing Duty Legislative Proposals* (U.S. Government Printing Office) June 1994.
7. See *World Trade* 1992 (U.S. Government Printing Office, Annex A).
8. Op. cit.
9. Op. cit.
10. John Jackson, *Restructuring the GATT System* (UK: RIIA, 1990) 114.
11. Robert Hudec, *Enforcing International Trade Law: The Evolution of the Modern GATT Legal System* (New York, MIT Press: 1993). The following pages summarize a piece of Hudec's analysis.
12. U.S. Congress (1990), 124.
13. UNCTC (1991), 9.
14. The Subsides Agreement also includes a special provision for economies in transition from centrally planned into a market economy. These economies have seven years to eliminate Article 3.1 (9a) "export subsidies" and 3.1 (b) "domestic sourcing subsidies" are exempted from the valorem cap on subsidies under Article 6.1.
15. Petersmann, *supra,* 1161.
16. Op. cit.
17. *Backgrounder USTR* U.S. Government Printing Office (19 December 1997)
18. Op. cit.
19. James McIlroy, "American Enforcement of Intellectual Property Rights," *Journal of World Intellectual Property* (May 1998): 447.
20. See in *American Journal of International Law* (1993): 1996.
21. John H. Jackson, "Editorial Comment: The WTO Dispute Settlement Understanding-Misunderstandings on the Native of Legal Obligations," *American Journal of International Law* 91 (1997): 60.
22. Op. cit., 60.
23. Op. cit.
24. See Schoenbaum and Arnold, "Judicial Review of Law Decisions: A Comparitive Analysis," in Hilf and Petersmann (editors), *National Constitutions and International Economics Law* (Amsterdam: 1993): 475-501.
25. Op. cit.
26. Op. cit.
27. See Buchanan, *Supra,* in passim.
28. Hudec, *Supra,* note 11.
29. Op. cit.

30. Patrick Low, *Trading Free: The GATT and U.S. Trade Policy* (Twentieth Century Fund, New York 1993), 28.
31. *Financial Times* 2 February 1998, 1(A).
32. Petersmann, *Supra*, 1017.
33. *Toronto Star*, 9 November 1998, 3(D).

Part III
Inevitable Issues

Chapter Six

Chinese Torture?
A Scrutiny into the Inscrutable

World trade and the WTO face enough grueling challenges without adding China to the WTO prematurely. This chapter will explore the "second-image" domestic structures and dispute settlement obstacles in China that have impeded the road to membership. It is now possible to glimpse a workable accession of China to the WTO.

This writer remembers the Chinese delegate-observer's visit to the Canadian tent pitched outside the casino hosting the formal GATT negotiations in Punta del Este, Uruguay. The month was September. The year was 1986. He politely reminded us that China made its official application for the resumption of GATT contracting party status on July 10 and he offered evidence of increasing market pricing in his country. He wanted us to support him when the time came for China's reentry to GATT as a developing nation. He didn't engage in debate. He simply stated a desire. Over fifteen years later, his wish had yet to be granted.

Meaningful reforms have occurred in China since 1986. Yet their commercial and administrative law regimes still remain largely inscrutable. What appears to be intense bias on the part of these bodies could, of course, unleash a host of frustrations from disputants against China on dispute settlement bodies in the WTO. Two results – very quickly – are prone to occur. One is Chinese departure once it joined. The other is U.S. or EC departure because of the number of DSU decisions it could not abide. The inevitable result would be the collapse of the WTO itself.

China had been a founding member of GATT in 1947. When the government of Chiang Kai-shek fled to Taiwan in 1949, it took China's GATT seat with it. As a result, the People's Republic of China (hereafter China) was forbidden relations with the remaining GATT members. In

1986, China had formally notified the GATT contracting parties of its decision to regain membership in the organization. In 1992, it was granted observer status.

The U.S. and EC trade relationship with China will bedevil the global trading system in the next decade. Indeed, if enough major disputes between the United States, EC and China were hauled before the WTO, the organization would either collapse under the weight or be pushed into paralysis. The solution, of course, is to ensure that China's entry balances the "voluntarist" desire to incorporate it into the WTO with the "realist" insistence on first getting maximum alignment in trade systems. Finally, some assessment in a "realist mode" of how much compromise would really be needed to make it work might keep the whole juggling act in business. The full benefits that the United States. and China have negotiated bilaterally will flow to the United States. when the U.S. Congress extends permanent normal trade relations (NTR) to China.

In April 1999, observers fixed on the U.S. textile and steel demands which stymied U.S. acceptance of China's WTO entry during Chinese Premier Zhu Ronghi's visit to North America. Chinese resentment sprang from the fact that Japan and Korea entered GATT in 1949 with more concessions than the United States offered China. It appeared to Zhu that the United States. insisted that China continue to be subject to textile and clothing quotas no longer subject to WTO phaseouts.

The central concern of this chapter is the status of China's trading system and the USTR's view of it. Along the way, it offers a look at the mechanisms in China vis-à-vis dispute resolution (as compared with those of the new WTO) and notes China's aversion to adjudication and favoring instead consultation or "friendly negotiation." Although Chinese and WTO provisions appear somewhat similar in their formal surfaces, in reality they are still far apart. Combined with other aspects of China's trading system, this provisional gap puts the realists in the driver's seat with international voluntarists in the trunk – especially when it comes to the question of China's timed entry to the WTO. Until late 1999, it was never clear if the negotiating entity of the Chinese government could bend other departments of government in China. Asserting more comprehensive authority over those departments allowed the Chinese premier to maximize and solidify the binding effect of trade negotiators before his 1999 state visit to the U.S. capital.

Robert Ross in an article in 1997 entitled "Enter the Dragon"[1] argued that because of favorable domestic economies of scale and a nearly unlimited supply of cheap labor, China "could become a major export power capable of prevailing in the domestic markets of its economic competitors." He argues that current trade practices in China "are at wide variance with the WTO obligations assumed by the world's major trading powers."

Ever the realist, Ross pushes for China to change its second-image economic system to complement the WTO's rule-based order:

> If this process is delayed, China will develop sufficient economic power to resist pressures for reform. The U.S. faced this situation in its relations with Japan. By the time Washington actively sought change in Japan's trading system in the 1980s Japan had developed the economic power to resist U.S. pressure. Washington failed to act when it had maximum leverage.

Against this backdrop, Ross found the "carrot" of WTO entry only mildly effective when negotiating with the Chinese. His viewpoint is "realist:"

> Given China's current ability to access markets, the benefit of WTO membership is primarily prestige. Beijing has determined that prestige is of little use in making China strong or in raising the standard of living of the Chinese people.

As we recalled earlier, the initial GATTs were not without huge admixtures of realism and compromise. During the Cold War, countries including the United States and Canada allowed their NATO allies significant "graduated protectionism" in various sectors of the economy. This generosity allowed huge amounts of protectionism to persist in places like Japan and South Korea. In the meanderings of the Uruguay Round, the United States initially mused over an eventual "zero reduction" of Japan and Europe's total agricultural subsidies. This short-lived position at Punta del Este never came close to being worked into the final accord. In essence, GATT may have gained great stability during the Cold War precisely because it accommodated the basic interests of Europe and Japan. In return, these nations supported the system.

The same accommodation will no doubt have to be done for China. Realism and "soft law" will have its day here too. The task at present is to know how and when to press for maximum Chinese reform. Greg Mostel in a 1997 article acknowledged the potential third-image liberalizing effect if China joins, but advocated that in negotiations WTO membership for China, "is likely to improve the life of the average Chinese citizen, make China a more formidable trading partner, increase trade opportunities and stimulate economic growth worldwide. China's membership is not, however, urgently required."[2]

According to this reasoning, bilateral arrangements can work in the interim. The reader will see how the threat of trade sanctions has led to a whole series of adjustments in China's approach to trade. For example, it can be argued that protections for intellectual property are superior in European-Chinese and U.S.-Chinese bilateral agreements than available through the WTO at present.

On the trade front, insofar as progress has been made on a number of specific U.S.-Chinese and EC-Chinese bilateral negotiations, why should we care about China's eventual accession to the WTO? Well, all of us should care because China is one of the fastest-swelling economies in the world, with growth rates averaging around 10 percent in recent years. Possessing the world's largest population, China may have the world's largest economy by 2010.

Today, the land that Mao Tse-tsung once wanted to make a self-sufficient communist island is the world's tenth largest exporter-importer and the United States' fourth largest trade partner. In approximate terms, U.S. exports to China have nearly quadrupled over the past decade, and the United States has become China's largest export market: U.S. imports from China comprise more than 20 percent of China's exports to the world. By contrast, U.S. exports of goods to China are less than one quarter of what it imports from China. The U.S. trade deficit in goods and services with China surpasses its deficit with Japan.

Like so many things in a world with China's influence, the large trade deficit with China, what D. H. Lawrence would call "a vast and ghastly intricacy" is the result of countless factors. The most important factor, however, is China's failure to provide increased market access. This is demonstrated by the 2 percent growth in U.S. exports to China in each year in the late 1990s. Contrast this with the average 25 percent growth in China's exports to the U.S. each year in the late 1990s for example. Pat Buchanan's "unequal access" argument has force when applied to China.

Despite China's gradual movement away from a centrally planned economy and towards a quasi-market system in recent years, the U.S. trade representative still points to the People's Republic as an unpenetrated fortress.

> China's markets still remain relatively closed. China is pursuing an export-led growth strategy while protecting its domestic markets through high tariffs, quotas, restrictive standards and activities of state trading enterprises. In addition, China's failure to meet fundamental international norms – such as national treatment, transparency, or the right

to import or export freely – deprives U.S. exports of a level playing field on which to compete.

The Administration trade policy with China is clear. First, we will continue to pursue market opening initiatives on a broad scale for U.S. goods, services and agricultural products through the WTO accession process and bilateral initiatives and agreements. U.S. businesses should have access – and the necessary protection for their properties – in China's market, equivalent to that which China enjoys in the U.S. market.

The second fundamental principle of our trade is to ensure that China accepts the rule of law. We seek to encourage China to develop trade and economic policies that are consistent with international trade practices and norms. The rule of law is an important part of ensuring that China provides meaningful market access and underpins our bilateral and multilateral agreements.[3]

Both China, the United States and the EC agreed that the former's accession to the WTO had to be "commercially meaningful" for both. While bilateral trade agreements cover specific segments of U.S. trade, negotiations on China's entry to the WTO has provided an opportunity to address trade issues comprehensively and systematically for all sectors of the U.S. economy. China's accession to the WTO offers a perfectly reasonable focus for efforts to expand market access for U.S. exports, justifiably bringing China into the parlor of international rules-based trade.

The diverse elements of China's WTO accession negotiations can be broadly divided into a periodic table of two categories. The first concerns rules and general principles like national treatment, transparency and elimination of nontariff measures and compliance with such WTO pacts as the Agreement on Application of Sanitary and Phyto-Sanitary Measures. Ever expanding, this category would also include any transition periods and provisions created to address particular aspects of China's trade regime (e.g., antidumping rules and safeguards). The second broad category concerns market access details for industrial and agricultural goods and services. Greater flexibility in China's tariff and services schedules is an integral part of any protocol. All elements of this package (market access for goods, agriculture and services, acceptance of rules, safeguards and timing) must fuse for China's accession efforts, if accession is to move forward.

Early in 1997, negotiators came together in a sweet – if brief – display of unity, in identifying a series of needs related to WTO rules:

commitments related to national treatment (trading rights and non-discrimination), transparency, the TRIPs agreement and agriculture export subsidies. On the market access front, China announced that it intended to join the Information Technology Agreement as soon as possible and that it would agree to further cuts to its tariff levels.

Here is a recent U.S. trade representative's "top six" list of achievements vis-à-vis rules and the summit announcements:

> *Trading Rights* (the right to import and export): In March [1997], China agreed to increase progressively the availability of the right to import and export products so that at the end of three years all foreign individuals and companies and all companies in China will have the right to import and export all products throughout China. This commitment represents a major change in China's trading system since only a comparatively few companies in China now have the right to import goods directly from U.S. companies. This is an important step in providing national treatment to U.S. exports.

> *Non-Discrimination*: China has agreed to eliminate other practices that discriminate against imported goods and foreign producers of goods in China. For example, China will eliminate its system of dual pricing for products and services related to production, distribution, marketing and sale of goods in China. Under the old system, foreigners would be charged much more for air or rail freight or preferential access to these services would be granted to a domestic producer. China has already begun to dismantle its system of dual pricing, thus putting U.S. invested companies on a more equal footing.

> *Transparency*: China has committed to making information available to other governments and to people engaged in trade on all of the issues covered in the WTO. Translations of laws and regulations will be available and WTO members will have the opportunity to comment on proposed laws and regulations before they become effective. Furthermore, China has agreed that it will enforce only those laws and regulations that they publish.

> *Judicial Review of Administrative Decisions*: China will have independent tribunals for the review of administrative actions relating to implementation of the WTO Agreements and grant the right to seek judicial review of these administrative actions. Both steps will help address corruption and encourage development of the rule of law in China.

Intellectual Property Rights: China has committed to implement the Agreement on Trade Related Aspects of Intellectual Property Rights (TRIPs) upon accession.

Agriculture: China has agreed not to use export subsidies for agriculture products.[4]

Formidable as the list may be, accession or not, a great deal of work still remains to be done on market access and implementation of the WTO's rules and safeguards. Typically in 1997, according to U.S. trade representative spokesperson Susan Esserman, China had not yet presented an acceptable offer on market access issues despite its progress in other areas. China needed to improve the timing of tariff cuts and the number and level of tariff peaks. Moreover, "we need to reach agreement on the cuts on U.S. priority products," she wrote. There was no agreement on acceptable phaseout periods for China's remaining quotas, licensing and tendering requirements. Other issues still await proper consideration: issues like China's application of mandatory standards for imports, customs valuation and corporate licensing, that all affect access of exports to this Asian market.

On agriculture, for example, intensive discussions have taken place around market access for key export products. These discussions deal with sticky politics: tariff levels, administration of the tariff rate quotas that China wants to enforce, the activities of state trading enterprises and the details of China's implementation of the WTO Agreement on Agriculture. WTO members are also urging China to implement the Agreement on Sanitary and Phyto-Sanitary Measures fairly and effectively.

Control of consumer services is another particular concern to the United States. and other WTO members; China's commitment to trading rights is only the first step in ensuring that U.S. exports reach customers in China. The ability to engage in all elements of distribution, including after-sales maintenance and repair, is key to establishing long-term relationships in the market and thus real market access for goods. Significant commitments from China are necessary in a number of other service sectors, including telecommunications and financial services like insurance.

During the key November 1997 summit, China made two announcements that could be interpreted as more than seductive overtures in its courtship of the WTO. First, China expressed its intention to join the Information Technology Agreement (ITA) as soon as possible. The ITA calls for elimination of tariffs on all information technology products hopefully by the year 2000, although extended staging may be allowed for a limited number of products not beyond the year 2005. China must negotiate, and all ITA participants must agree, to any staging beyond the millennium. The ITA permits countries and (separate customs territories in the process of acceding to the WTO) to participate in the agreement. As a result, China can participate in the agreement prior to completing the WTO accession process. Countries accounting for approximately 95 percent of world trade are now signatories in the agreement. Its participation is an authentic break-through in terms of ITA's reach and universality. China's market for ITA products is growing rapidly. One estimate places China's total imports of ITA products at $24.5 billion in 1999 and other estimates are higher. According to industry estimates, China imports about 15 percent of its information technology products from the United States. China's announcement on the ITA is also significant, as it is the first time that China has decided to participate in a zero-for-zero initiative.

The second key announcement China made at the summit was that it was willing to make substantial cuts to tariffs. Previously, China's applied tariff rate averaged 23 percent. On October 1, 1997, China announced reductions in its tariffs that result in an overall average tariff rate of 17 percent. Offering further tariff reductions (catalyzing a substantially lower average tariff rate). Ultimately, effective assessments of the tariff reductions will depend on whether China meets requests on priority products and satisfies other key criteria.

China also gave the United States a new written services offer, an indication that China is taking the politics of service market access more seriously. While some improvements in the offer were made, U.S. requests in important areas like distribution, telecommunications and financial/professional services were not addressed to American satisfaction. For example, China's offer covers a number of service sectors generally, but provides for foreign control only on a very limited or "experimental" basis. What's more, this limited access is frequently restricted to certain geographic regions.

Bilaterals continue to be a crucial mechanism in addressing specific sectoral problems that require immediate action. Monitoring and enforcing current accords is equally essential. In these contexts, the U.S. administration has demonstrated its willingness to wield sanctions as part of its campaigns to achieve its objectives. Another important result of U.S.-Chinese bilateral initiatives is that they often complement and reinforce the multilateral aspects of U.S. trade policy. For example, bilateral agreements on intellectual property rights, provided the foundation for China's commitment to implement the TRIPs agreement immediately upon accession to the WTO. Similarly, effective implementation of agreements on the rule of law are a principle that underlies both bilateral and multilateral pacts.

The Clinton administration reached an agreement with China that provides an interim solution to a longstanding problem regarding regulation of those American companies that profit from providing financial information to the Chinese market. The interim solution secures important market access for foreign financial information companies operating in Asia, such as Dow Jones and Reuters, while ensuring that Chinese companies and financial institutions maintain access to U.S. information services. While the agreement is a Band-Aid, further commitments are still sought from China to provide expanded market access and national treatment for financial information services in China's wounded WTO accession negotiations.

A second development involves the insurance services sector. While the United States is requesting that China make significant improvements in its GATS schedule on insurance services, China has announced that a select number of U.S. companies will be licensed to provide insurance within its borders. Many highly qualified U.S. companies are seeking to enter China's growing market for insurance products. Moreover, the United States has indicated it will continue to press China to expand access to other insurance companies angling for a piece of the transpacific action

The United States and China signed an agreement on space launches in late 1997 which solidifies effective price discipline in some of the more rapidly-growing areas of commercial space launch activity. The agreement puts new provisions into effect as part of the 1995 U.S.-China space launch accord, a pact that clarifies conditions included in the pricing of launch services. More information and greater certainty will consequently be provided to industries interested in participating in this market.

Thanks to a boom in the establishment of bilateral agreements, United States access to China's market is greater now than it has ever been. Monitoring implementation and enforcement of these agreements is one way to expand access and build a foundation for future agreements. An examination of a few significant bilateral agreements offers invaluable insight into the so-called "free market" of the modern People's Republic.

Intellectual Property Rights

In 1995, the United States reached an agreement with China on intellectual property rights enforcement, specifically copyrights and trademarks, and improved market access for U.S. firms in the computer software, motion picture, publishing and sound recording industries. Culturally, this introduction of American entertainment media brought a greater awareness of the Western world to China – and more money to U.S. corporate wallets. In the 1995 agreement, China committed to put a basic structure in place for enforcement at the central and provincial level and in major cities. China also undertook improved customs enforcement at the border and strengthened protection for well-known trademarks.

Over the last years of the 1990s, the U.S. trade representative carefully monitored China's implementation of the agreement. While China created enforcement task forces and did pursue enforcement initiatives, overall piracy rates remained extremely high. American companies were frustrated in their efforts to achieve market access. In May 1996, the Clinton administration threatened to take action against China for its failure to satisfactorily implement commitments from the 1995 agreement. In June 1996, after steps were taken by the United States to verify their claim, it appeared that the Chinese had actually taken a "critical mass" of enforcement actions in connection with the agreement. There has been continued progress and continuing problems ever since. Intellectual protection enforcement is now part of China's nationwide anticrime campaign. China has put in place a functioning enforcement system, based on the agreements to protect intellectual property. On the labor front by 1998, Chinese authorities had shut down forty one factories with fifty eight CD/CD-ROM production lines, radically cutting back on pirated sound recording production in South China. China's judicial system has become involved in combating piracy and the number of decisions and the severity of penalties have increased.

Despite China's increased efforts; problems remain, particularly in the area of end-use piracy of business software. Piracy rates of entertainment software (game CDs) are also high. In the summer of 1999, for instance, the blockbuster movie, *Star Wars: Phantom Menace* was being sold in video-digital form in Chinese marketplaces within days of its commercial theatre release.

Besides enforcement activities, copyright industries have made some limited headway on market access. For example, access for foreign sound recordings, stagnant at 120 titles in 1994, reached approximately 1,000 titles in 1996. The elimination of quotas should pave the way for Chinese record companies to sign licensing arrangements that capitalize on the companies' entire catalogues.

Textiles

Economic spheres beyond the entertainment industry have been affected negatively and positively as well. The textile industry is one example. The February 1997 bilateral textiles agreement builds and improves on a similar 1994 agreement with China. For the first time, the bilateral contract provides market access for U.S. textiles and clothes in China's market. China has also agreed to ensure that nontariff barriers do not impede effective market access for textile and apparel exports originating in the United States

Under this bilateral agreement, China will lower tariff rates over four years. For certain high-priority products, China agreed to accelerate tariff reductions, the first cuts became effective on October 1, 1997.

The issue of illegal transshipments of textiles from China has been a significant concern. In the 1997 agreement, China's quotas in fourteen apparel and fabric product categories were reduced when and where transshipment violations of the 1994 agreement were conceded. Moreover, a special safeguard mechanism for textile imports will remain in effect until four years after the WTO Agreement on Textiles and Clothing has terminated.

Market Access Agreement

The quest for effective implementation of the October 1992 Market Access Agreement was another project in the Clinton administration's continuing mission for market openings. In that agreement, China committed to making significant changes in its import regime, i.e., to eliminate import substitution policies, publish its trade laws in an official journal, apply the same testing and standards requirements to domestic products and imports, decrease tariffs on certain products, apply sanitary and Phyto-Sanitary measures based only on scientific principles and eliminate licensing and quota requirements for production of more than 1,200 units.

In broad summary it is fair to conclude that China has taken some significant steps toward the implementation of the 1992 agreement. Its trade regime is now more transparent. The nation has lowered tariffs on many products and has eliminated well over a thousand nontariff barriers. While China has removed a substantial number of these barriers, some concern has been generated regarding its notorious habit of substituting other barriers for the ones removed. On some products in the medical-equipment sector, for example, China has replaced a quota with a tendering and registration requirement – full market access, then, is still a distant goal.

A number of other market access problems remain, in particular for agricultural products. As previously described, China promised in 1999 to eliminate all unscientific sanitary and Phyto-Sanitary restrictions used as market barriers. The vow has yet to be honored: over the last few years, measures have been enacted that permit the importation of live horses, apples, grapes, cattle, swine and bovine embryos.

Unjustified sanitary and Phyto-Sanitary (SPS) restrictions on exports of citrus, wheat, stone, fruit, beef, poultry and pork products still exist according to the U.S. trade representative. While China has granted some access for beef, poultry and pork products through certification and import quotas for individual processing plants, China still does not provide the international community with a system-wide certification of foreign plants or quota elimination.

China has ordered government departments and institutions to sever their links with 20,000 professional agencies now under their control. They must end links with accounting and auditing offices, financial consultants, tax-filing offices, lawyers, assets evaluation agents, pricing assessment agents and project cost audit agents. The government has also ordered the military to sever its ties to many business enterprises. The State Council, China's cabinet, will oversee the campaign to reduce the influence of government and eliminate corruption.

The China Securities Regulatory Commission is moving disclosure requirements for listed companies closer to international standards. A checklist released in 1998 demands that listed companies give detailed accounting of assets and operations, create provisions for account receivables and inventory losses and for short and long-term investment losses. In their financial reports, companies must detail how WTO membership will affect their operations. Any major changes in ownership and asset structure must be reported immediately.

China's entry into the WTO will lead to reductions in import tariffs for farm produce and open more of the agricultural sector to foreign investment, according to Xinhau. Access for commodities such as corn, cotton, wheat, rice, barley and soybean will be expanded, a key demand of U.S. negotiators. China's Ministry of Agriculture wants to boost grain output to 540 million tones by 2020 and increase output of meat and milk. It also plans to increase irrigated farmland by 56.7 million hectares. China needs advanced agricultural technology and foreign investment to meet these goals.

There will be significant changes as a result of China's bilateral agreement with the United States leading to WTO membership. China will eliminate all quotas and quantitative restrictions on imports of industrial goods, granting full distribution rights to foreign firms. In the auto sector, U.S. companies gain distribution and trading rights. Foreign capital will be allowed into the Internet services sector and other areas of telecommunications. Foreign banks will be permitted to take on auto financing and to handle local currency in China two years after the WTO accession. Foreign investors will be permitted to hold up to 33 percent in securities fund management joint ventures, rising to 49 percent within three years. Foreign movie companies gain distribution rights in China on a revenue-sharing basis and joint ventures in video and sound recording will be permitted. The United States has agreed to phase out quotas restricting imports of Chinese textiles with some safeguards to prevent dumping of cheap goods.

Some Tentative Comparisons to the 1980s

According to academic observer, Yunlong Man, China's admission to the IMF and the World Bank in 1980 signified the beginning of the Asian superpower's return to the world economic community.[5] As mentioned, in 1982 China was granted observer status in GATT, a privilege that has carried over into the WTO. We saw that in 1986 China applied to resume its membership in the treaty and banish the limbo it has been floating in since the nationalists had withdrawn.

The fundamental challenge of the China-WTO marriage is the legacy of the prereform era (pre-1978), a nonmarket trade regime which is even more incompatible with GATT's market-based principles than what has been described as "Organized Liberal Regimes" in chapter 1. As we have seen, China's prereform system did not respect GATT principles of nondiscrimination/transparency, and its systems were lousy with nontariff barriers. China's tariffs have indeed been very high, averaging 44 percent in the mid-1980s, as compared with an average of less than 10 percent imposed by the major western GATT contracting parties.

When it comes to essential direction, however, we have seen that China has introduced a series of reforms, which have fundamentally transformed its foreign trade operation from a closed nonmarket to a considerably open and increasingly market-driven system. The ultimate goal of China's economic reform is to establish something the regime describes as a "socialist market economy," an objective announced in March 1993 by Article 7 of the Amendments to the Constitution of the PRC. This delineates the state's power to make and implement "the economic plan," and changes the role of the state from micro-control to macro-management through the making and enforcement of laws and regulations. In accordance with this subtle yet crucial shift toward a market economy, China also adopted concrete measures to reform major areas of its foreign trade system.

By virtue of the heavy use of government subsidies for exports in accordance with the arbitrary national plan, tariff rates were created without the slightest heed of the goods' actual value in the world market. Between 1956 and 1977, China's foreign trade amounted to less than 4 percent of its national product, a ratio well below those of not only developed countries, but also other large developing countries such as Brazil and India.

Under central planning a web of ministries and administrative commissions spun by the central government managed all of China's foreign trade. These ministries and commissions combined business and administrative functions. They had full discretion to translate any administrative objectives directly into business decisions, allowing negligible scope for government regulation on foreign trade.

In 1980, what used to be called the Customs Bureau of Foreign Trade Ministry was elevated to a ministerial-level entity, the General Administration of Customs. It became responsible for the formulation and administration of tariffs. In 1987, a new Customs Tariff Commission was established. At the same time, China made an effort to promulgate laws and tariff schedules to make foreign trade policy more transparent. The National People's Congress enacted a comprehensive customs law to replace the interim law that had governed customs since 1951. The new law explicitly stipulated that all "customs schedules shall be published."

In 1983, China joined the Customs Cooperation Council. Unfortunately for the corporations who seek to profit off Chinese importation, efforts to reduce tariffs have not been as successful as Chinese reforms to the foreign trade management system. By 1987, the weighted average tariff rate had been reduced to 39 percent and 31.9 percent in 1992. This was similar to Brazil (31.9 percent) and Pakistan (35.9 percent), higher than those of Argentina (17.1 percent) and Colombia (15.1 percent), but much lower in the end than India's (54.8 percent). By the final days of 1995, China reduced its average tariff rate to 23 percent, one of the lowest percentages among major developing countries.

Under the heading of nontariff barriers, one-third of most imports in the 1980s and 1990s were estimated to be subject to canalization control via designated National Foreign Trade Corporations (NFTCs). Adding to these canals or fences, import planning (whereby state subsidies are attached to goods deemed "essential" either for the people's livelihood or national economic development) was applied to 18.5 percent of imports. The central government gradually dismantled the import planning system and decentralized foreign trade management. By 1991, government subsidies to exports were abolished, and each NFTC became responsible for its economic performance. Since then, import licensing and import/export quotas have not been obviously more prevalent in China than in other Western nations embracing freer trade, and thus could not be seen as obstacles to Chinese GATT/WTO membership.

Article III of GATT enshrined a key principle: internal taxes and regulations "should not be applied to imported or domestic products so as to afford protection to domestic production." However, Chinese enterprises with foreign participation were subject to entirely different tax treatment from domestic enterprises. This despite the fact that hardly any discrimination against enterprises with foreign participation existed. The dual tax system created numerous problems for foreign investors because of its complexity. China began to draft a new tax code in 1990 and enacted a law on transnational corporate taxation in 1991. The unification of the tax system (an important step toward a capitalist market economy) has brought China's tax law regime into compliance with GATT's national treatment requirement.

As pointed out in 1993 by the GATT Working Party on China's application, the Chinese dual-rate currency mechanism was a key obstacle to membership. The People's Bank of China administered two exchange rates. First it set an official rate for tourists and priority imports under the state plan. Second, the bank allowed local swap center administrators to peg a daily swap center rate, which was allowed to float within a limited range. By 1993, foreign exchange swap centers handled about 80 percent of current account transactions within China. Enterprises with foreign investment relied on these centers to acquire Chinese currency to pay local costs, and to exchange domestic earnings into hard currency for repatriation.

American and European criticisms focused on two aspects of the dual-rate exchange system, which they considered to be a nontariff barrier. First, the dual-rate system worked as a government subsidy for some Chinese import companies. By allowing the military and certain state-owned enterprises to pay for imported commodities at an overvalued official rate, the government absorbed a currency loss. Second, the dual-rate system was described as a hidden tax on currency trades. The central bank could target foreigners by forcing them to register their earnings in China at the official rate while repatriating profits at the swap center rate.

Only days after the conclusion of the Uruguay Round in December 1993, China made the surprising announcement that it was abolishing the dual-rate exchange system and was implementing a unified foreign exchange rate starting on January 1, 1994. The new rate adopted the former swap center rate.

In May 1994, the Standing Committee of the 8th National People's Congress drafted a Foreign Trade Law (FTL), which followed three proclaimed principles, all of which exude the unmistakable aroma of GATT influence. First, China's foreign trade policies and regulations must conform to the basic principles laid out in the FTL (i.e., they must be openly published and freely available). Second, bans or restrictions on imports and exports must conform to GATT rules and be transparent. Third, domestic industries must be protected through legal proceedings against unfair imports and not by administrative measures. The FTL strikes a balance between unity of policy and decentralization of operation in foreign trade by defining the role of the Ministry of Foreign Trade and Economic Cooperation as abolishing strict macromanagement and micromanagement.

During the 1980s, China gradually reduced the role of foreign trade planning. In addition to the outright abandonment of the export plan, the import plan (constituting 40 percent of China's imports in 1986) was reduced to cover only 18.5 percent of imports in 1992. Reflecting its drafters' determination to abolish all FTL plans, the draft is conspicuously silent on foreign trade planning. The FTL does retain the licensing system for the import and export of selected commodities and technologies, but licensing is treated as a temporary necessity, a mechanism to be disassembled in parts. Although the FTL fails to abolish quotas in foreign trade, it does a list of quota-bolstered commodities to be published. Significantly, the enactment of the FTL prompted China to publish the rules for export quota bidding and conducted public bidding for four agricultural products subject to export quotas. In prescribing measures dealing with trade surge, dumping and subsidies, the FTL directly borrows the solutions provided by GATT.

In March 1994, China submitted a proposal to the WTO for tariff reduction, which would commit the People's Republic to a ceiling of 40 percent in tariffs on industrial products. This rate would be reduced to 35 percent by 1998 and 30 percent within five years of China's entry to GATT/WTO. On NTBs, China agreed to gradually eliminate import quotas and licenses and shrink quantitative restrictions on imports from the current 1,247 tariff categories to 240, all by the year 2000. These objectives were significantly achieved through the reduction of average tariff rates to 23 percent on April 1, 1996. After these changes, many observers have assessed that China's foreign trade regime should be very much like those of most other market economies. Even before they were made, China's foreign trade regime under the 1994 FTL was more liberalized than those of the centrally-planned economies of Romania, Hungary and Poland when they were admitted to the GATT in the 1960s and 1970s.

Without the influence of the GATT/WTO framework and bilateral agreements reached by the United States and EC with China, it is impressive to imagine China's foreign trade regime having achieved this much free-market transmutation. Because the reformist Chinese leadership is unable openly to follow the practices of Western countries, they turn to international organizations for guiding market principles. The influencing power of GATT/WTO is not limited to the legal regime of Chinese foreign trade. Many practices, like the unification of tax rates, were first introduced in foreign-related economic activities and then applied domestically. The laws on protecting intellectual and industrial properties closely resemble those of European nations, especially Germany. The Corporation Law of December 1993 adopts a combination of the Anglo-American and Continental European systems. Adopting GATT/WTO practice early in the legal restructuring of its economy has enabled China to establish a legal system based on many commonly accepted international norms. This is all sweet music to the ears of third-image voluntarists and second-image realists in the capitalist economies as their trade with China expands.

Notes

1. Robert Ross, "Enter the Dragon," *Foreign Policy* (February 1997).
2. Greg Mostel, *Far Eastern Review* (spring 1997).
3. S. Esserman, *Office of the U.S. Trade Representative* (1998).
4. Op. cit.
5. See Yunlong Man in *UCLA Pacific Basin Law Journal* (fall 1996).

Chapter Seven

Dispute Settlement "Chinese Style"

As for dispute resolution, Jun Ge, in "Mediation, Arbitration and Litigation: Dispute Resolution in the People's Republic of China"[1] describes Chinese dispute resolution devices and evaluates their effectiveness in light of recent developments. As this book emphasizes, dispute resolution is critical because the maintenance and expansion of economic ties between China and the rest of the world depend largely on how the former handles business disputes with the latter. This is engrossing to those attuned to the heart of this book, dispute settlement for trade among sovereign nations.

Ge advances a highly optimistic view of existing Chinese dispute resolution devices, extolling the virtues of a model which "enables a population of 1.2 billion to live in harmony." It is argued that the overly litigious West has much to learn from the PRC's methods and philosophies. The limits of the Chinese model are not directly addressed. Although the author admits there is a need for some fine-tuning, he argues that China is fast becoming a "law-oriented country" and that its dispute resolution mechanisms meet current world standards.

Strongly rooted in Confucianism, this Chinese tradition is based on the idea of "mediating disputes by smoothing away discords." The focus is on upholding virtue and communal values rather than strict legal principles. It is one of the few aspects of the traditional Chinese legal system which was not completely abolished by the communist regime. And in the past two decades, the Chinese mediation system has become the largest in the world. Currently, more cases are brought to mediation committees than to the Chinese courts. The author is glowingly positive, extolling the advantages of new rules "perfected" for this system. He focuses on the successes of these committees in dealing with a wide array of domestic cases; limitations are not dealt with.

A distinctive feature of Chinese arbitration proceedings is the combination of arbitration with mediation. All manner of arbitral organs, including CIETAC (China International Economic and Trade Arbitration Commission), are required (or at least permitted in CIETAC's case) to attempt mediation before proceeding to arbitrate. A recent survey indicated that approximately 30 percent of the international arbitration cases accepted by CIETAC were solved by mediation. In recent years, steps have been taken to further facilitate the use of mediation during arbitration. Under CIETAC Arbitration Rules, as revised in late 1995, mediation is permitted if both parties have a desire for mediation or one party so desires and the other party does not object when consulted by the tribunal.

China is also credited with having invented new mediation methods in international arbitration, such as "joint mediation." Under the joint mediation device, a Chinese party may apply to CIETAC while the foreign party applies to a corresponding arbitral organ in their own country. This serves to alleviate some concerns about the bias that would exist where all mediators are Chinese nationals.

This is a feature of Chinese civil procedure for domestic cases. According to Ge, in 1986 alone, the Chinese courts solved approximately one million civil and economic cases through mediation, 61.5 percent of the total number of cases handled that year. Along with the growth in trade since the adoption of the "open-door" policy, arbitration relating to international business transactions has developed nicely, witnessing the emergence of new arbitral forums, rules and regulations.

Since September 1995, a unified and independent domestic arbitration system has operated in China. According to Ge, this brings Chinese proceedings of domestic arbitration in line with prevailing world practices. Among other things, the 1995 reforms mean that foreign parties in a domestic arbitration are not restricted to representation by Chinese counsel. Foreign counsel may appear in such proceedings. In addition, decisions are completely binding. The author argues that the reform of this system negates the compulsion and influence from the Chinese government and ensures the impartiality of Chinese domestic arbitration. This system is expected to grow as market mechanisms in China strengthen.

Since its inception in 1988, the number of cases submitted to CIETAC has grown. [2] Moreover, the range of cases tends to be more complex and linked to larger claims than in the past. The author credits the success of CIETAC to the enforceability of its awards both in China and in over 100 1958 New York Convention countries. In March 1994 and September 1995 major changes were made to CIETAC's arbitration rules to bring them in line with recognized international standards. Its scope of jurisdiction has been greatly enlarged. Of the eighty-one articles in the 1994 CIETAC Arbitration Rules, thirty-eight are entirely new

Key developments in the new CIETAC rules that are billed as "benefits" for foreign corporations include the inclusion of foreign diplomats in the arbitration panel, permission to carry out arbitrations in English (or another foreign language agreed on by the parties), the ability of foreign parties to use their own (non-Chinese) attorneys, a nine-month time limit for a tribunal to conduct a hearing/render its award (extensions possible where "really justified"), the affirmation that final arbitration awards made by CIETAC are binding, and the possibility of fast-tracking (at the request of one party if dispute involves less than RMB500,000 yuan, or at the request of both parties if the amount exceeds this figure). Ge expects CIETAC rules to be refined even further.

Can One Litigate?
Although traditionally discouraged, traditional litigation has developed in China nonetheless. Modern economic reform since the late 1970s has in fact created an ultimate "need" for litigation mechanisms.

Part IV of the Civil Procedure Law (enacted in 1991) is devoted to regulating cases involving foreign laws and foreign disputants. A party from another country now ostensibly has the same rights and obligations as a Chinese party, unless the foreign party's country does not follow the international rule of reciprocity. This law also specifies particular principles relating to jurisdiction, service of process, provisional security remedies and judicial assistance.

It is worth noting that amendments to the Arbitration Rules of China International Economic and Trade Arbitration Commission (CIETAC), which came into effect on April 10, 1998, made a significant change in CIETAC arbitration procedures which will allow disputes among foreign investment enterprises (FIEs) and Chinese entities to be submitted to CIETAC arbitration.

This change has solved a problem, which has long troubled foreign investors and lawyers: under the previous CIETAC rules, only disputes arising from contracts with "foreign elements" may be submitted to CIETAC arbitration. As a result, it was uncertain whether disputes arising from a contract between a wholly foreign-owned enterprise (or a Chinese-foreign joint venture) as a "Chinese legal person" and a local Chinese company could be arbitrated through CIETAC. Foreign investors were left with little choice but to be subjected to uncertainty and Chinese court jurisdiction.

China's system for enforcing arbitral awards still has its share of kinks and problems. Most notably, the CIETAC rule change has not eliminated the dichotomy between the domestic Economic Contract Law and Foreign Economic Contract Law. Nevertheless, this change reflects CIETAC's latest effort to become more consistent with international practices (and to be more competitive; 700 cases were submitted in

1997), and will allow FIEs to have more certainty in establishing contractual relationships with local businesses.

Perhaps the most significant effect of the CIETAC rule amendments is the allowance of what were previously regarded as "domestic contracts" as "international contracts" for arbitration purposes. A subtle ploy, this change makes it possible for parties to such contracts to submit disputes to foreign arbitration bodies for resolution outside of China. Although the Arbitration Law and the Civil Procedure Code should also be amended to clarify a number of ambiguities, the amendments to CIETAC rules have fundamentally broadened the definition of "international contracts." This is a crucial phase synchronizing the system with an international trend to favor alternative dispute resolutions and contracting parties' choice of forum. As a member of the New York Convention and a nation whose Supreme People's Court ruled for stricter adherence to this convention's requirements, China is expected to improve its alternative dispute resolution environment. This is a truly a welcome change which will clearly benefit foreign investors and exporters.

It is further expected that the CIETAC amendments will prompt contract reviews by major foreign investors in China, with contracts pertaining to local enterprise amended to take advantage of this change. Typical contracts subject to review are sourcing agreements with local suppliers, agency agreements and service and repair agreements. Because the amended Article 2 of the CIETAC rules features a very broad definition of CIETAC's jurisdiction, some lawyers also believe that noncompete agreements, IP agreements and even certain labor contracts may also come within CIETAC's jurisdiction. (See Appendix B of this book for the Arbitration Clauses outlined).

Let us remember another trade policy context. China and the United States, of course, are members of the twenty-two-nation Asia Pacific Economic Forum. What is the forum? It certainly is not a deregulated trade zone. As a minister of trade, one remembers attending briefings on APEC one month before their 1993 meeting and noting how vague the links binding the forum together really were. In fact, the United States later warned the conference that unless it could deliver solid results in bringing down import barriers sooner in East Asia, it risked losing American support. This led to an Australian proposal for "concerted liberalization" which offered a plan by November 1995 for lowering barriers to deregulated trade and corporate investment – especially politically sensitive tariff and nontariff structures. Some understandings stretching past the millenium have been approved by the members of the forum, but nothing approaching a trade agreement (let alone a dispute settlement mechanism) is in place.

APEC deliberations offer not only an opportunity to decrease trade protections but a forum for dialogue on developing domestic trade laws among all members with similar content (provisions made, of course, for more advanced economies). In 1988, nominally the minister responsible for rewiring Canada's tariff system into the worldwide harmonized tariff system, this writer was surprised to learn that there was in place already a framework for a "collectivized" system. There are harmonized definitions for most goods and services that seem to be inter-subjectively agreed upon across nations.

Therefore, an urgent need for harmonized domestic trade laws does exist, and can be built with the WTO's specific treaty requirements. It could very well be put into statute books without much delay. Indeed, APEC should be a forum for this as well as for discussion/review of tariff and nontariff reductions. Once this is done, dispute settlement bodies (including above all the WTO's) would be left with simpler disputes about whether domestic trade law is being administered properly, as the rules would be more conducive to transparency and thus, credibility.

Into the Future

As we have seen up until the late 1970s, foreign trade and corporate investment played an insignificant role in a country nearly autonomous within its domestic economy. Pat Buchanan's vision of "America the self-reliant" in fact flourished as a reality in China until recently. As we have seen, with the rise of Deng Xiaoping and the death of militant Maoism, however, China reversed its economic policy and emerged as an economic power. Its so-called "open-door" policy has made it one of the world's largest trading powers, not to mention a target for observers calling for global human rights.

First the reality. In the foreseeable future, China must comply with its own trade laws or it will gain nothing but enemies in the world trading regime. Here, the experience of the original FTA may be helpful under a number of systems: the WTO, DSU, an ad hoc bilateral or perhaps an APEC-organized panel. A side accord type of committee could be formed simply to ascertain if compliance with one's own laws is happening.

In China, the dual influences of Confucius thought and communism is still infectious. The leverage of these philosophies affects both the composition of panels and the possible apprehension of panel bias. One could see these philosophies' fingerprints all over the resolution with the United States over software piracy and other disputes in 1994.

The inherent difficulties surrounding Chinese corporate dispute settlements are compounded by an unspoken Asian assumption that all of a nation's economic, political, legal and social institutions exist to serve the ruling class. This of course is reminiscent of some "civil society" protesters' assumptions in Seattle. As a result, Chinese leaders start with skepticism about getting an equitable hearing from a non-socialist country. If a country is not socialist in ethos, it will not have the same policies as China and will, by definition, be at odds with the Asian superpower. It is not surprising that outsiders believe, given the Chinese government's historic role in business and the economy, that its political views shape the result of international trade disputes. Recall that in China's domestic dispute settlement arrangements, an individual's needs take a back seat to the Party's needs and policies. This mentality of suspicion of individualistic capitalist outsiders haunts foreign contractors when they deal with or compete with the government-controlled business sectors.

In spite of all this, China's dispute settlement techniques function on a set of underlying principles that just might not be too distant from those of the WTO's DSU. The Confucian-communist-Deng tradition will not disappear overnight, yet the potential exists for both the DSU and ad hoc bilateral (or potential APEC) understandings to settle disputes, perhaps using even NAFTA as a model.

As we have seen in all the previous chapters, dispute settlement mechanisms have the purpose of helping provide a stable-trading environment where members can be certain of their rights and obligations. Yet, in order for any contract to mean anything, the rights and obligations under these agreements must be enforced. Many trade agreements lack the "teeth" to do this. However, as earlier chapters outline, the dispute resolution provisions have been institutionalized to provide a specific framework of rules and procedures.[3]

It is these dispute resolution procedures that may be the fundamental "stumbling block" to China once it rejoins the WTO. We have reviewed earlier the several recognized barriers to China's entry to the WTO. Among them are foreign trade policies, its tax system and the country's general lack of transparency.[4] We have itemized how China has begun to restructure its laws as a precondition to entering the WTO. Beginning in 1992, China abolished export subsidies and adjustment taxes on imports, and reduced the categories of goods requiring import/export licenses and quotas.[5] Too often ignored is the status of China's dispute resolution practices: While in theory it appears that the provisions are the same, a comparison of China's mechanisms with WTO reveals that they are still far apart.

On February 26, 1995, the United States and China successfully avoided a trade war that would have cost both countries billions of dollars. At the center of the dispute was the lack of enforcement in China against copyright infringers of U.S. products. As a result of the dispute, a variety of imported goods from both countries were facing massive increases in tariffs.[6] The trade war would have been very costly to both countries, not just in monetary terms, but in the crippling of their overall trading relationship. If China successfully acceded to the WTO before the dispute arose, the opportunity to witness the new dispute resolution provisions may have been provided by the intellectual property rights disagreement.

Always influenced by Confucius,[7] Chinese society has found adjudicated settlement of disputes to be offensive. While legal avenues were always open for adjudication of conflict, conciliation and mediation were the real preferred methods. Today, mediation and conciliation remain the predominant forms of civil and commercial dispute settlement in China, regardless of whether the dispute arises from domestic or international causes.[8]

The principal government dispute resolution body in China is known as the China International Economic and Trade Arbitration Commission (CIETAC).[9] The vast majority of various domestic and international contracts refer to CIETAC as the dispute resolution body, which will mediate the hearing. As a surgeon to her scalpels, CIETAC has its own set of comprehensive rules and procedures governing dispute resolution.[10]

In China, there are three formulae for nonarbitrary settlement of disputes. "Settlement through friendly negotiation" requires that the parties engage in direct negotiations without the aid of an official arbitration organ. "Consultation" involves the CIETAC "assisting" parties in finding a solution among themselves. Finally, "conciliation" requires that the arbitration organ make a concrete but nonbinding suggestion to the parties.[11] These definitions bring to light the first problem plaguing dispute settlement in Asia's largest economy – the concepts of dispute settlement are defined differently there.[12] What China refers to as "settlement through friendly negotiation" is known to the West as "consultation;" whereas Chinese "consultation" is Western "conciliation," and finally, Chinese "conciliation" is Western "mediation." Furthermore, these terms are not explicitly defined in the GATT. This leaves open a highly elastic interpretation of these concepts.

A common Western lexicon might define arbitration as a proceeding between two parties in which a neutral third makes a binding decision. Arbitration, as a method for resolving domestic and international disputes, has been around in China as early as 1954.[13] However, only recently have the decisions by Chinese arbitration organs been published.[14] This makes it now less difficult to analyze and to draw comparisons.

The changing politics in China with the advent of Mao and the Communist Party changed the way that mediation was employed in China.[15] Traditional mediation purposely avoided the levers of state machinery in resolving disputes. On the other hand, the communist style of mediation directly involves representatives of the state and the Party's ideology. No longer was mediation used to reharmonize the disputants – instead, it became a political tool. Chinese judicial reports make clear the party's intention to use dispute resolution as a political instrument to mobilize support for the Party among the peasantry: dispute resolution techniques serve to articulate Party principles; disputes are suppressed rather than resolved (since ideological principles come before individual principles and needs); and finally, dispute resolution is a means of control.[16] Mediators apply mediation principles that stress commitment to the party and to the national goals of "the collective."

In China, because there has always been a cultural aversion to formal methods like arbitration for resolving trade conflict, the majority of international disputes are therefore resolved informally, through consultations and conciliations. Even when enforced settlement becomes necessary, the Chinese lean strongly – and uniquely – toward mediation. The roots of this preference may lie in the belief that applying foreign law often results in all-or-nothing resolutions. This conflicts with the Confucian philosophy that disputes should be resolved by compromise, with an eye to mutual benefits. Clearly, this preference is evidenced by China's standard form contracts for foreign trade and investment. They all stipulate that the governing arbitration body is CIETAC, unless the parties agree to go abroad:

> Parties to a joint venture shall apply for arbitration in accordance with the relevant written agreement. They may submit the dispute to the China International Economic and Foreign Trade Arbitration Commission of the China Council for the Promotion of International Trade in accordance with its arbitration rules. With the mutual consent of the parties concerned, the arbitration can also be carried out through an arbitration agency in the country where the sued party is

located or one in a third country in accordance with the arbitration agency's procedures.[17]

Let us see how this aligns with WTO's DSU. As we have seen, the WTO has a permanent body charged with governing trade conduct. The mandate of the WTO is to:

> [P]rovide the common institutional framework for the conduct of the trade relations among its Members in matters related to the agreements and associated legal instruments included in the Annexes to this Agreement.[18]

Among the "associated legal instruments included in the Annexes to this Agreement" is Annex 2, the *Understanding on Rules and Procedures Governing the Settlement of Disputes* (hereinafter "DSU"). Specific responsibility for administering the DSU is given to the WTO.[19] Within the structure of the DSU, a dispute settlement body (DSB) is established to administer the relevant rules and procedures.

As outlined in chapter 3, the basic structure of the dispute settlement techniques employed by the DSU are as follows:[20] First, consultations are undertaken to "accord sympathetic consideration" to other members' concerns.[21] If the consultation does not result in "satisfactory adjustment of a matter," a panel is automatically established.[22] Second, "conciliation and mediation" are voluntary procedures that may be engaged in before a panel is convened and may continue during the panel process.[23] Third, after hearing submissions from each party, the panel will issue an interim report at which time the parties, if they choose, can "request . . . . a review [of] precise aspects of the interim report."[24] After hearing arguments, the panel issues a final report.[25] Lastly, the panel report is open to appeal. The appellate body can "uphold, modify or reverse the legal findings and conclusions of the panel." Finally, the report of the appellate body is adopted by the DSB – unless there is a unanimous decision not to do so by all members.[26] A valuable insight can be extracted from all this seeming intricacy: arbitration has a very limited role in the DSU and is referred to as an "alternative means of dispute settlement."[27]

As discussed earlier, the reforms of the DSU include the expedition of decisions, the automatic right to a panel and the right to have reports automatically approved and not blocked (unless the right to appeal is invoked).[28] The DSU provisions are now subject to ministerial review, as the deadline of January 1, 1999 [29] has arrived.

The plot thickens: China wants to reenter the WTO as a developing nation in order to receive special allowances, especially with regard to jettisoning the power of governments to set priorities in market policy. Originally, the United States. blocked China's entry with this status.[30] However, with the resolution of the intellectual property rights dispute in 1994, the United States has officially removed its objection.

The significance of China entering the WTO as a developing country is twofold. First, it enables the People's Republic to receive full benefits accorded to members, but releases it from some key obligations imposed on other members. Second, there are special rules with respect to dispute settlement procedures for developed countries. These require that members "exercise due restraint in raising matters under these procedures" and "exercise due restraint in asking for compensation and suspension."[31] In addition, conciliation and mediation are mandatory procedures before a panel will be convened.[32] If China was a member of the WTO and the U.S.-China trade dispute had resulted in sanctions, China could have taken refuge in these provisions to explain why it was not enforcing copyright laws.

Not surprisingly, the rules and procedures outlined by the DSU are infinitely more comprehensive than those of CIETAC. However, there are similarities in the general structure of both: their common jurisdiction over international trade matters,[33] their insistence on having a standing number of members from which panels are struck [34] and their strict time requirements regarding everything from panel selection to rendering decisions.[35] Practically (and again similarly), both bodies allow for the consultation of experts for clarification of certain questions.[36]

Another point of comparison concerns the organizations' underlying principles of dispute settlement. Within the framework of the DSU, the same phrases are repeated. For example, "maintenance of a proper balance between the rights and obligations of members";[37] "achieving a satisfactory settlement of the matter";[38] "secure a positive solution to a dispute";[39] and "solution mutually acceptable."[40] These jack-in-the-box words indicate an overriding WTO principle of conflict avoidance and universally acceptable solutions that do not jeopardize "security and predictability in the multilateral trading system."[41]

Analogous phrases occur in the Chinese law as well. For example:

> The representative of the Contracting Parties, upon request by either of them, shall in the spirit of co-operation and mutual understanding discuss measures aimed at broader economic and trade relations between the two countries and solution of problems connected with the implementation of this Agreement.[42]

or,

> The contract should be made in conformity with the principles of equality and mutual benefit, and of achieving unanimity through consultations.[43]

Arbitration, by definition, does not balance the interests of the parties involved; it decides who is right and who is wrong. "Positive solutions" and "unanimity" are viewed and valued differently from the claimant's and defendant's point of view. Moreover, "acceptability" and "equality" are not part of arbitration. What appears to be happening in the DSU is an adherence to the Chinese concepts of friendly negotiation, consultation and conciliation. These like principles may help ensure that China and its would-be fellow WTO members are starting from the same premises with respect to dispute settlement.

Despite the similarities between the DSU and CIETAC, the significant difference between their rules and procedures cannot be ignored.

The Arbitration Commission consists of:

> 15-21 members to be selected and appointed by the China Council for the Promotion of International Trade for a term of one year from among persons having a special knowledge and experience in foreign trade, commerce, industry, agriculture, transportation, insurance and other related matters as well as in law.[44]

Although not specifically stated, the Arbitration Commission consists *of Chinese nationals* who meet the necessary prerequisites of knowledge and experience. Given nationalistic concerns, one wonders whether a Chinese arbitrator can really work independently of the Chinese party negotiating in the dispute. Will the foreign party be engaging in a useless procedure?

In contrast, the DSU provides that:

> Panels shall be composed of well-qualified governmental and non-governmental individuals, including persons who have served on or presented a case to a panel, served as a representative of a Member or of a Contracting Party to the GATT 1947 or as a representative to the Council or Committee of any covered agreement or its predecessor agreement, or in the Secretariat, taught or published on

international trade law or policy, or served as senior trade
official of a Member.[45]

The contrast between the DSU and CIETAC is clear as crystal. Panel
members of the DSU may come from a diverse spectrum of experience
and nationalities. Furthermore, it is provided that "panelists shall serve in
their individual capacities and not as government representatives, nor
representatives of any organization."[46] In essence, there can be no
apprehension of bias as clearly existed with CIETAC panelists. There is
now an expectation that non-nationals will soon participate in CIETAC
panels.

There is no right to appeal as outlined by the Provisional Rules of
CIETAC:

> The award given by the Arbitration Commission is final and
> neither party shall bring an appeal for revision before a court
> of law or any other organization.[47]

However, China's Law of Civil Procedure contains provisions with
respect to the enforcement of arbitration awards, provisions that
effectively amount to an appeal. If a Chinese corporation does not agree
with a CIETAC decision, it could ignore the terms of the award knowing
perfectly well that the foreign party would have to plead to the court in
the defaulter's jurisdiction. If this occurs, the court can refuse to perfect
the award on the following grounds: first, if no valid arbitration
agreement exists between the claimant and the nonperformer; second, if
the award is found to contravene the social or public interest of China;
third, if the party against whom the award is made can prove that the
award deals with matters (a) not within the scope of the arbitration
agreement or (b) which the arbitration institution has no power to
arbitrate. Finally, the court can refuse to use its perfecting power if the
parties have concluded an arbitration agreement, which is void or
incapable of being performed.[48] The defaulter would simply argue one of
these grounds and the court would rule that the award is unenforceable.
Obviously, this is an ethically questionable method for bypassing the
"no-appeals" provision of CIETAC.

Article 17 of the DSU provides for disputants' right to an appeal, but
not for third parties.[49] Furthermore, areas of appeal are "limited to issues
of law covered in the panel reports and legal interpretations developed by
the panel."[50] (In other words, the appeal is constrained to a judicial
review of the panel's decision and no new issues may be raised.) Once
the appellate body has made its decision, it is binding. It's also

automatically adopted by the DSB.[51] There is no avenue of appeal after a final decision has been rendered. And once China accedes to the WTO, the nation will be unable to resort to its civil law to avoid carrying out the DSB's ruling – whatever that ruling may be.

CIETAC handles almost all the arbitrations arising between China and its array of various disputant foreign parties. However, once an award has been granted, it is up to the Chinese court system to enforce payment. Chinese law binds its courts to recognize CIETAC arbitration awards:

> The award of the Arbitration Commission shall be executed by the parties themselves within the time fixed by the award. In case an award is not executed after the expiration of the fixed time, the People's Courts of the People's Republic of China shall, upon the request of one of the parties, enforce it in accordance with the law.[52]

Furthermore, China is a signatory to the 1958 *New York Convention on the Recognition and Enforcement of Foreign Arbitral Awards*.[53] This requires that the courts must also recognize arbitration awards made by foreign tribunals.

These Are the Rules. Do They Work?

Despite these legal provisions, a number of obstacles make it effectively impossible to always enforce the rules. Local courts have placed regional interests ahead of foreign claims and have been alleged to have even gone so far as to misrepresent bank account statements in order not to have the local corporation pay the outstanding award to the foreign claimant.[54] There is an obvious lack of coordination between CIETAC and the local courts. Whether this will be ameliorated as a result of the PRC's *Foreign Trade Law* of 1994 and the judicial review undertakings at the Clinton-Jiang 1997 summit remains to be seen.[55]

Furthermore, civil procedure law offers an array of justifications for the already recalcitrant regional evading their responsibility to execute the awards. Loopholes allow the courts to review an arbitration award and independently rule on its enforceability.[56] The provisions provide very broad grounds for the local courts not to uphold the arbitration award.

In the WTO, enforcement awards falls under Article 22 of the DSU, entitled "Compensation and Suspension of Concession":

> Compensation and the suspension of concession or other
> obligations are temporary measures available in the event the
> recommendations and rulings are not implemented within a
> reasonable period of time. However, neither compensation nor
> the suspension of concession or other obligations is preferred
> to full implementation of a recommendation to bring a
> measure into conformity with the covered agreements.[57]

This provision articulates the overriding principle of GATT: conflict avoidance. To this end, the complaining party must enter negotiations for a "mutually acceptable compensation" before seeking DSB permission to suspend its trade obligations to the recalcitrant state.[58] If the defaulting state fails to follow the recommendations of the panel or appellate body, it will then (and only then) face sanctions.

For the Chinese, this means that foreign parties would have no recourse to the People's Court, where the possibility of local judiciaries overturning the arbitration award would seem very likely. This may be a bitter pill for Chinese officials and businesses to swallow. However, this is also a matter for the Chinese government to resolve internally; its conclusion will surely be that enforcing arbitration awards in the long term is a small price to pay for membership in the WTO. Moreover, if it enters as a developing country, China will benefit from applicable special rules. Theoretically, this will result in other members having to exercise due restraint before beginning to exercise their rights under the DSU; consequently, China ought to be handed fewer complaints and less awards to enforce.

As Thomas Yunlong suggested, China's level of transparency is vitally important to the current members of the WTO. Knowledge of laws and regulations, import and export systems, domestic regulations with respect to trade and market-driven internal prices are essential for a trading regime that financiers can look to as an engine for profits. With regard to its foreign trade system, China's government regulates trade through administrative orders. This makes it difficult for foreign trading partners to be informed of changes in China's trading policy. However, in order to meet the WTO requirements, the Chinese government has started to promulgate PRC laws.[59] The number of state-owned enterprises is still substantial, of course. Nevertheless, government procurement contracts in China will be placed under scrutiny once China accedes to the WTO. There are no provisions in the Procedural Rules of CIETAC that relate to government procurement practices, but compared to some of the other challenges facing China's WTO entry, this omission may not be a huge obstacle.

One of the included trade agreements of the GATT is the Government Procurement Agreement (GPA). The parties to the GPA recognize:

> that laws, regulations, procedures and practices regarding government procurement should not be prepared, adopted or applied to foreign or domestic products or services and to foreign or domestic suppliers so as to afford protection to domestic products or services or domestic suppliers and should not discriminate among foreign products or services or among foreign suppliers.[60]

This provision is akin to the national treatment principle requiring countries to accord the same treatment to foreigners as their own residents. Equal knowledge and application of laws is necessary to avoid discrimination against foreign parties, or special treatment for domestic investors.

A problematic aspect of the GPA is that it binds only signatories; and being a signatory of the GPA is separate from being a signatory to the WTO.[61] Therefore, unless the PRC chooses to be bound by the GPA provisions, it will not be held to the obligations under it. Considering existing corruption in China,[62] it would clearly be preferable if China voluntarily participated in the GPA. Perhaps mandatory participation in the GPA should be an issue for the next round of trade negotiations.

The DSU is applicable to the administration of the GPA. There are, however, a few special rules specifically provided for in the GPA with respect to dispute settlement.[63] The main deviation from the general rules, which ensures that the effect of a GPA dispute will not flow over into other parts of the GATT, is clear:

> any dispute arising under any Agreement listed in Appendix 1 to the Dispute Settlement Understanding other than this Agreement shall not result in the suspension of concession or other obligations under this Agreement, and any dispute arising under this Agreement shall not result in the suspension of concessions or other obligations under any other Agreement listed in the said Appendix 1.

To enforce advancement in administrative fairness and transparency, it is clear that World Bank and perhaps IMF "soft power" requirements may be also needed to buttress progress.

Conclusion

The evolution of China to WTO membership is clearly a case of domestic evolution from a closed nontransparent, nonmarket regime to something less closed, more transparent, more market oriented. So we see emerging conditions for a third-image "rules-based legal momentum" acceptance are taking place on the mainland of China for accession to the WTO. It is clear that "realist" negotiations (mostly by the United States and the European Community but also by domestic lobbies) have helped to move China to this threshold. Voluntarist acts of faith based on the assumption that "soft power" public opinion had readied China for membership would have been folly. There is a need for further "soft power," and public pressure in pushing for more transparency in China, perhaps accelerated by transnational voices on the Internet and "hard power" negotiations. The dispute settlement regime of China and that of the WTO are not so different that accession would spell collapse for the DSU if China did join.

Also softening China's early going once it joins the WTO is, as we have seen in an earlier chapter, some tendency in the United States and others in the WTO's membership to not put developing nations to the test of every WTO obligation. We have seen that the incubation of Internet-driven "soft law bias" in favor of more openness and objectivity can also ease transitions to the new trade systems in China.

To ease that passage it might also be worth considering an interim arrangement whereby bilateral dispute settlement (i.e., encouraging enforcement of domestic law) might provide a happier, healthier introduction to the WTO. This can be a solvent, as the Canada-U.S. and NAFTA experience shows. It can lower political temperatures and can be especially effective on routine antidumping disputes. Whether this would be a mere diversion from the WTO/GATT ambition can be honestly debated. Ultimately, it is significant that in the evolution of the FTA to NAFTA, bilateral dispute settlements were far more than smoke and mirrors. They lowered political temperature at times and furthered a better dispute settlement mechanism. Whether enforcement of sovereign environmental and labor laws could be enhanced through side accords as was done in NAFTA, is also an intriguing question.

China as WTO Preserver?

Another remote possibility, seldom explored by American or European "China observers," is that China's accession to the WTO could enhance the WTO by adding a major player that could mediate U.S.-EU differences. When these two trade behemoths start slugging it out, there is no one member of the WTO that commands enough trade respect to help them resolve their disputes. Japan is unable or unwilling to play this larger role because of its domestic economic malaise, and its current aging leaders hardly demonstrate a vision for global liberalization of trade.

The good offices of the director general of the WTO have yet to be occupied by a leader with the stature and persuasive force to command the attention of American and European trade officials who are generally excessively confident in their own case. Imagine then, a China as a respected WTO member, and leaders like Chinese Premier Zhu Rongji, who exercise true statesmanship. When a dispute between the United States and the European Community threatens to rip apart the WTO, the Chinese statesman could host settlement negotiations in Beijing. Settlement under the shadow of the Great Wall certainly would not be reached every time, but "it may be difficult for the disputants to reject a fair deal mediated by this kind of China" writes Raj Bhala .[64]

Bhala writes

> China will be involved in many WTO cases, sometimes as a complainant, sometimes as a respondent. Perhaps, China might serve as a welcome example and not be as litigious as the U.S. and the EU. But, given the volume of China's overseas transactions, we can surely expect a level of participation at least comparable to that of India. Each case in which China will be involved that is not settled through consultations will result in a decision by a WTO panel and, if that decision is appealed, by the WTO Appellate Body. The conventional wisdom is that these decisions are not "binding" precedents for future cases. In fact, they are a source of authority, an international common law of trade. With Chinese participation in the WTO dispute resolution process, we can expect a growing body of precedents (for example, on key issues such as the meaning of most-favored nation or national treatment in particular contexts). These decisions will provide legal authority for other nations as they formulate their own trade policies.[65]

Notes

1. *UCLA Pacific Basin Law Journal* (Fall 1996).

2. See Joseph Meehan, *Dispute Settlement In China vs The GATT* (April 10, 1995) for research behind the next 12 paragraphs.

3. Jeffrey Schott, *The Uruguay Round: An Assessment* (Washington: Institute for International Economics, 1994), 8.

4. Guigo Wang, "China's Return to GATT: Legal and Economic Implications," 28 (June 1994): *Journal of World Trade* 51.

5. Mark O'Neill, "US-China trade war edges closer: Negotiators leave Beijing without agreement on copyright protection" *The Globe and Mail*, 30 January 1995, B3.

6. Rod Mickleburgh, "US, China avert trade war: sanctions avoided by 11th-hour deal" *The Globe and Mail*, 27 February 1995, B1.

7. The Confucius philosophy promotes the concepts of harmony and understanding in society. Compromise and social conformity are stressed to avoid friction between individuals. Laws and its institutions have no role in Confucianism since resort to these mechanisms exposes one to loss of virtue. Ralph H. Folsom and John H. Minan, eds., *Law in the People's Republic of China* (London: Martinus Nijhoff Publishers, 1989), 4.

8. Ibid., 85.

9. *Decision of the Government Administration Council of the Central People's Government Concerning the Establishment of an Economic and Foreign Trade Arbitration Commission within the China Council for the Promotion of International Trade*, adopted on 6 May 1954 at the 215th Session of the Government Administration Council, English translation in National Council for the United States-China Trade Special Report, no. 4. *Arbitration and Dispute Settlement in Trade with China* (1974) 48-57. This writer follows here the research of Joseph Meehan in 1995 into CIETAC's operations.

10. Ibid., Article 12: Rules Concerning the Procedure of Arbitration shall be made by the China Council for the Promotion of International Trade. See also, the *Provisional Rules of Procedure of the Economic and Foreign Trade Arbitration Commission of the China Council for the Promotion of International Trade*, adopted on 31 March 1956 at the Fourth Session of the China Council for the Promotion of International Trade.

11. Gene T. Hsiao, *The Foreign Trade of China: Policy, Law and Practice* (Berkeley: University of California Press, 1977), 154.

12. See for example, the *Dictionary of Canadian Law* (Scarborough: Carswell Publishing, 1990) and the *Dictionary of International Law and Diplomacy* (New York: Oceana Publishing Inc., 1973).

13. This is the founding date of the Foreign Trade Arbitration Commission, the original name of CIETAC.

14. Op. cit., 9, 148.

15. Ibid., 95.

16. T'ai-hsing Report, 1946, Stanley Lubman, "Mao and Mediation: Politics and Dispute Resolution in Communist China" in Folsom and Minan, eds., *Law in the People's Republic of China* (London: Martinus Nijhoff Publishers, 1989), 96.

17. *Regulations for the Implementation of the People's Republic of China on Joint Ventures using Chinese and Foreign Investment*, Article 110. Promulgated by the State Council on 20 September 1983.

18. *Agreement Establishing the World Trade Organization*, 15 April 1994,

19. Ibid. at Article III(3).

20. The DSU incorporates, by reference, Articles XXII and XXIII of *GATT 1947*. See Appendix C of this paper.

21. *The Understanding on the Rules and Procedures Governing the Settlement of Disputes*, 15 April 1994, Final Act Embodying the Results of the Uruguay Round of Multilateral Trade Negotiations, Article 4(2).

22. Ibid. at Article 4(3) and 4(7).

23. Ibid. at Article 5(1), 5(3) and 5(5).

24. Ibid. at Article 15.

25. Ibid.

26. Ibid. at Article 17.

27. Ibid. at Article 25(1).

28. Op. cit., note 5, 126-28.

29. Op. cit., note 5, 14.

30. Madelaine Drohan, "Davos Notebook," *The Globe and Mail*, 28 January 1995 B5.

31. Op. cit., note 23 at Article 24(1).

32. Ibid. at Article 24(2). Contrast with Article 5.

33. Op. cit., note 12 at Rule 2; *Supra*, note 23 at Article 1(1).

34. Op. cit., note 12 at Rules 2 and 3; *Supra*, note 23 at Article 8(4).

35. Op. cit., note 12 at Rules 9, 11, 14 and 30; *Supra*, note 23 at Appendix 3(12).

36. Op. cit., note 12 at Rule 27; *Supra*, note 23 at Article 13.

37. Op. cit., note 23 at Article 3(3).

38. Op. cit., note 23 at Article 3(4).

39. Op. cit., note 23 at Article 3(7).

40. Ibid.

41. Op. cit., note 23 at Article 3(2).

42. Op. cit., note 13, Trade Agreement between the Government of the Republic of the Philippines and the Government of the People's Republic of China, Department of Industry, Republic of the Philippines.

43. *Foreign Economic Contract Law*, Article 3.

44. Op. cit., note 11 at Article 3.

45. Op. cit., note 23 at Article 8(1).

46. Ibid. at Article 8(9).

47. Op cit., note 12 at Rule 31.

48. Law of Civil Procedure, Article 260, and Promulgated 9 April 1991.

49. Op. cit., note 23 at Article 17(4).

50. Ibid. at Article 17(6).

51. Ibid. at Article 17(4).

52. Op. cit., note 11.

53. 10 June 1958, 330 U.N.T.S. 3.

54. Matthew Bersani, "The Enforcement of Arbitration Awards in China," *Journal of International Arbitration* 49 (June 1992): 49-50.

55. See comments of U.S. Trade Representative Esserman, in chapter six and Thomas Yunlong Man, chapter six for descriptions of these issues.

56. Op. cit., note 50 at Article 260.

57. Op. cit., note 23 at Article 22.

58. This is where the United States can invoke its "Super 301" provision.

59. Op. cit., note 6 at 58.

60. *Agreement on Government Procurement*, 15 April 1994, Final Act Embodying the Results of the Uruguay Round of Multilateral Trade Negotiations, Preamble.

61. Ibid.

62. Op. cit., note 8. Chinese premiers have often startled the world by admitting that corruption was a serious problem in the Chinese government.

63. Op. cit., note 62 at Article XXII.

64. Raj Bhala, *American Lawyer* (April 27, 1999).

65. Ibid.

Chapter Eight

The Future of "Free Trade for the Americas" and the Dispute Settlement Rules

Third Image Disciplines in a Regional Setting

"Free Trade for the Americas" is not exactly dead. It moved slowly because the Democratic party's votes in the late 1990s for "fast-track" authority for the president to negotiate were in too short supply in Congress. Still, technical discussions with future signatory countries continue into the new millennium. Republicans have vowed to try to restore fast-track authority to President George W. Bush. In the drive to create a Free Trade Area of the Americas (FTAA), trade ministers have produced a heavily-bracketed draft agreement. President George W. Bush is a strong supporter of the FTAA in spite of formidable substantive challenges on trade rules, treatment of foreign investment and labor and environment regulations. We have seen that civil society protestors pounce on FTAA summits as readily as they did at Seattle. This chapter reminds us too of the essential ingredients of NAFTA that may be difficult to export to the FTAA: the panel dispute-system and its oversight of domestic trade agency determinations. While the media will center during any negotiations on the range of trade it might include, this book reminds us of another vital dimension. This chapter looks at the present regional agreements in North America with the focus on dispute settlement, this writer's notion of the key to any successful trade agreement.

The United States' trade problems and trade potential are as regional as they are global. U.S. trade with the Americas, South and North, outstrips its trade with Europe or Japan or China. Usually, Japan or some European nation gets the billing as America's most important customer. This is not the case. Canada is by far the United States' biggest trade partner. In fact, the U.S.-Canada trade relationship is the biggest exporter-importer relationship in the world. Canada-U.S. trade dwarfs U.S. trade with Latin America, Japan or any European country. To most Americans, the North American Free Trade Agreement (NAFTA) is about Mexico. However, in bulk trading terms, it is far more about Canada-U.S. trade.

NAFTA and its predecessor the FTA (Free Trade Agreement of 1989-93 between Canada and the United States) have served, according to respected observers, as a useful trade liberalizing laboratory for the WTO itself and as a platform for expanding liberalized trade beyond to the Americas. To the attentive NGO and civil society community on environment and labor issues it also serves as the first ever attempt to relate labor conditions and environmental disciplines to a trade agreement. These side accords on environment and labor can be a useful laboratory for the WTO if it considers linking these concerns in a non-protectionist way to the trading system.

U.S.- Canada reciprocal trade pacts had trouble getting any applause in the early going. Many American observers complain that Canada "snookered" the United States by achieving the FTA back in 1988. Canadians generally refuse to be convinced the agreement was positive for Canada, even though access to the U.S. market has propelled Canada's economy to new heights in the nineties. Since there has been almost no increase in domestic demand for goods and services in Canada, access for its exports to the United States explains the increased Canadian GDP. Canada has also won more panel disputes than the United States. Still, about half of all Canadians, in any poll, seem to view NAFTA with indifference, even hostility. Most Americans attentive to NAFTA view this relationship as a healthy marriage: sometimes bumpy but otherwise fine. Conventional wisdom says that CUSTA (The Canada-U.S.Trade Agreement of 1989) or FTA (Free Trade Agreement as it was called in Canada) smoothed the way and was later enhanced by adding Mexico under the NAFTA (North American Free Trade Agreement) and by implementing the side accords on labor and the environment. Naysayers abound, of course in all three nations. The critics believe wrongly that a tight superstructure has been put in place with little wiggle-room available in the interstices of the pact, to protect domestic producers and other values.

The vast majority of trade in North America now takes place in accordance with the clear and well-established rules of the NAFTA and the WTO. Nonetheless, in such a large trading area, disputes are bound to emerge. In such cases, the NAFTA directs the governments concerned to seek to resolve their differences amicably through the NAFTA's committees and working groups or other consultations. If no mutually acceptable solution is found, the NAFTA provides for expeditious and effective panel procedures.

One of the principal elements of the NAFTA is the establishment of a clear set of rules for dealing with the settlement of disputes. Dispute settlement provisions for countervailing duty and antidumping matters are covered under Chapter 19 of the NAFTA. Chapter 20 of the NAFTA includes provisions relating to the avoidance or settlement of all disputes regarding the interpretation or application of the NAFTA. There are also special rules for disputes under Chapter 11 and Chapter 14. Administrative support to Chapter 19 and Chapter 20 panels is provided by the Canadian, U.S. and Mexican national sections of the NAFTA secretariat.

Prior to the entry into force of the Canada-U.S. FTA and then the NAFTA, only antidumping, countervailing duty and injury final determinations could be appealed. In the case of a United States final determination appeals went to the Court of International Trade; in the case of a Mexican final determination, appeals went to the Tribunal Fiscal de la Federacion; or in the case of certain Canadian final determinations to the Federal Court of Appeal; or for some Revenue Canada decisions to the Canadian International Trade Tribunal (CITT).[1]

As of February 2001, there were four active Chapter 19 cases reviewing Canadian government antidumping decisions on imported products from the United States. There were seven cases in which a United States decision was being appealed by Canadian producers. As well, a Canadian agency's decision on hot-rolled carbon steel plate from Mexico was appealed and a Mexican decision was being appealed by Canadian producers. One case, involving the review of a Canadian agency's decision in an antidumping case on concrete panels from the United States that was requested in 1997, was completed during 1998. There are also a number of cases involving trade remedy actions by Mexico and the United States not involving Canadian firms.

Chapter 20 is invaluable in ensuring that Canadian trade relations with the United States and Mexico are based on an established set of rules as opposed to economic or political power. As such, the objectives of the Chapter 20 provisions are similar to those of the dispute settlement provisions of the WTO.

There have been relatively few applications of the NAFTA Chapter 20 dispute settlement provisions compared with activity under Chapter 19. Canada was a respondent in a case brought by the United States regarding tariffs on certain U.S.-origin agricultural products. United States and Mexico have also used this procedure regarding a United States safeguard action on corn brooms. In 1998, Canada took action under Chapter 20 on producers on meat labeling and on certain measures by United States restraining Canadian exports of grain and livestock. As well, several consultations were held in 1998 under Chapter 20 concerning Mexico-U.S. disputes on sugar, bus and trucking services, in which Canada participated as a third party. On bus and trucking services, following NAFTA Commission meetings in 1998 convened to address theses disputes, Mexico requested arbitral panels under

Chapter 20 to have them resolved.

For investment disputes relating to obligations of NAFTA parties under Chapter 11, the NAFTA sets out dispute resolution procedures to resolve complaints between the investor and the host state. Complaints that are subject to NAFTA Chapter 11 are resolved by arbitration, based on the arbitration rules of the UN Commission on International Trade Law (UNCITRAL) and the International Center for the Settlement of Investment Disputes (ICSID). A roster of potential panelists was established for Chapter 11, whose members have expertise in investment law or practice.

As of March 1999, several cases involving Mexico and the United States are before arbitral tribunals under the investor-state dispute settlement provisions of NAFTA Chapter 11. For financial services concerns, the NAFTA establishes a mechanism for the settlement of disputes by providing that Chapter 20 shall apply, with modifications.

There is considerable evidence of domestic producers losing in the FTA or NAFTA after initially winning domestic agency protection in their own jurisdiction. This can be viewed as evidence of third image legal momentum influencing trade determinations. This writer's reading of the FTA and NAFTA is not prone to complete "third image" optimism, but it is still similar to the reading of GATT and WTO. When it comes to "wiggle-room," or perhaps "scope for realist compromise," NAFTA is definitely not a straitjacket, despite its obligations on its members.[2]

There are three reasons for a less-than-total "third image" reading of this regional agreement. First, neither the FTA nor NAFTA presume to align member law with objective standards, other than consistency with WTO agreements. NAFTA is essentially about recognizing each nation's sovereign right to make trade law while insisting that a persistent pattern not to enforce existing domestic law on trade or environmental or labor matters be brought before a panel. Let us not forget that this regional agreement is a fairly elegant joining of a sensitive sovereignty (second image) strategy with a voluntarist (third image) regional attempt to bring "order" to dispute settlement. The sovereign right for the signatories to make trade or environment or labor policy, is not restricted by this agreement, but adherence to dispute panels is expected.

Second, the sovereign right to amend or enact new domestic trade law regardless of the agreement has already been used by the United States after a panel decision occurred on softwood lumber adverse to U.S. interests. This ruling seriously undermined Canadian confidence in the FTA and NAFTA structure. This puts before us the example of the U.S.-Canada *Softwood Lumber* dispute. This dispute is outlined in the next chapter. There is nothing in the agreement strictly forbidding trade law changes, but obviously a residual psychological and political disrespect for the accord can infect it if its spirit is obviated in this way too many times in too many highly politically visible cases.

The third caveat is that the heart of the agreements beats with a weak understanding of how much deference FTA panels were, and NAFTA panels are, to pay to domestic trade agencies determinations on disputes. Third image advocates would say: "Domestic agency determinations should be subject to objective review." Second image advocates would say: "Domestic agency determinations should be subject to review only in the context of it's own received domestic process . . . of judicial review of administrative action otherwise this would be an invasion of sovereignty." Disagreement on this issue is a profound and classic debate between the schools of "second image realist sovereigntist" and "third image legal momentum" views of NAFTA.

This writer remembers when Canada's ministerial delegation negotiating the FTA in 1987 decided to leave the Washington D.C,-based proceedings – probably for good. The negotiations between our two countries had bogged down over an issue vital to the Canadian side. Canada needed a clear time-bound dispute settlement mechanism to settle antidumping and countervailing duty law determinations of U.S. administrative agencies. Otherwise, the huge cost of reaching a decision on appeal of these determinations would mean that the jurisdiction able to extract the most time and expense, and having the most convoluted but seemingly legitimate litigation process would prevail. That side would prevail simply by wearing out the appellants, in terms of time and expense. Moreover, a biased administrative agency determination could act as a "chill" on the trade in question.

Our side agreed that the determining law of the country's agency would apply, "chill-effect" or not. We simply wanted a binational panel review of whether the agency's decision was consistent with its own law. That was all. We were not seeking agreement on some new abstract test, only an official answer to this essential question. Meanwhile, our ministers were attacked back home, not for leaving the negotiations, but for trying to erect a system upholding U.S. trade law as the ultimate focus of any panel reviewing an U.S. agency determination. Frankly, our negotiators and our government were largely comfortable with the content of most of U.S. trade law: it was reasonable and modern, from our point of view. It was its administration that bedeviled us. This nuance was difficult and remains difficult to explain in a politically-charged atmosphere to an American or Canadian electorate.

A number of creative proposals to reduce the application of anti-dumping and countervail trade remedies were discussed in late September of 1987. At the end of the negotiations the Canadian request for a common FTA set of laws covering these issues or for suspension of their application to Canadian exporters to the United States was clearly too much for the U.S. Congress to agree to. As it then stood, the agreement largely dealt with tariff lowering which would be to Canada's disadvantage because Canadian tariff walls were somewhat higher than those of the United States. The package negotiated up to October 1, 1987 was clearly too little for Canada. Canadians were determined to get some kind of dispute settlement arrangement, which would deal more fairly with issues such as *Softwood Lumber* that had bedeviled Canada-U.S. trade relations from 1981 through to 1987. That dispute was informing our view of what kind of dispute we thought should be subject to a rules-based dispute resolution regime both countries could agree to.

So on October 1, 1987, lacking agreement on a better trade remedy and a dispute settlement regime, Canada was left primarily with a tariff-reducing agreement. The prime minister had stipulated that any agreement should clearly be better than a tariff-only agreement. When his chief of staff, Derek Burney, reported to him that the agreement was "*not* better," the prime minister ordered his negotiating team home that day. On October 2, the chief U.S. negotiator said to Mr. Burney that President Reagan wanted to speak to Prime Minister Mulroney. The advice to the prime minister was that there was no point in talking to the White House if nothing new and substantive was put on the table.[3]

Former secretary of the treasury, James Baker, admits today that "the agreement came close to not happening." The negotiations were "protracted and painful and on the verge of complete collapse;" he allowed in remarks some 12 years later, June 4, 1999. "We were aware of the political limits and dynamic in our own country" but "there is a tendency in the U.S. to take Canada for granted, to forget that Canadian politics are also complex. We were slow at the beginning to grasp Canadian sensibilities."[4]

Derek Burney recalls that provincial premiers and federal ministers were called to Ottawa on October 2 to be told there was to be no agreement. As a minister, this writer can remember wondering "What were to be our talking points? What were we to say about why the deal failed? Where were we going next on dealing with a protectionist U.S. Congress?"

These ruminations were not all negative. Failure to do a deal could be in a sad way a bit of a relief. It would be easy, and not bad from a political point of view, to say "we fought and fought for a good deal, but we are not patsies, the U.S. offer is not enough. We will not sacrifice Canadian interests." These ruminations were short-lived. Within twelve hours we heard that our key negotiators had been directed by the prime minister to return to Washington. The fast-track deadline was October 3 at midnight.

James Baker recalled the unease the U.S negotiators felt about the agreement's constitutionality. As Chuck Roh (an assistant undersecretary at the time) put it "Congress won't like 'international panels' overruling our judges. This will look unconstitutional."[5] In fact, days later as Clayton Yeutter and James Baker remind us, the Senate committee deciding on 'fast-track authority' for these negotiations October 3 was deadlocked at ten-to-ten. This tie was perverse because the nay votes didn't have so much to do with Canada or with Roh's constitutional point, recalled Yeutter.[6] They were prompted instead by the Senate wanting to send a message to President Reagan about its dissatisfaction over other trade matters, such as Japan's protectionism, so-called slave labor in China and so on. Baker recalls that the president himself telephoned a number of committee members to get their support for the FTA outline. A senator who was out of the country had to be called to vote. Success on the fast track was finally narrowly secured.

So the Canada-U.S. trade agreement was signed and the novel panel power to settle disputes put in place. In the final analysis then, individual political leaders, the first image (not anonymous macro-economic forces), made this agreement a reality.

The FTA 1989-1994 and NAFTA Since

If one is concerned about panel members' success not in acting on national lines but as a third image solvent of disputes, how well did binational panels under the FTA work out in practice? How well do they work under NAFTA? Critically do panels actually end up slavishly deferring in most cases to original national agency determinations?[7]

In order to analyze what has transpired since 1989, we must ask whether panels took a fresh look at agency decisions or merely redundantly followed the ruling and method of domestic determinations. Our answer is that the panel decisions did not and do not reflect deferential review; in fact, deference gives way to close scrutiny under the guise of malleable tests originally designed to restrict review.

As noted, the primary goal of the Canadian government in negotiating the Free Trade Agreement was to maintain or improve market access, an aim it could achieve by mitigating the application of U.S. trade remedy laws to Canadian exporters (specifically, antidumping and countervailing duty CVD).[8] As we have seen, while an exemption from American trade remedy laws or harmonization of U.S. and Canadian antidumping and CVD standards would have been preferable, the Canadian government was able to win binational dispute settlement as a compromise between its objectives and a complete breakdown of the bargaining process. Marvellously thorough studies of these negotiations especially by Michael Hart and Gordon Ritchie, outline how this all happened.[9] Under Chapter 19 of the FTA, binational dispute settlement panels were to exist for five years, or until such time as the United States and Canada could develop a substitute system of rules in both countries for antidumping and countervailing duties as applied to their bilateral trade.

However, while the panels may have been dreamt up as temporary solutions to a bargaining impasse, they have since found favor with trade law power-brokers in both countries. Subject to some minor modifications, they have become a permanent institution under NAFTA Article 1904.[10] The composition of panels are as follows: five members are drawn from a list of twenty-five citizens "of good character, high standing and repute, [who have been] chosen strictly on the basis of objectivity, reliability, sound judgement and general familiarity with international trade law." Moreover, "[a] majority of the panelists on each panel shall be lawyers in good standing." (Most of those lawyers who currently sit on panels have practiced in international trade.) Added to NAFTA Annex 1901.2, is the further commitment to "include sitting or retired judges to the fullest extent practicable" on their rosters, with each country choosing panelists from another nation.

NAFTA Article 1904.1 provides that "the Parties shall replace judicial review of final antidumping and countervailing duty determinations with binational panel review." The purpose of a panel review is to ensure that final determinations of the appropriate agencies are consistent with the substantive laws of that country, and in accordance with that country's laws relating to judicial review of administrative action. Article 1904.8 authorizes the panel to affirm or remand a determination, in whole or in part. Panel decisions are not appealable to the parties' domestic courts and are binding upon the agency from which the determination was issued. In certain instances, however, decisions of the panel are subject to an extraordinary challenge procedure under Article 1904.13.

The constitution of a "final determination" is provided for under the country-specific definitions of NAFTA Annex 1911. Essentially, the panel review system filters all the major decisions made by appropriate administrative agencies under the applicable domestic antidumping and countervailing duty laws. Thanks to the adoption of GATT Antidumping and Subsidies Codes, a real similarity can be seen between the legislation and the institutions governing antidumping and countervailing duty matters in Canada and the United States.

Antidumping actions begin with a finding that foreign produced goods have been dumped in the domestic market, predicated on evidence of international price discrimination. (This is often the characterization by trade lawyers but the real issue is predatory pricing. Investigating authorities include Revenue Canada (RevCan), now called Canadian Customs and Revenue Agency, or the International Trade Administration (ITA) of the United States Department of Commerce.) Countervailing duty actions commence with the finding (by RevCan in Canada or the ITA in the United States) that goods imported into the domestic market have been subsidized directly or indirectly by the exporter country. The initial finding of dumping or subsidy must be followed by a determination of resulting material injury made by the Canadian International Trade Tribunal (CITT) or the United States International Trade Commission (ITC), respectively.

The ITA and the Canadian equivalent are both administrative agencies, hierarchical in structure, bureaucratic in staffing and organization. Each authority is responsible in its country for the administration of trade remedy law.

A further source of U.S. trade law is found in the procedures and practices of the U.S. agencies which make factual determinations in trade cases, largely proceedings on dumping and countervailing. The determination of whether a foreign importer has engaged in dumping or has *received a subsidy* is made by the I.T.A. The determination of whether there has been *injury or a threat of material injury to American producers* is made by the International Trade Commission (ITC). These agencies have developed a substantial body of procedural rules concerning their hearings, as well as a substantial body of methodological rules for determining the existence of dumping and subsidies or injury, as the case may be. This is a marvelous political solvent (if a nation can afford it!); to dilute the angst of domestic producers but its determinations can be appealed. The final source of U.S. trade law is found in the procedural and substantive decisions of U.S. federal courts, most importantly the Court of International Trade (CIT), which reviews the agency determinations. The CIT makes decisions on the appropriate standard of review, and in some cases substitutes its approach for that of the agency.

Early on, Canadian negotiators grasped what the problem with the U.S. trade regime was not: it was *not* specific legislation, but application of that legislation by the ITA and the ITC. For example, U.S. legislation, like Canada's, on the subject of dumping and countervailing duties has been drafted so as to conform to GATT. Accordingly, U.S. antidumping and countervailing duty laws are very similar to those of Canada, and each comply with the relevant international obligations. However, the rules developed by the U.S. and Canadian agencies for their factual determinations often appear to violate the spirit of these same international obligations. These rules are complex, frequently one-sided and often have the effect of making it very difficult (if not impossible) for foreign exporters to prove they are not dumping, or being subsidized and, in either case, of threatening to cause material injury to their American competitors.

Although U.S. law is also similar to Canadian law in providing for judicial review of administrative agency determinations, judicial review has been generally ineffective in remedying unfair decisions by the ITA or the ITC. A major reason for this is that under U.S. law, due to the expertise of the organizations involved, agency decisions are entitled to a high degree of curial deference.

Pursuant to Chapter 19 of the FTA, companies affected by agency determinations in Canada and the United States could seek review of these determinations by ad hoc binational panels. If panel review was sought, domestic judicial review was excluded, subject to some residual jurisdiction in U.S. federal courts in respect of U.S. constitutional matters. The theory behind panel review is that panel members will have greater familiarity with trade law issues and greater expertise than the national courts in either country; consequently, their review of agency decisions are expected to be more rigorous, intensive, and impartial. This panel apparatus has been extended under Chapter 19 of the NAFTA.

As we have seen, obtaining impartial binational review of U.S. agency determinations was an important objective of the Canadian government when agreeing to the FTA. The United States was concerned that the bi-national panels might usurp constitutional functions reserved to superior courts in the United States; the United States also worried that binational panels might use a different standard of review than American courts. Accordingly, chapter 19 requires any panel to apply to the domestic law of the country from which the review derives, while clearly denying any panel authority to develop unique substantive trade law as between Canada and the United States. The sensitivity of the situation prohibited the panels from interpreting the U.S. Constitution – or Canada's.

Surely a "a second-and third image" test of whether the panels are exercising their powers would not ask the panels to alter any domestic trade law. Nor would the test enquire whether these panels are expressly overruling legislation, which they cannot and do not do. The real test is to ascertain whether panels are overruling agency determinations in a way that compels the agencies to conduct their hearings in a manner different from what they have become accustomed to doing. The question is: are they aiming to compel domestic administrative agencies to use different rules when they make their fact-finding determinations, and when they interpret domestic trade law in accordance with principles of free trade as embodied by the FTA and the WTO?

The experience of the panels over a decade indicates they have developed their powers by construing their jurisdiction quite liberally. In this regard, a panel is no different from any other tribunal or court, which seeks to expand its powers by expanding its jurisdiction. Theoretically, a panel has two choices in defining its jurisdiction and hence its power: it can defer to the agency's determination unless the agency has made an unreasonable interpretation of fact or law, or it can require the agency to approach its task as would the panel if the panel were deciding the matter itself.

As we have seen, Chapter 19 of the FTA determined the operation of binational panels. The most important provision was from Article 1902 (1), empowering each party to apply its antidumping and countervailing law to goods imported from the other country. It is admitted this fell short of a new regime of rules to deal with unfair pricing and government subsidization that Canadian negotiators were seeking. A mutual understanding to reexamine this effect existed under the FTA and was to be formally reexamined under NAFTA. Unfortunately, this never happened.

The composition of the binational panels was established in Annex 1901.2. Panel members were to be chosen from a roster of fifty candidates, twenty-five from each country.

The central role of the panel, is to review "the administrative record to determine whether such determination was consistent with the trade law of the importing country."[11]

Panels must base their review on the administrative record, defined as "all documentary or other information presented to or obtained by the competent investigating authority" prior to reaching their final determination. Conveniently, this definition blocks the introduction of new evidence. In undertaking such a review, the FTA stated that the panel shall employ the standard of review employed in the importing country and that the general legal principles of the court of said country. For example, when a U.S. final judgement is reviewed by a FTA (now NAFTA) panel, it will find unlawful any determination that lacks substantial evidence or violates its own law. In Canada's case, section 28 (1) of the *Federal Court Act* was to be applied. The *Federal Court Act* may set aside determinations in which the Canadian International Trade Tribunal or the antidumping/countervailing division of the Department of National Revenue misinterpreted law or based a decision on capriciously-found facts, without regard to the applicable material.

A panel may determine that an error of law has taken place at the administrative level and, secondly, of particular significance, a panel may find, in the case of U.S. administrative determination, that there is not substantial evidence on the record to support it and, in the case of a Canadian determination, that the decision is "based on a finding of fact made on a perverse or capricious manner without regard to the material before it."

In either case, a panel returns the case to the competent investigating authority "for action not inconsistent with the panel's decision." This is called a "remand." Therefore, under Article 1904 (8), while a panel cannot overturn a decision made by the administrative agency, the agency is compelled to act in conformity with the panel's decision or face the serious political repercussions that would otherwise ensue.

One can agree with scholar Michael Hart and Andreas Lowenfeld on this agreement that critics of Chapter 19 were "overly pessimistic" before they had sufficient panel history. The critics unduly discounted the key role the panels can play in "reducing the abuse of application of trade remedy laws."[12] A major concern of exporters prior to the FTA was not the substance of the law, but the abuse of its application. .U.S. experience showed that the standard for review binding the CIT did not reveal a uniform interpretation of the law within the CIT. Furthermore, examples of varying interpretations by different CIT judges were not uncommon. Hart also notes that the panels had access to information to reach different conclusions from the CIT, though the use of the "substantial evidence" test. This was overlooked by early critics. In *Matsushita Electric Industrial Company* v. *the United States*, the following definition of substantial evidence was adopted: "substantial evidence is more than a mere scintilla. It means such relevant evidence as a reasonable mind might accept as adequate to support a conclusion." What the CIT considers "sufficient evidence" may be deemed inadequate by a panel. Composed of trade lawyers and other experts in the field of trade law, the panel may conceive of what "a reasonable mind might accept as adequate to support a conclusion" more accurately than judges with less enriched backgrounds. This is established U.S. administrative law. One former ITC Commissioner is trenchant on this subject:

> It is fatuous to suggest that the decision-makers (panelists) are mere ciphers. Surely no matter what the review standard, the reviewer necessarily makes some difference. . . American standards for judicial review of administrative decisions are by no means so clear, continuing, or deferential as the argument for ineffectuality supposes.[13]

During the early months of the FTA, the authority of the panels was questioned in academic literature and many journalistic and political circles. Critics questioned where a panel could look for guidance. Where does a panel stand in the review of hierarchy? If one considers the panels to be equivalent to the CIT in the eyes of U.S. law, it follows that a panel may treat CIT decisions as helpful and respected, but not binding. Some literature also suggested that a panel could be compared to an appeal court, that previous panel decisions could be considered, but would not be a canon whose word informed all decisions.

An equally provocative debate in academic and political circles centered on the question related to what panelists accepted as evidence, especially "substantial evidence." There seemed to be a difference between American standards of review and those in Canada. The most significant test of "substantial evidence" for a panel to remand an agency decision is that it must claim it found "insufficient evidence to supports an agency's determination." In other words, a panel would not change the law if it remanded a determination; it would simply imply that the agency's determination on a particular issue was based on "insufficient evidence" given that the test involved a "reasonable mind." Key to the evidence test is the presence of trained and experienced trade lawyers on the panels. This implies prima facie that these panels should be less deferential to an agency than, for example, the CIT, as knowledge may very well be brought to the panels which the CIT judges may not possess. Here, we see that the "substantial evidence" test is the foundation for the argument of whether a decision by an agency leading to a panel was or was not correct. Similarly, the substantial evidence test is the foundation for arguing for correctness when the panel itself makes a decision.

Some observers of panel decision making also noted the processes of discontinuity on domestic agencies. Frequent references were made to inconsistencies in alignments between the judges of the CIT. This can be attributed without doubt to the fact that a single judge sits on a CIT case. Many observers argued that panels of three or five people would be more consistent in reasoning, simply because more minds offer more consideration of the issues and the law."

Some may regret that (third image) multilateral disciplines may be weakened by panels which allow different rationales in their decision in NAFTA. These people must remember instead that one key tenet of the process is that a panel is able to build its rationalization, in part, on the need for GATT consistency. In so far as GATT standards approximate a virtually universal or WTO version concept of "trade" justice, some observers wonder if this is a subtle way of introducing an element of natural justice into the decision calculus. A trickle of "third image discipline" perhaps?

Responding to the need for greater harmonization of United States law with international trade law, superior courts in the United States have been prepared to accept changes in American law as it applies to international trade obligations. Continuing this development, one notes the tradition in the United States where a court, when interpreting a statute, may refer to the legislative record. (This notion is foreign to Canadian review.) As a result, with respect to the FTA and GATT, there are consistent American legislative pronouncements about the need for binding dispute resolution mechanisms in GATT and the FTA. All of this provides a rationale for accepting an evolving standard of judicial review.

It is possible to identify decisions reached by FTA panels that demonstrate that the effect of U.S. law was redirected through panel decisions (a proposition which would seem to contradict the obligations undertaken in the FTA). Or conversely, does one find decisions reached by panels, although created and based on evidence not admitted in an ordinary court but part of the administration record, are still consistent with U.S. and Canadian law.

A powerful review of all of these issues is deliberated in an article by Michael H. Greenburg, a member of the New York Bar and the Bar of the Court of International Trade. Greenburg served as chairman of a Chapter 19 panel (Chapter 19 of the FTA.)[14]. Greenberg asks whether findings by a panel will be legally binding on both governments. He queries whether the panel should have jurisdiction to determine that the law was properly applied. Under Chapter 19, if it is found by a panel that the administering authority erred on the basis of the same standards applicable to review of administrative action as would be applied by a domestic court, the panel can send the issue back to the administrative authority to correct the error and make a new determination. (Administrating authorities might include the Department of Commerce or the International Trade Commission in the United States, or the Department of National Revenue or the Canadian Import Tribunal in Canada.)

Greenberg found after four years of FTA experience that the binational panel review set up in the FTA was a favorable development that represents another step toward the goal of the true internationalization of trade laws. His article addresses the development of Article 19 in the FTA, the potential for NAFTA to supersede the FTA and the implications this will have for Chapter 19. He predicted that the panel process will become permanent rather than languish with a time limit, as it did with the FTA. (The panels gained permanency under NAFTA.) He guessed that there would be no "study committee" to replace any dumping and countervailing duty laws. On this subject, he was proven wrong, but the committee was deadlocked. This so-called "study committee" conducted subsequent to an agreement negotiated by the Chretien government with the Clinton administration, produced no substantive change. Greenberg also argued that there would be a move to change panelists, substituting experienced judges for trade practitioners, a prediction which in fact came true under the NAFTA.

In addressing the standards of review, the author looks at the question of whether panels strayed from the U.S. or Canadian trade law. Greenberg concluded, "from a legal perspective the panels are strictly circumscribed."[15] One can maintain that panel decisions do not seem to have varied the domestic laws they are mandated to uphold. One can support this by highlighting that there had been only two extraordinary challenges, both supporting the panels involved. (Case support for the panels was also manifested in a third instance, the softwood lumber appeal of 1994.[16]) Quoting from the international law section of the American Bar Association, Greenberg is trenchant:

> While at first glance, the Chapter 19 system may appear to be flawed in the sense that it is the law rather than its administration that may be objectionable . . . it has also permitted the disengagement of the respective national bureaucracies to some large degree and allowed aggrieved interests in each country to make their cases without any overhanging linkage to any other issues."[17]

Canadian observers had long complained before the FTA was negotiated with the United States that CIT was too deferential to the Commerce Department and the ITC. Greenburg and Hart's contention is that this practice should be put to rest. As it happens, the CIT has displayed a growing willingness to remand where agency determinations lacked substantive and rational support.[18] In international circles, there was also a fear that the FTA would establish idiosyncratic anti-dumping/countervailing duty standards for exclusive U.S.-Canada trade use that would differ from trade law with other nations. Greenburg argues that this has not happened.

Additionally, Greenburg also addressed the question of whether the CIT could refer to a panel decision that was well reasoned and persuasive in making its own evaluation. He argues that there is no reason why this should not happen. Indeed, he demonstrated that there is already citation of panel decisions by other panels, concluding that although domestic law was being applied under the FTA, there is evidence of some internationalization of American law:

> The panel's examination and exegesis of the GATT anti dumping and countervailing duty codes may well lead to a greater uniformity of interpretation across national boundaries of the international guidelines to domestic unfair trade practice legislation . . . a panel reviewing a US anti dumping or countervailing duty final determination is constrained by the statutory requirement that US law take precedence if there is a conflict. The effort to harmonize US law and the GATT codes

wherever possible however is furthered by bi-national membership on the panels. [19]

Thomas W. Bark, an American judicial scholar, concludes that the FTA binational panel dispute resolution system, in practice not just theory, was undoubtedly constitutional. He addresses Article III of the U.S. Constitution, which states that Congress may grant adjudicatory authority in a non-Article III review of a U.S. agency determination. The concerns he addressed pertained to whether the presence of Canadian members on the panel would violate constitutional appointments (i.e., that the president must appoint all officers of the United States). Bark also questions whether a panel review could adequately preserve the litigant's "due process" rights under the Fifth Amendment. (Court-established rights fundamental to due process consist of the following: 1, the right to a hearing before a fair and impartial decision maker and 2 the opportunity to be heard in a timely and meaningful manner.)

Interestingly, Bark's discussion confirms the flexibility of due process: "The requirements of due process are not fixed but depend upon the context of the situation and the nature of the deprivation." "Due process is flexible and calls for such procedural protection as the particular situation demands" and "due process, unlike some legal rules, is not a technical conception with a fixed content unrelated to time, place and circumstance."[20]

Bark also traces the increased receptivity of U.S. courts to international arbitration in international commercial disputes. Presenting case law, he expresses his certainty that invalidating an agreement to submit a dispute to arbitration would "reflect the extremely parochial concept that all disputes must be resolved under our laws and in our courts." [21] Furthermore, he writes that "[w]e cannot base trade and commerce and world markets and international trade exclusively on our terms as governed by our laws and resolved in our courts."[22] The U.S. Supreme Court has also supported the legitimacy of commercial domestic arbitrations almost without qualification, knowing the purpose of the parties was to set up a private adjudicatory system that circumvents the established judiciary and, even more important, the dreaded civil jury, a constitutional icon.

Addressing the thorny question of whether a U.S. court's standard of review is appropriate for application by binational panels, Bark quotes a 1948 case :

> Recognizing that this determination involved Congress' and the President's combined authority over foreign commerce and international relations, the court stated that decisions about foreign affairs are wholly confided by our constitution to the political departments of the government, Executive and

Legislative. They are delicate, complex and involve large elements of prophecy . . . they are decisions of a kind for which the judiciary has neither aptitude, facilities nor responsibility in which has long been held to belong in the domain of political power not subject to judicial intrusion or inquiry. [23]

Similarly, with regard to the concept of *stare decisis*, he states that "its decision does not create a new source of US law but is binding only with respect to the matter before the panel."

Bark's article is effective not only as a constitutional primer and "third image" buttress, but also as a catalyst for key points on the independence of panels informed by American judicial concepts. It is clear too from a review of the *Red Raspberry* panel that the standard of review does not force panels to interpret U.S. law in the same manner as the CIT. The authors agree with critics of Chapter 19 of the FTA, who note that panels are bound by the laws and precedents of the country in which the administrative determination was made. Critics are mistaken, however, in extrapolating that panel decisions would be no more beneficial to foreign exporters than previous decisions of the CIT. Variation of course stems from the reality that U.S. trade laws are not so precise that their content can never evolve through interpretation.

It is also clear that what constitutes "substantial evidence" is at least partly a matter for expert opinion. Even though the U. S. Court of Appeals has defined the term for the federal circuit, the definition lacks precision and leaves room for varying interpretation. As a standard of review it leaves a great deal of discretion to the reviewer. ITC Commissioner Cass writes "American standards for judicial review of administrative decisions are by no means so clear, continuing or deferential, as they are human.."[24] Further, it is clear that panelists will naturally draw upon their collective experience in a way, which the judiciary at the CIT could not, considering its inadequate resources and expertise. Andrew Stuart argued in the *Northwest Journal of International Law and Business* in 1991 that:

> [T]hough it is a close call, constitutional considerations and judicial economy are probably not hefty enough to outweigh the need for uniformity in the interpretation and application of GATT law. In law courts the separation of powers, judicial economy and the need for uniformity, all combine to support deference to administrative agencies on legal and mixed questions. In the GATT, however, only non-deference on such questions can avoid inconsistent interpretations among the municipalities. For this reason and because the panel's case load appears manageable under the current approach *de novo* review

makes sense with respect to legal as well as mixed questions that
are case-specific. [25]

Stuart then points out that the CIT of 1988 had a much lower affirmation
rate (40 percent) on final antidumping/countervailing duty determinations
than the national rate affirmed by federal courts panels of NAFTA (75
percent). This makes it evident that under the old GATT, panels of experts
familiar with their treaty's requirements will be even more prepared to look
at review on a near de novo basis. Moreover, they will be less deferential to
domestic agencies. "Unlike the US courts there is no presumption of
correctness accorded to the Commerce Department actions."[26] One court
case, the panel had to construe a U.S. statute, which was previously
unexplained. The panel addressed the "substantial evidence" standard
directly and created a burden on the ITC. The record had to show more than
a "possibility of injury," as the panel said to the ITC. In the end, the paned
remanded, with direction, thereby inferring a rule of finality.

Panel treatment of the "substantial evidence" test offers firm discipline
on the ITC and Revenue Canada in its methodology. The "substantial
evidence" test was:

> used to sanction the ITC's failure to rely on micro economic
> theory. Without the use of consistent and coherent economic
> theory there is no rational connection between reasons and
> conclusions, therefore, such conclusions are not supported by
> substantial evidence.[27]

Equally important, the requirement under the FTA that disputes be
resolved gives evidence of another significant limitation on administrative
agencies. Stuart reminds us that:

> [T]he ITC was restrained both from reopening the record beyond
> very narrowly defined issues and from continuing to assert its
> impugned conclusion of threatened material injury beyond a
> second remand. Both of these limitations of ITC procedures were
> imposed in order to insure a more expeditious conclusion to the
> case.[28]

Extraordinary Challenges

It is also instructive to note that the "extraordinary challenge" committees
created to review panel decisions have not been interventionist – as a result,
panel effectiveness has not been limited in the slightest.

The "substantial evidence" test has been used to reduce trade barriers by placing greater restrictions on administrative agencies. In the case of *Red Raspberries*, the agency was shown to have failed in providing sound reasoning, proof that the conclusion followed from the facts of the case. In the *Steel Rails* case, the panel did not require the administrative agency to provide sound reasoning or show a rational connection between the facts and the conclusion. This, argued Hart, was the "only anomalous" panel decision of the FTA. In panels on *Pork* there were findings of five separate incidents of the ITC failing to provide adequate reasoning to justify its conclusion. All five issues were remanded to the ITC.

Hart summarizes the first nine cases like this: in 1992, "six show a strict application of the 'substantial evidence' test by the panels. The data and facts relied on must be accurate and the reasoning of the administrative agency must be clearly stated and be rationally connected to the conclusion reached." [29]

Furthermore, U.S. trade lawyers Gary Horlick and Amanda deBusk found that FTA dispute resolution was more than twice as expedient as U.S. judicial review. The FTA panel review process must be completed within 315 days while the average time from instigation to completion of CIT cases, over the 1980-90 period, was 126 months. They also discovered that arriving at FTA remands were almost twice as fast as CIT remands. In addition, that time period had seen only one appeal to an extraordinary challenge committee. The time limits within which such an appeal must be completed meant that the issue would be resolved almost five times faster than appeals from the CIT in the past. The two advantages "reflect a system that results in a more fair and impressionable hearing; a perception that can be found among interested persons in government, the law, and business." Horlick and deBusk conclude with a ringing endorsement: "The FTA panels have been working admirably . . . the efficiency of the FTA panels is widely acknowledged in the international legal community." [30]

Distinguished international law scholar Andreas Lowenfeld has concluded that the FTA binational dispute settlement history was a kind of cement, binding Canada and the United States together on their common venture in free trade. He cited a major test, the first extraordinary challenge review allowed of a FTA panel decision. The extraordinary challenge committee itself saw a danger in being seen as an appellate forum, and in fact rejected being treated as such.

Lowenfeld and members of the group discussing his paper in 1992, clarified that the panel's reference to "due process" as a principle in the FTA was a departure from due process as it was interpreted under U.S. law. Panels seem to resist the notion that a body of jurisprudence was building up as a result of the panel decisions. Still, Lowenfeld concluded: "I think there is no real conflict between the GATT as a method of construing the FTA and

United States law [as a method]." It is obvious though that the FTA panels have made a series of departures from the "substantial evidence" standard of review in order to accomplish that "lack of conflict."[31] In fact, to quote Lowenfeld's summary, "the *Pork* panel did not rely fundamentally on U.S. law, but followed the decision of another panel precedent." In addition, the Pork panel "essentially created a new specificity test. This burden shifting is not found in United States law." On the question of two conflicting sets of laws, GATT and United States law or FTA and United States law, he concluded that "there ought to be . . . harmonization."[32]

Gary N. Horlick and F. Amanda deBusk, both American trade lawyers, explain how Chapters 18 and 19 panels functioned over the first two and a half years of operation of the FTA. They support the panel decisions, calling them well written and thoughtful. What's more, they claim that the process of establishing the panels has functioned smoothly and that both countries have given binding effect to the decisions. They add this paradox:

> It is odd that the U.S. negotiators on the FTA insisted on imposing a more onerous standard on U.S. parties seeking to appeal a Canadian decision than on Canadian parties seeking to appeal a U.S. decision . . . perhaps the FTA panel interpretations of the standard of review can be instrumental in bringing the U.S. and Canada standards closer to concordance. [33]

This may improve Canadian administrative law treatment on trade issues.

And this telling note on expedition of decisions:

> FTA dispute resolution is more than twice as fast as US judicial review. One reason is that decisions can only be challenged by government whereas any party can appeal the CIT decision. Also, Court of Appeals for the federal circuit conducts a *de novo* review while the extraordinary challenge committee standard of review of a FTA panel decision is very narrow. [34]

This serves to greatly comfort the "third image" "legal momentum" view of these matters as NAFTA appears to follow FTA in its practice on these matters.

A worrisome principle in FTA dispute settlement at the beginning of the experience under the FTA was the question of this exotic new idea of an extraordinary challenge committee and its power over a panel's decision to create a rule of finality. ("The show is over. The fat lady has sung.") In the *Pork* case, the extraordinary challenge committee indicated that the binational panels had broad authority, while the ITC had argued that the panels could only give open-ended remands and that the panel went too far in creating a rule of finality. The extraordinary review committee disagreed, holding that "there are no restrictions on the panel's power to remand with or without instructions to the competent investigating authority." By upholding the panel's authority to limit remands, the committee recognized the FTA's goals of speedy and inexpensive review. It is interesting to note that the two authors referred to the dispute settlement panels under the FTA as a model for the steel consensus arrangements by indicating that they believe the GATT panel dispute resolution could be improved by incorporating some aspects of FTA panels. This in fact occurred when the Uruguay Round decisionmakers limited severely the time horizons for WTO panels.

Michael Hart draws a similar conclusion in referring to the *Pork* panel and the *Red Raspberry* panel, both of which involved panels ordering the ITC to change their methods:

> These cases have established the authority of the panel procedure and placed the two tribunals on notice that panels expect a very high standard to be pursued in the application of these US statutes to Canadian products. They have achieved these results more quickly than would have been possible in the US courts and they have impressed regal observers on both sides of the border with the thoroughness and quality of their reviews.[35]

GATT standards were invoked in the FTA preamble: "To build upon the mutual rights and obligations under the GATT" (p. 24, Article 1902). That led to an agreement among the two nations not to hunt for changes to their antidumping laws that would or could prove inconsistent with GATT. A second panel on replacement parts stated that CIT decisions should be viewed as a "valuable though non-binding precedent." With respect to previous decisions at the appellate level, the panel did not address the issue, stating that there is no reason why panels could not consider themselves equal to the Federal Court of Appeal and therefore not bound by appeal decisions. Panels could show creativity in getting around previous court of appeal decisions if they do not like them. The approach to replacement parts forwarded by the second panel is an example.

The authors end on a powerful note by quoting the then recently departed vice-chairman of the ITC, Commissioner Cass, who found the panels might be instrumental in promoting stronger, more thoughtful ITC decisions in years to come:

the scrutiny of ITC decisions by Chapter 19 panels . . . well might offer incentives to clearer, better reasoned decisions that track more closely the dictates of U.S. law and also of international agreement to which the U.S. is a signatory party.[36]

An FTA Third Image Scorecard

No commentary this writer could find felt differently from the general view that during the FTA, Chapter 19 panel decisions and subsidy dumping agreements were largely well reasoned, thoroughly researched, professionally administered and rarely divided along national lines. FTA Chapter 19 cases were resolved expeditiously, and decisions did not serve to create a body of trade law jurisprudence divergent from that which existed in either Canada or the United States.

From the perspective of Canadian exporters, Chapter 19 binational panel review appears to have provided an effective, albeit limited, remedy to the application of U.S. trade remedy administrative review determinations by inducing a more disciplined administration of those laws. By contrast, from a U.S exporter's perspective, the FTA Chapter 19 system failed to provide substantive relief from injurious Canadian agency determinations. This asymmetry in results, and, more important, the way in which Canadian panelists have examined certain U.S. agency final determinations, have together caused significant controversy in U.S. trade legal circles. The asymmetry was largely attributable to disparate standards of judicial review.

Chapter 19 panels routinely found that the American ITA had misapplied U.S. antidumping and countervailing duty law. Still the ITC for the most part upheld ITA final injury determinations. According to Michael Hart's close study of decisions, panels consistently found that both Revenue Canada and Canada's CIT had properly interpreted and applied Canadian trade remedy law.

Of the thirty cases in which FTA panels rendered decisions, fourteen involved review of final ITA determinations.[37] Panel decisions forced the ITA to reduce or remove duties in nine instances. For Canadian exporters this result represented a substantial improvement over appeal to the CIT, which overturned agency determinations less frequently.

In stark contrast to their Canadian counterparts, U.S. exporters challenging Revenue Canada final antidumping determinations enjoyed little success under Chapter 19. In three of four cases, Revenue Canada duties were not only approved, but increased by the panel rulings. In the fourth, the duty was affirmed. Perhaps because the Canadian side in these cases prevailed and because Canadians seem to refuse to believe trade disputes are ever won versus the United States, this writer is not aware of this ever being reported in any prominent way in the Canadian media.

Both Canadian and U.S. exporters were relatively unsuccessful in overturning final affirmative injury determinations. U.S. exporters were universally unsuccessful in appealing four determinations. Canadians won on *Pork* and *Softwood Lumber*, but were unsuccessful in three other cases.

Between 1980 and 1988 *before* the FTA, the United States initiated twenty two antidumping cases and eleven countervailing duty cases against Canadian exports, resulting in the application of definitive duties in nine and six of these cases respectively. In this period, Canada initiated fifty antidumping and one countervailing duty actions against U.S. exports, resulting in the application of definitive duties in twenty-four and one cases respectively.

Where binational panels issued decisions reviewing U.S. agency final determinations, those three-person panels frequently agreed on whether a final determination warranted affirmation or whether it needed to be remanded to the administering U.S. agency for redetermination. In the nineteen cases, a total of thirty-five panel opinions were delivered, all but four unanimously. The four cases in which dissenting opinions were delivered involved disagreements concerning the applicable standard of review. In three other cases, panelists, while not dissenting, issued statements of "additional reviews" in which they departed from the panel majority as to the applicable standard of review. Panelists generally divided along national lines: in *New Steel Rails,* one dissenting Canadian argued that the standard of review applied by the majority was overly deferential to the U.S. agency. In *Corrosion-Resistant Carbon Steel Products,* one Canadian dissented from the majority's affirmation of a ITA finding, contending that the ITA's determination contradicted the express language of the statute. In *Live Swine,* one dissenting American argued that the standard of review applied by the majority was too strict and that the ITA was entitled to greater deference. In *Softwood Lumber,* the two dissenting Americans argued that the majority had applied an overly-stringent standard of review which contravened U.S. judicial practice. Thus, only one of thirty-five panel opinions, *Softwood Lumber*, had a split along national lines in which two panelists dissented from a finding against the United States.

In a detailed and fascinating review of the lessons from the NAFTA experience, John Mercury found that in the eleven cases in which panels examined CITT or Revenue Canada final determinations, seventeen panel decisions were rendered (two with "additional views" concurring in the result, but not the approach taken). Ten were unanimous. In five cases one U.S. panelist dissented from rulings upholding Revenue Canada or CITT determinations, arguing that the majority's standard of review was overly deferential. In the remaining two cases (*Tufted Carpets, Hot Rolled Steel Sheet*), one U.S. panelist, accompanied by one Canadian, dissented by taking a position adverse to the U.S. interest.

The average duration of panel review was 511 days, longer than anticipated, but still an improvement over the status quo ante, when CIT cases lasted an average of 734 days.

Of cases resulting in remands, only one of the six against Canadian agencies were remanded for a second time, while seven of the fourteen American cases were (two were still active at the time of writing) and one (*Softwood Lumber Injury*) was remanded three times. What follows draws on John Mercury's research and analysis and that of David Lopez in an extensive review published in 1997.[38]

(The reader can skip the details for the next ten pages if they want to move to the summation.) [39]

Explaining the Disparity of Results

First, the standard of review applicable to Revenue Canada findings appears similar to the standard of review relevant to U.S. agency final determinations, but the standard applicable to final Canadian Import Trade Tribunal (CITT) determinations is more deferential than the general U.S. standard. This is because the existence of a "privative" clause in the *Special Import Measures Act* (SIMA), explicit language seeking to protect the substance of agency determinations from judicial review. This has insulated CITT determinations from the same type of exacting review given to U.S. agency determinations and Revenue Canada findings. In essence a panel cannot remand without showing Canada's CITT determinations to be "patently unreasonable."

In Canada, the *Federal Court Act* (FCA), section 28(1), sets out the standard of review which is to be applied by reviewing bodies to Revenue Canada and CITT final determinations. A reviewing court can set aside an agency determination if the agency:

a) failed to observe a principle of natural justice or otherwise acted beyond or refused to exercise its jurisdiction;
b) erred in law in making its decision or order, whether or not the order appears on the face of the record; or
c) based its decision on an erroneous finding of fact that it made in a perverse or capricious manner or without regard to the material before it.

During the FTA years, the standard of review that Canadian courts would apply to final CITT determinations was different from that which applied to final Revenue Canada findings because of the privative clause mentioned above. The Supreme Court of Canada in a 1992 case, *United Brotherhood of Carpenters and Joiners of America, Local 579* v. *Bradco Construction Ltd.*, outlined the standard of review to be applied to administrative tribunal decisions in the presence of such a clause: "Where the relevant legislative provision is a true privative clause, judicial review is limited to errors of jurisdiction resulting from an error in interpreting a legislative provision limited to errors of jurisdiction resulting from an error in interpreting a legislative provision limiting the tribunal's powers or a patently unreasonable error on a question of law otherwise within the tribunal's jurisdiction."

U.S. exporters were unsuccessful in appealing CITT final determinations for three main reasons. First, because it is difficult to categorize a CITT mistake as one of jurisdiction, panels reviewed most alleged errors as "errors of law." Second, because of the existence of a privative clause, alleged CITT "errors of law" were reviewed using the highly deferential "patently unreasonable" test. Third, panels did not consistently attempt to articulate and apply a stringent version of the "patently unreasonable" test.

The power of a privative clause is evident in the case of *Cerlain Beer* originating in the United States. The CITT found that a concentration of dumped U.S. imports had caused material injury to the beer industry in the province of British Columbia. The U.S. petitioners contended that the CITT had exceeded its jurisdiction under FCA's 28(1)(a) . They asserted that as a result of this violation, the binational panel was required to employ the "correctness" test. This test, enumerated in a 1988 Supreme Court of Canada case, *U.E.S., Local 298* v. *Bibeault*, means that if an expert tribunal has inquired into matters not authorized by statute, the agency's determination will be deemed incorrect and will be remanded for redetermination. The "correctness" test is very demanding on the agency under review.

In the first of its two opinions, the panel rejected the Canadian industry's request to frame the U.S. exporters' allegations as "errors of law," and thereby precluded application of the deferential "patently unreasonable" standard of review. Instead, the panel attacked the tribunal's findings by applying the more stringent "correctness" test on the ground that the agency had failed to conduct the type of inquiry required by the SIMA. The panel held that the SIMA had not authorized the tribunal to make an inquiry as to the existence of a causal link between extraneous factors (nondumping factors) and material injury. This issue was remanded, as the panel concluded that the Tribunal had transgressed the "correctness" standard. In a concurring opinion, the American panel chairman warned that when a reviewing body is deciding whether an issue is to be classified as an "error of law" or as a "breach of jurisdiction," Canadian law requires that the administering agency be given the benefit of the doubt. The chairman remanded the determination by finding that it was "patently unreasonable."

On remand, the CITT substantiated its original determination, but again took into account extraneous factors. The panel majority upheld this redetermination by finding that it was not patently unreasonable. With regard to the standard of review issue, the panel held:

> The scope of this Panel's inquiry in a review of the Determination on Remand is much narrower than was the scope of its review of the Tribunal's original Determination. The panel's inquiry in reviewing the Determination. The panel's inquiry in reviewing the Determination on Remand is thus limited to deciding whether the Tribunal addressed the question that the Panel directed to it, followed the panel's instructions, an in so doing reached a result that is not patently unreasonable and is supported by at least some evidence in the Tribunal's investigative record.

The panel offered no explanation of why it had changed the application standard of review. The *Beer* case illustrates how the presence of a privative clause helped insulate the CITT from rigorous binational panel review.

Panels reviewing CITT determinations have been inconsistent on how much deference to show to that tribunal under the "patently unreasonable" tab. *Tufted Carpets for the United States* is a good case example. In the first of three panel opinions concerning this matter, the majority made a thorough attempt to trace the evolution of the "patently unreasonable" test. It concluded that the conventional approach applied by Canadian courts was restricted to ascertaining whether or not a tribunal's determination could be sustained by "any evidence." The majority conceded that this type of judicial review effectively precluded reviewing bodies from examining whether agency results flowed logically from supporting evidence. But the majority then suggested that recent decisions concerning the "patently unreasonable" test had broadened the mandate of reviewing bodies. Instead of being restricted to examining whether or not a tribunal result could be sustained by "any evidence," the panel concluded that reviewing bodies were now required to ensure that the methodology employed by the administrating agency was reasonable. For authority, the majority cited the Supreme Court's 1990 decision in *Lester* v. *U.A. Local 740*, which stated: "Courts should exercise caution and deference in reviewing the decisions of specialized administrative tribunals. This deference extends both to the determination of the facts and the interpretation of the law. Only where the evidence, viewed reasonably, is incapable of supporting a tribunal's findings of facts, or where the interpretation placed on the legislation is patently unreasonable, can the court interfere."

After citing a number of other recent judicial propositions supporting a more active judicial role, the panel formulated its own version of the "patently unreasonable" test:

> If a reviewing Panel finds that the decision of a specialized tribunal cannot be sustained on any reasonable interpretation of the facts or where the evidence viewed reasonably is incapable of supporting the tribunal's findings of fact, the tribunal's decision will be deemed patently unreasonable. Put another way, if a rational or logical relationship does not exist between the evidence and the decision of the tribunal, such decision will be deemed patently unreasonable.

Once the panel employed this relatively exacting approach to the CITT's final determination it found that nearly all of the tribunal's conclusions were not rationally connected to supporting evidence. The two dissenters, one American and one Canadian, disagreed with the strict standard of judicial review formulated by the majority and would have affirmed the CITT determination. Where the majority had cited *Lester* to justify a more expansive role for reviewing bodies, the dissent drew upon another statement in the same case to support the orthodox approach:

> If there is any evidence capable of supporting a finding . . . the court will defer to the board's finding even though it may not have reached the same conclusion. However, absent any such evidence, the decision must fall.

In the panel's second opinion, the majority and dissent again diverged on the applicable standard of review. The panel majority in the second opinion, composed of the two original dissenters and a newly appointed Canadian panelist (due to a withdrawal), chose not to reapply the rigorous standard of review employed in the first decision, substituting a more deferential approach. On the matter of past and present material injury, the majority rejected the tribunal's analysis. The panel found that the tribunal had not addressed the concerns of the initial opinion. These issues were again remanded. The majority affirmed, however, the agency's "future injury" finding. The panel held that there existed evidence in the administrative record to support the tribunal's findings. The sole dissenting panelist, a U.S. member of the majority in the first opinion, refused to affirm the tribunal's future injury finding. The panelist argued that the "patently unreasonable" standard required that each tribunal conclusion be sustained with supporting evidence.

In its second redetermination, the tribunal concluded that there existed no past and present material injury to the Canadian industry. The Canadian Carpet Institute sought review of these findings, while the U.S. petitioners asked the panel to reconsider its previous affirmation of the CITT's future injury finding. In its third opinion, the panel unanimously affirmed the tribunal's findings and refused to reconsider the future injury determination.

Had the panel been able to apply the standard of "reasonableness" to the alleged error of law – as it would have for a Revenue Canada determination – the panel might have remanded the future injury finding. The case demonstrates how panels reviewing CITT determinations have been inconsistent in determining how much deference is required by the "patently unreasonable" test. Rather than reaffirm the initial decision's strict standard of review, the panel majority in the second opinion opted for a more lenient version. Although such an outcome was unfortunate from the perspective of U.S. exporters, any deviation from this approach would have violated Canadian administrative law and tradition. In the other five cases reviewing CITT findings, panels accepted the traditional "any evidence/curial deference" approach to the "patently unreasonable" test.

The Revenue Canada Standard of Review

Revenue Canada final determinations, like those of the CITT, can be appealed on any of the three grounds listed in the *Federal Court Act*. Hence, if Revenue Canada exceeds its jurisdiction, or commits an error of law or fact, the agency's final determination can be remanded for redetermination. The absence of a privative clause with respect to Revenue Canada final determinations is most significant in relation to alleged errors of law. Whereas CITT errors could only be reviewed by way of the "patently unreasonable" test, alleged Revenue Canada errors of law may be examined by way of the "reasonableness" standard. If there is more than one reasonable interpretation of the SIMA, a reviewing body must not substitute its judgement for that of Revenue Canada unless the agency is not reasonable, or is clearly wrong.

Panels applied the reasonableness standard rigorously. This contrasts with the generally deferential approach which panels took to CITT final determinations, and approximates the manner in which panels examined U.S. agency final determinations. In each of the four cases reviewing Revenue Canada determinations, panels rejected the agency's interpretation of the SIMA as "unreasonable," and remanded to the agency for redetermination.

Cases Reviewing United States Agency Determinations

The standard of review to be applied in Chapter 19 panel review of a U.S. agency final determination has been statutorily framed: "The court shall hold unlawful any determination, finding, or conclusion found . . . to be unsupported by substantial evidence on the record, or otherwise not in accordance with law." A review of judicial decisions shows that U.S. appellate courts have been unable to articulate clearly how much deference must be accorded to final agency determinations. Determining what constitutes "substantial evidence" and what may be deemed an "error of law" involves subjective judgement. Chapter 19 panels have used the latitude which exists in U.S jurisprudence to formulate a relatively unyielding standard of review in contrast to reviews of Canadian Tribunal determination, but not unlike Revenue Canada determination.

Under the U.S. Supreme Court's 1984 *Chevron* decision, a reviewing court must determine whether the agency's conclusion is based on a "permissible" construction of the relevant statute. Although this deferential principle has been followed regularly when aggrieved foreign exporters have challenged ITA and ITC final determinations before the CIT, U.S. courts have more recently weakened this approach. For example, in the 1990 *Dole* case, the Court remanded an agency conclusion because it had been reached without using "the most natural" interpretation of the statute at issue.

As for "substantial evidence" in U.S. law this has been defined by courts as "such relevant evidence as a reasonable mind might accept as a adequate to support a conclusion." The test requires broad deference, but reviewing bodies must consider the body of evidence opposed to the agency's view. Determinations may be remanded if they lack of "reasoned" basis and a reviewing authority may not defer to an agency determination premised on inadequate analysis or reasoning.

The Fresh Chilled and Frozen Pork from Canada case is a good example of a less than deferential panel approach to agency determination in the United States. The *Pork* panel recognized that U.S. jurisprudence required "great deference" to be accorded to the findings of administrative agencies, but surveyed leading cases in U.S. administrative law to articulate a relatively strict "substantial evidence" test:

> In assessing the evidence, the Panel must consider the Record as a whole, including evidence on the Record which detracts from the substantiality of the evidence relied on by the agency making its determination . . . The proscription against a Panel reweighing the evidence does not foreclose a Panel from ever deciding that an ITC determination is unsupported by substantial evidence; nor is the deference properly owed to the ITC's

> determination without limits. The Panel may not permit the agency "under the guise of lawful discretion or interpretation" to contravene or ignore the intent of Congress.

The panel's analysis undermined a significant portion of the ITC's reasoning.

In its redetermination on remand, the ITC reopened the administrative record and admitted new evidence as to the threat of material injury. The second panel opinion rejected the ITC's new rationale for lack of evidentiary support and ordered the ITC to find that Canadian pork imports posed no threat of material injury to U.S. industry. Although it complied the ITC alleged that the panel had egregiously intruded into its factual decision-making capacity, "impermissibly" reweighed evidence, and clearly violated the FTA's mandate by applying a standard of review inconsistent with that required by U.S. law.

The United States trade representative requested the formation of an extraordinary challenge committee (ECC) to assess whether or not the panel had applied a de novo standard of review instead of the correct standard of "substantial evidence on the record." The ECC unanimously concluded that so long as a panel made a conscientious attempt to articulate and apply the U.S. standard of review, it would not interfere with a panel's conclusion.

Pork illustrates why Canadian exporters have enjoyed such a high degree of success in the Chapter 19 process. First, the panel demonstrated that the U.S. standard of review could be formulated and applied in such a way as to force U.S. agencies to support their conclusions with substantial reasoning. Second, the panel formulated and applied an unyielding standard of review in both its initial opinion and in its subsequent review. This contrasts with the panel review of CITT determinations discussed above. Third, *Pork* demonstrated that the ECC would not function as an ordinary appellate court. Although the committee did not identify what level of panel misconduct would constitute a "manifest" breach of mandate, the decision reinforced the notion that panel decisions were dispositive.

While *Pork* showed how the "substantial evidence" test could be used to overturn a U.S. agency final determination, *The Live Swine* case exemplifies how panels can employ the "errors of law" test. The Chapter 19 panel articulated the same strict standard of review and held that "Commerce does not perform a proper de facto analysis if it merely looks at the number of companies that receive benefits under [a] program." "It is not the sheer number of enterprises receiving benefits that dictates whether or not a program is countervailable." [citing a 1991 CIT case] Rather, Commerce must examine all relevant factors to determine whether "if, in its application, the program results in a subsidy only to a specific enterprise or industry of specific group of enterprises or industries." [citing *PPG Industries*] To fulfill this requirement, Commerce must comply with its own proposed regulations, as expressly approved by the Court of Appeals for the Federal Circuit in *PPG Industries*, and it "must exercise judgement and balance various factors in analyzing the facts of a particular case in order to determine whether an 'unfair' practice is taking place." The panel found that the ITA determination resulted solely from an application of one of the criteria of the proposed regulations and that the ITA had failed to consider the other factors. The panel remanded the final determination, declaring it "not in accordance with U.S. law." The ITA reaffirmed with virtually no consideration of the other factors which the panel had ordered the agency to assess. The panel majority again rejected the ITA's conclusions:

> It appears that Commerce has taken a unidimensional, mathematical approach to the determination of specificity, despite the Agency's statement in its "Background" to its Proposed Regulations that "the Department must exercise judgement and balance various factors in analyzing the facts of the particular case." Commerce also stated that "the specificity test cannot be reduced to a precise mathematical formula." Yet Commerce, in our judgement, has resorted to just such a "precise mathematical formula."

One of the U.S. panelists wrote a dissent in which he charged the majority with seriously breaching its mandate. He stated that the ITA's interpretation was reasonable and therefore in accordance with U.S. law:

> this panel's decision is breathtaking. The panel shows no recognition of the limitations imposed by United States law on reviewing bodies confronted with a highly technical, fact-intensive record, and no consideration of the impact of its decision on the binational process. While panel decisions are not binding on United States courts, they do influence other binational panels; if given precedential respect by other panels, this panel's decision would cause a fundamental change in the way United States countervailing duty law is administered in cases involving Canadian products.

The United States trade representative requested the formation of an extraordinary challenge committee (ECC) to assess whether or not the panel had manifestly exceeded its powers and authority. The committee was satisfied that the panel majority had accurately articulated the applicable standard of review. It concluded that the panel may have "erred" in its finding that the ITA's determination was neither in accordance with law, nor based on substantial evidence. Nevertheless the committee was not persuaded that the panel had failed conscientiously to apply the properly articulated standard of review. In failing to establish the point at which an error in the application of the standard of review becomes so serious as to constitute a "failure to apply the appropriate standard," the committee failed to clarify the limits of a Chapter 19 panel's jurisdiction.

Softwood Lumber from Canada and Deference to Agencies

Before the *Softwood Lumber* panel, the ITA argued that once it found that a subsidy had been conferred upon a limited number of users, it was not required under U.S. law to examine the other factors in its Proposed Regulations. In the alternative, the ITA contended that it had considered all the criteria, but had decided that only one – the limited number of users – was required. The panel stated its standard of review: "While this panel is obligated to show deference to the agency's expertise, we are entitled to ensure that the agency's interpretation of the statute is reasonable." As in *Live Swine*, the panel rejected the assertion that an affirmative finding of "specificity" could be grounded on consideration of only one factor in the Proposed Regulations. The panel reasoned that if the ITA had considered the other factors, it might well have found differently. It based its repudiation of the ITA findings on solid jurisprudential support:

> the Court of Appeals for the Federal Circuit has stated in [a 1992 case] that Commerce must consider all of the factors in the Proposed Regulations 'in light of the evidence in the record in determining the specificity in a given case.' Nowhere in either of the Preliminary Determination nor the Final Determination is there a reference to any record evidence regarding government action, disproportionate use, or government discretion.

In its redetermination, the ITA found that Canadian users constituted one large group. In addition, the agency provided data showing that this group was a disproportionate user of stumpage. The panel majority's second decision again canvassed the U.S. stand of review. The Court of Appeals for the Federal Circuit's intervening decision in *Daewoo* found that reviewing agencies were required to give deference to the ITA's choice of analytical and empirical methodology. The panel majority, however, concluded that the "general" statements in *Daewoo* articulating "deference" did not have the effect of overturning the prior "specific" pronouncements of U.S. courts. It held that the ITA was still legally obliged to consider all four criteria and to apply the test in a reasonable and rational manner. Noting that "a contrary conclusion would result in the evisceration of the purpose for reviewing agency determinations, rendering the appeal process superfluous," the panel majority scrutinized the ITA's findings using the same rigorous standard of the first opinion. *Daewoo* in its view did not create a "new" or "expanded" standard of deference.

The majority stated:

> The complete lack of reasoned analysis whether or not the number of industries using stumpage is too few, and the mechanical, mathematical way in which Commerce decided that the users of stumpage are too few to be non-specific, is contrary to law and legal precedent . . . [T]he analysis of dominant or disproportionate use . . . is either irrelevant or perverse . . . we therefore remand this issue to Commerce for a determination that the provincial stumpage programs are not provided to a specific enterprise.

The dissenters, the two American panelists, asserted that the majority had misconceived and misapplied the appropriate standard of review. The dissent alleged that the majority had failed to provide the amount of deference required by *Daewoo*, which had reinforced the "posture of deference" accorded to agency determinations by U.S. administrative law. It argued that the majority was engaged more in statutory and regulatory amendment than judicial review, and had clearly violated the requirements of U.S. law.

The United States trade representative requested the formation of an extraordinary challenge committee (ECC) to assess whether or not the panel had manifestly exceeded its powers, authority and jurisdiction by ignoring the U.S. standard of review. The two retired Canadian judges in the ECC majority upheld the decision. In their view, the panel majority had not failed conscientiously to apply the standard of review required under U.S. law. The dissenting opinion of retired U.S. Circuit Judge Malcolm Wilkie concluded that *Daewoo* simply reaffirmed that U.S. administrative agencies were to enjoy discretion when choosing and applying methodology: "I believe that this Binational Panel majority may violate more principles of appellate review of agency action than any opinion by a reviewing body which I have ever read." Going on to indict the entire Chapter 19 process, Judge Wilkie noted:

> The record shows that five (or in this case three) distinguished "experts" have shown no deference whatsoever to the "experts" in the ITA of the Commerce Department. Psychologically, why

should they be expected to show the deference to administrative agency action which is required as a fundamental tenet of United States judicial review of agency action? The panel members are experts; they know better than the lowly paid "experts" over in the Commerce Department, and they have felt inclined to say so. Repeatedly, most vividly in this particular case, they seem to have substituted their judgement for that of the agency. They have not hesitated to say that the agency was wrong on its methodology, wrong in the choice of alternate economic analyses, wrong in its conclusions, and that the Panel of five experts knows far better how to do it. All of this of course is directly contrary to long-standing United States law concepts of review of agency action. [40]

Cases Brought Against U.S. Agencies – Conclusions

Binational panels in these cases used the "substantial evidence" test and "errors of law" requirement to force reversal of unsubstantiated U.S. agency conclusions and to ensure that those agencies were consistent in their choice and application of methodology. In the domain of trade remedy law, where the calculation of dumping and subsidy margins is intrinsically tied to methodology it has promoted, methodological consistency has furthered the pro-competitive objective of the FTA and NAFTA.

Judge Wilkie's dissent in *Softwood Lumber* asserted that Chapter 19 binational panels have, at times, exceeded their jurisdiction by applying an "incorrect" standard of review. In written testimony before the House Ways and Means Committee Subcommittee on Trade, Judge Wilkie elaborated on these conclusions. He contended that the FTA Chapter 19 system had "failed" because panelists lack accountability; are too prone to conflicts of interest; cannot avoid the temptation to "redo" the work of the administering agencies; and have no experience with judicial review. On the last point, Judge Wilkie insisted:

> The ad hoc panels have no feeling for the unique standards of judicial review, which in many respects is a unique American institution. There is no sense of deference to the expertise of the administrative agency, which the CIT does have. More damaging to the fairness of the system, foreigners, even Canadians, lack an essential knowledge of United States law, both substantive and procedural, or perhaps are unwilling to apply it against the traditions of their own law. [41]

These criticisms appear to many academic legal scholars to be misplaced for three reasons. First, to suggest that a panel has applied an incorrect standard of review implies that there exits a correct standard. Yet, beyond the limited guidance provided by the statutory "substantial evidence" and "errors of law" tests, the applicable standard of review is not ascertainable with ease. Instead, it is composed of a number of different elements including conflicting judicial propositions. Second, it has been suggested that Chapter 19 panelists lack an essential understanding of U.S. procedural and substantive law. This and other studies have found that panelists have proven adept at interpreting and applying complex trade remedy laws, as well as the requirements of United States and Canadian administrative law, during review of final determinations. Nonetheless, there is a subjective element to determining what constitutes United States law on any given matter and, as a result, it is possible to conclude that Chapter 19 panelists have failed properly to interpret procedural and substantive United States law. What is indisputable is that there has been a general consensus among commentators that FTA Chapter 19 panel decisions have been of high quality. Third, it is far from clear that Chapter 19 panels have delivered decisions that uniformly diverge from the opinions which would have been rendered by the CIT. FTA Chapter 19 panels for the most part produced uncontroversial decisions and outcomes which could well have fallen within the range of opinions rendered by the CIT.

Subsidies and Dumping Dispute Settlement under NAFTA

A number of amendments to the FTA system in NAFTA have been made. Under the FTA the only recourse available to the United States or Canada if they were concerned with the other country's effective implementation of Chapter 19 was abrogation of the entire agreement. NAFTA Article 1905 permits a party to suspend operation of Article 1904 (binational panel review) with respect to a government that has failed to meet its Chapter 19 obligations.

NAFTA has also mandated that the roster of panelists "shall include judges or former judges to the fullest extent possible." Judges, by training, are more attentive to questions of jurisdiction, and are less likely to challenge agency determinations with the same degree of rigor as have FTA panelists.

Under the FTA, an extraordinary challenge committee's (ECC) responsibilities ended with ensuring that a panel did not engage in gross misconduct, biased deliberation, breach of fundamental procedures or action that manifestly exceeded its mandate. Under NAFTA, an ECC is explicitly authorized to examine a panel's analysis of substantive law and underlying facts and is given ninety rather than thirty days to deliberate. The ECC can now vacate or remand a panel opinion if it finds that the panel "failed to apply the appropriate standard of review." This makes the ECC resemble an appellate court.

An important amendment has also been made to the Canadian standard of review. Effective January 1, 1994, the SIMA the CITT's privative clause was repealed. The Supreme Court of Canada, however, in the 1994 *Pezim v. British Columbia (Superintendent of Brokers)* case, held that even in the absence of a privative clause, "considerable deference" should be given to an expert tribunal's determination. Two recent NAFTA Chapter 19 panels reviewing CITT final determinations applied this *Pezim* standard. The *Baler Twine* panel explained that:

> the Tribunal's decision is not protected by a privative clause, there is no right of appeal from its decisions. The only right that arises is one of judicial review. There is no reason, in logic or in law, to conclude that it is entitled to anything less that "considerable deference." While that deference does not extend to the point of patent unreasonability, it resides close to that end of the spectrum of deference. [42]

Thus, even without the privative clause, U.S. exporters cannot expect over-rigorous panel review of alleged CITT errors of law.

Dispute Resolution Under NAFTA Chapter 20

Trade Other than Subsidy and Dumping
Chapter 20 of NAFTA constructs a three-stage dispute resolution process involving: consultation; a meeting of the Free Trade Commission (cabinet-level officials deciding by consensus); and nonbinding arbitration. After a complaining party formally requests consultations with the offending party, a thirty-day time limit must expire before a party may ask for a meeting of the Free Trade Commission. The commission convenes within ten days. After another thirty-day time limit, any disputant can request the formation of an arbitral panel. In controversies involving two parties, the parties are to agree on the chair of the panel within fifteen days and, within fifteen days thereafter, are each to designate two panelists who are citizens of the other disputing party. In a dispute involving all three parties, the disputants agree on the chair of the panel, then the party complained against selects two panelists (a citizen of each of the two complaining parties), and, finally, the complaining parties jointly select two panelists who are citizens of the party

complained against. Subject to the agreement of the disputants, the panel may seek advice from experts or request a formal written report form a scientific review board. Chapter 20 guarantees the disputants the right to make written submissions and to have at least one hearing before the panel.

Within ninety days after the last panelist is selected, the panel is to present to the disputing parties an initial report, on which written comments may be submitted within fourteen days. No later than thirty days after the initial report, the panel must deliver its final report for transmission to the Free Trade Commission. Minority opinions can be issued but only anonymously. Unless the commission decides otherwise, the final report shall be published fifteen days after transmission. If, within thirty days after receiving the final report, the disputants have not resolved the controversy, the complaining party may suspend NAFTA benefits to the offending party until a resolution has been reached. The suspended benefits should be roughly equivalent to the harm incurred as a result of the offending party's misconduct and should be in the same trade sector(s) as are affected by the measure at issue.

By the late 1990s, eight disputes had formally entered the Chapter 20 consultations phase. This first stage of dispute resolution resolved only one of these disputes, a Canadian concern about a U.S. uranium purchase agreement with Russia. One dispute was still in the consultation phase, one was resolved outside it, and five went on to stage two, the meeting of the Free Trade Commission. In two cases, despite the commission's failure to resolve the dispute, no party asked for panel proceedings. In the case of the joint Canadian-Mexican complaint concerning the Helms-Burton Act, President Clinton's suspensions of the private right of action component led to neither complaining country pursuing the panel option. Mexico did institute stage three, the panel procedure, in December 1996 on the issue of *straw broom* exports. The only panel decision reviewed by the article, however, is that instigated by the United States, concerning tariffs applied by Canada on agricultural imports of dairy, poultry and egg products.

In July 1995, after the Free Trade Commission's efforts to resolve this dispute failed, the United States formally requested that a Chapter 20 arbitral panel be convened to adjudicate the matter. Although four panelists were selected by October, the parties did not agree on the chairperson, an English jurist, until January 1996. Oral arguments were presented by mid-April 1996. The panel should have issued an initial report by no later than April 1996 (ninety days after the last panelist was selected) and a final report by no later than May 1996 (thirty days after the initial report). In the event, the panel did not present an initial report until July 1996 and a final report until December 1996. All five panelists, including the two Americans, ruled that Canada's tariffs conformed to the provisions of NAFTA. Because the panel found in favor of Canada, no further action by Canada was necessary, and the dispute did not advance to the implementation phase.

Dispute Settlement under NAFTA on Subsidies and Dumping

Unlike Chapter 20's dispute resolution mechanism, which covers disputes concerning the interpretation, application or breach of NAFTA, Chapter 19's dispute settlement mechanism applies solely to antidumping and countervailing duties. Chapter 19 requires that "each Party shall replace judicial review of final antidumping and countervailing duty determinations with bi-national panel review." Under Chapter 19, private persons entitled to commence domestic judicial procedures to review such national determinations are allowed to appear and be represented by counsel before the panel.

A panel is immediately formed upon request by a NAFTA party. Within thirty days, the involved parties each select two panelists and, within twenty-five days thereafter, agree on the selection of the fifth panelist. A majority of the panelists and the chair of the panel must be lawyers in good standing. By no later than 315 days after the request, the panel must issue a (binding) final decision. This can either uphold the antidumping determination or remand it for reform.

From January 1994 through November 1998, Chapter 19 arbitral panels were requested to resolve forty-two disputes, twenty-seven of which had come to a conclusion. Ten ended prior to any panel decision. Six panels affirmed government rulings. One case ended with the panel, with two Americans and one Mexican in the majority, ordering Mexico to rescind completely prior dumping and material injury findings, as well as antidumping duties imposed on two U.S. steel companies. Nine other cases resulted in decisions affirming in part and remanding in part.

Conclusion

Robert Howse in a thoughtful paper examining NAFTA is much less sanguine about its utility now that the WTO has new agreements on subsidies and on dumping which offer in his view, "increasingly precise definitions of concepts such as 'subsidies', 'dumping' and 'material injury' providing benchmarks against which U.S. agency determinations can be scrutinized that are not bound by U.S. judicial interpretation."[43] In particular, he notes "clearer criteria now exist for the definition of countervailable subsidy." He explores dispute settlement weaknesses such as in a few FTA panel cases, the high legal costs, time delays and of course the near interminable *Softwood Lumber* case. Still he concedes binational panels have certainly disposed of routine appeals more expeditiously than has the CIT and the quality of legal and economic analysis employed by the panels has been high. According to Howse, the NAFTA Chapter 19 process "seems to have worked particularly well in antidumping actions" and he notes that the Uruguay Round Agreement's dumping provisions provide fewer bases for challenging domestic agency "determinations under the WTO rules than does for example the agreement on subsidies."

In essence, our argument is that FTA (now NAFTA) panels will influence the future evolution of U.S. and Canadian trade law and administration. All of this implies that panels are, in fact, changing the evolution of the law and its execution. From this perspective, one is able to say that the law is not so much contracting as evolving through panel decisions.[44] Mexico, by entering into a free trade agreement with the EC raises the question if NAFTA would be more meaningful if all the partners had to agree before one of them could enter into a trade agreement with another country, potentially nullifying the benefits of the agreement. Perhaps the United States, Canada and Mexico should focus their energies on strengthening NAFTA, not neglecting it.

NAFTA and WTO Dispute Settlement Compared

The similarities between the mechanisms created under NAFTA's Chapter 20 on dispute settlement and the WTO's dispute settlement understanding "are substantial and are much greater than the differences." Both are designed to provide a speedy process. Both require the issuance of reports to show the rationale for decisions. Both contemplate a process that is protected from public scrutiny of review until completed. However some differences are worth noting. Where "non-violation" or "nullification and improvement" actions occur, only NAFTA is capable of providing binding decisions. There seems to be a less prompt choice of panelists for NAFTA than the WTO. NAFTA cases include nationals as panelists, a WTO case cannot; WTO cases provide the complaining party with an opportunity of enlisting the support of non-NAFTA nations. Not so under NAFTA.

These differences aside, third image legal momentum behind settling disputes is apparent in both. A troublesome difference between NAFTA and the WTO, but not fatal for third image legal momentum, is of course the frequently heard American opinion that under the WTO the implementation of panel reports is less than perfect. New mechanism advanced the instances in which implementation of an adverse panel report has been completed were substantially outnumbered by those in which implementation is pending," whereas under NAFTA the prevailing party is specifically authorized to retaliate and may do so in thirty days.

Chapter 11 of NAFTA: A Potential Nightmare?

One nightmarish result of NAFTA not so much for the integrity of dispute settlement panels, but for NAFTA's ability to defuse political temperatures has only recently been glimpsed. This devil is in the details of a little known clause in the NAFTA agreement that attracted little or no media attention during the negotiations or in NAFTA's early years. Its impact has already been far more nightmarish for the signatory governments than the side accords relating to the substantive issues of human health and the environment probably ever will be.

This is Chapter 11, Article 1110, which prohibits a government from acting in such a way as taking actions tantamount to expropriation. It prohibits a government from, in effect, expropriating a foreign company's investment in its country unless it pays compensation.

Suddenly in 1998, and each year since, the clause has become the basis for a number of lawsuits against both the Canadian, Mexican and United States governments. Significantly the clause has been used to challenge environmental and health protection legislation. Simon Potter, noted Canadian trade lawyer, ruefully admits this is a potential bonanza for trade lawyers unless it is lightened in some way.[45] Others disagree. A "regulatory taking" is a difficult case to make under U.S. or Canadian law, but it is a most useful constraint on regulatory "do-gooders" pandering to their political masters who in turn pander to zealous and very vocal, focused interest groups. It is in effect a "third image" restraint on the "first image" opportunist.

For example, the U.S. government had a lawsuit filed against it on June 14, 1999 arguing that a plan by the State of California to phase out the use of a gasoline additive produced by Methanex Corporation of Vancouver was tantamount to an expropriation of its business and it sought $1 billion (U.S.) as compensation. California argued that the additive causes water pollution, possibly cancer and is of indeterminate benefit in cleaning car emissions. Methanex cited contrary scientific information.

Another example was a file against the Canadian government by Ethyl Corporation of Virginia protesting the government of Canada's ban on a gasoline additive it manufactures. The Canadian government admitted the weakness of its research supporting its claim and ended up having to pay US$13 million to Ethyl to settle the matter. The paradox is that Chapter 11 can be exploited by companies trying to negate well-intentioned health and environmental standards. As one who was involved in negotiating NAFTA one cannot remember this paradox being contemplated or debated during 1992-93. It does, however, checkmate many real or virtual expropriations.

Relevance for Free Trade in the Americas

The links among lower tariffs, freer trade and dispute settlement mechanisms are vital, as we have seen earlier. Fairer dispute settlement was the *sine qua non* for Canada in the FTA and for the United States in the new WTO. However, when the United States calls for a Free Trade of the Americas (FTAA), is it willing to have "multilateral" panels decide on U.S. agency determinations as it has in NAFTA and did in the FTA? This great equalizer for the smaller nation is its attraction for the smaller nations. If this is not in the agreement, then will the Latin American countries want to lower barriers to trade?

The experience of the United States and Canada with Mexico's agency determinations under NAFTA is not discouraging, but it does remind us of the legal and cultural challenges. Identifying and observing the Mexican process of agency determinations on such matters as subsidies and antidumping is complex and time consuming. Would it not be equally so in the case of the other countries of the Americas? "The similarity and transparency of the Canadian and United States systems look like a 'no-brainer' compared to other countries in the Americas," says Chuck Roh.

To call for freer trade in the Americas as President George W. Bush does, is to hearken back to what Clayton Yeutter and James Baker called their strongest asset in the "terms of the debate" against an American second image fortress. This will be perhaps the mantra of the Republicans in the 2004 elections. This third image "leap of faith" as President George Bush put it when defending NAFTA in 1992, is the most important arsenal against the first-and second image opportunists in Congress who could bring about the more serious nightmare of a return to a badly functioning WTO and NAFTA and the consequent nightmarish effect its malfunctioning will have on world financial confidence. As renowned nineteenth-century English Whig essayist Thomas Macauley put it, "If all our neighbors are poor, how can we get rich?"

Let us not, however, underestimate the price of freer trade. It requires necessary concessions to some third image disciplines. A perceived fair and objective dispute settlement mechanism in both the WTO and in any new FTAA is the price. The mechanism can work as we have seen in this book but it needs constant reinforcement and attention. It needs American and other member commitment to an incremental third image legal momentum transformation of the world-trading system. It also needs a similar level of commitment from other major players such as the European Community, Japan and China. Failing this concession, a cancer will grow at the heart of these trade agreements.

A voluntarist championing of "third image" legal momentum thinking would radically alter the playing field for the United States in any future FTAA under the WTO and NAFTA. In most cases to date in the WTO and NAFTA, the checkmate "second-image" defenders of domestic agency primacy, seemed themselves to be checkmated. But were they? Let us turn to the so-called *Achilles' heel* case under the agreement: the *Softwood Lumber* dispute, a case which opened the channel of legislative reordering in certain situation of trade conflict. Softwood also stands as the most strenuously conflictual of all United States-Canada trade disputes and is worth examining as an extreme case.

Notes

1. Before Chapter 19 of the FTA came into effect, the Federal Court of Appeals had exclusive jurisdiction to review AD/CVD determinations made by the Deputy Minister of Revenue Canada and injury determinations made by the Canadian International Trade Tribunal (CITT). Decisions of the Federal Court of Appeals could be reviewed by the Supreme Court of Canada. In the United States, AD/CVD determinations of the Department of commerce-International Trade Administration (DOC) and injury determinations of the International Trade Commission (ITC) could only be reviewed by the Court of International Trade (CIT). CIT decisions could be appealed to the Court of Appeals of the Federal Circuit (CAFC), and ultimately to the Supreme Court of the United States. After Chapter 19 of the FTA came into effect, AD/CVD/injury determinations could be reviewed by either binatinal panels or domestic courts.

2. Gullermo Aguilar Alvarez et al, "NAFTA Chapter 19: Binational Panel Review of Antidumping and Countervailing Duty Determinations," in William Robson, S. Dahlia Stein (eds), *Trading Punches: Trade Remedy Laws and Disputes Under NAFTA* (Washington: National Planning Association 1995), 32-33.

3. Speech at McGill Conference at the Tenth Anniversary of the first year of the Canada-U.S. Free Trade Agreement (Montreal), 7 June 1999.

4. Ibid.

5. Chuck Roh, McGill Conference.

6. Clayton Yeuter, McGill Conference.

7. See John M. Mercury, "Chapter 19 of the United States-Canada Free Trade Agreement 1989-95: A Check or Administered Protection?" *NorthWestern Journal of International Law and Business, Vol. 15, No.3 (Spring 1995), 573-74; James R. Cannon Jr.,* Resolving Disputes Under NAFTA Chapter 19 (Colorado Springs: Shepard's/McGraw-Hill Inc., 1994) 63-6 and see 17 & 24.

8. Gordon Christenson, Kimberly Gambrel, "Constitutionality of Binational Panel Review in Canada-U.S. Free Trade Agreements," *The International Lawyer,* Vol. 23, No.

2 Summer, 1989), 402:

James R. Cannon Jr., "Dispute Settlement in the Article 1904 U.S.-Canada Binational Panel Versus the Court of International Trade," Unpublished, 1990, 3-4; Homer E. Moyer Jr., "Chapter 19 of the NAFTA: Binational Panels as the Trade Court of last Resort "*The International Lawyer,* Vol. 27, No. 3 (Fall, 1993).

9, See M. Hart et al., *Decision at Midnight: Inside the Canada-U.S. Free Trade Negotiations* (U.B.C. Press, Vancouver 1994) and Gordon Ritchie, *Wrestling with the Elephant,* (Macfarlane Walter and Ross Toronto 1997). A helpful bibliography can be found U.S. Department of Commerce (fax: 202-482-4076) ask for NAFTA A Selected Bibliography April 1998.

10. NAFTA Article 1904.11 & 9.

11. Ibid.

12. See Michael Hart "Dispute Settlement and CUSTA" Occasional Papers, Carleton University, 1990 and Adreas Lowenfeld "The Free Trade Agreement Meets its First Challenge, *McGill Law Journal,* Vol. 37, 1992.

13. Quoted in Michael H. Greenberg, "Chapter 19 of the U.S.-Canada Free Trade Agreement and the North American Free Trade Agreement: Implications for the Court of International Trade, 25 <u>Law and Policy in International Business</u> 37 (Fall 1993), 34

14. Ibid.

15. Ibid., 40.

16. Ibid., 47.

17. Ibid., 48.

18. See Footnote 7 Mercury above.

19. See Greenberg Op, cit. his concurring opinion in the "Certain Beer" case in 1991 and Bark, "The Binational Panel Mechanism for Reviewing the U.S.-Canadian Antidumping and Countervailing Duty Determinations: A Constitutional Dilemma," *Virginia Journal of International Law* (1989): 699.

20. See Bark, Ibid. Literature on the constitutionality of Chapter 19 is extensive. Informative pieces include Gordon A. Christenson, Kimberly Gambrel, "Constitutionality of Binational panel Review in the Canada-U.S. Free Trade Agreement," *The International Lawyer,* Vol. 23. No. 2 (Summer, 1989); Demetrios G. Metropoulos, "Constitutional Dimensions of the North American Free Trade Agreement, "*Cornell International Law Journal,* Vol. 27, No. 1 (Winter, 1994); Stewart A. Baker, Shelly P. Battram, "The Canada-United States Free Trade Agreement, "*The International Lawyer,* Vol. 23, No. 1 (Spring, 1989).

21. Ibid. 707.

22. Ibid. 709.

23. Ibid.

24. R.A. Cass, *Economics and the Administration of the U.S. International Trade Law,* Ontario Centre for International Business Research Program Working paper 16, 1989, 31.

25. Vol. 11, 1991 see pages 621-42.

26. Ibid.

27. Ibid., 639.

28. Ibid., 640. See also Homer E. Moyer, Chapter 19 of the NAFTA-Binational Panels as the Trade Courts of last Resort, 27 *The International Lawyer,* 707 (Fall 1993). Robert Napoles, Dispute Resolution Under Charter 19 of the NAFTA: Antidumping and Countervailing Business as Usual, 10 *Arizona Journal of International and Comparative Law,* 459 (Fall 1993); Angel R. Oquendo, NAFTA's Procedural Narrow-Mindedness: The Panel Review of Antidumping and Countervailing Duty Determinations Under Chapter 19, 11 Conn. J. Int'l Law 61 (1995). Gustavo Vega-Canovas, SYMPOSIUM: NAFTA and the Expansion of the Free Trade: Current Issues and Future Prospects: Disciplining

Antidumping in NAFTA.

29. See Michael Hart, *A Vision of Canada-U.S. Free Trade* (Chapter for Trade Policy and Law, Carleton University) 1999 Part 10.

30. Gary Horlick and Amanda Debusk "Dispute Resolution Panels of the U.S.-Canada Free Trade Agreement," *McGill Law Review*, 307 (Fall 1991).

31. Lowenfeld, Op. cit., 312.

32. Ibid.

33. Horlick and DeBusk, Op. cit., 310.

34. Ibid.

35. See Michael Hart reference in David Lopez, "Dispute Resolution Under NAFTA: Lessons from the Early Experience," *Texas International Law Journal* 32 (1997): 163, and Mercury, Op. cit.

36. Cass, Op. cit.

37. See the articles referenced above by Mercury, Op. cit. passim; Lopez, Op. cit. passim; also all of Hart's research.

38. The following eleven pages summarize the research in the work published n footnote 37 above. Each quote or finding will not be repeated until page 191.

39. See J. Mercury, Op. cit. and D. Lopez, Op. cit. and the M.A. thesis by S. Matijasich (Carleton University, Ottawa), for a discussion of standards of review of GATT, FTA and NAFTA and for a fine list of sources on cases to be discussed in the next few pages.

40. Opinion of Judge Wilkey United States-Canada Free Trade Agreement Article 1904:13. Extraordinary Challenge Proceeding in the Matter of Certain Softwood Lumber Products Canada (ECC-94-1904:01 U.S.A.) 3 Aug. 1994, 56-7.

41. Ibid., 57

42. See William J. Davey, "Pine and Swine Canada-United States Trade Dispute Settlement – The FTA Experience and NAFTA Prospects," (Ottawa: Centre for Trade Policy and Law, 1996), 4-5.

43. R. Howse, "Settling Trade Remedy Disputes" (C.D. Howe Institute Commentary, Toronto 1998).

44. See Gilbert R. Winham, Anne M. Finn "Accession to NAFTA: The Implications of Extending Chapter 19 Dispute Settlement on Antidumping and Countervailing Disputes" in Joseph McKinney, Melissa Essary (ed), *Free Trade for the Americas: Issues in Economics, Trade Policy and Law* (Waco: Baylor University Press, 1995), 104.

Chapter Nine

Panels Matter, Politics Matter:
Case Histories under the FTA and NAFTA

"Softwood and Trucks"

Regional trade agreements are apples and oranges, chalk and cheese. No two regional pacts are alike. Some are deep and intrusive. The European Community (EC) is the best example of intrusive.[1] Others are more aspirational and "regional attention-getters" than anything else. APEC may be an example of this. NAFTA is far from achieving the depth of the EC, but one doubts that any of the inhabitants wish it to be as deep. Mercosur (the regional agreement for the cone of South America) is both aspiration and reality, but it lacks an acknowledged battery cell. Caricom is the same. The Organization of African Unity is neither African nor organized nor united, as one wit put it. It would be ill-advised to invest one's hopes in the potential of all regional trade liberalizing stepping stones leading to a more assured WTO. The FTA and NAFTA, however, have helped produce a more assured WTO so far. Still, several cases flaw NAFTA's record. Two stand out. The Mexican truck access and the change in U.S. trade law on softwood lumber. These may not cripple NAFTA, but they have reduced somewhat its image and credibility for decisiveness, and its image for bringing closure to disputes.

These reservations aside, as we have seen in an earlier chapter, there is a clear residue of promise for other nations if they wish to use FTA/NAFTA dispute resolution example for settling disputes. If other regional agreements used this formula, such as any future FTAA or a future APEC panel system, this would help to prevent overload of the young WTO. They could be fashioned to respect WTO primacy wherever required. The FTA experience is indicative here. It succeeded in not violating sovereignty, yet dissolved countless disputes without political interference, excessive controversy or the overloading of GATT. The FTA, now NAFTA, dispute settlement system can in some cases be bypassed for the WTO's, but this need not be frequent. NAFTA is not meant to prevent a signatory from changing its trade laws (as the

Softwood Lumber case shows), but such bold changes in law are rare and if used after a panel loss too often would cripple trade partners' confidence in the overall agreement. Above all, as we have seen in the previous chapter, NAFTA panels can generate decisions that don't always defer to domestic review. NAFTA combines a pinch of "third image" voluntaristic progress with a dash of "second image" realist deference to domestic administration of trade law.

Mexican Trucks into the United States

The most prominent recent NAFTA disappointment is not a reflection on the workings of the NAFTA dispute resolution system. Instead it is a reflection on the lack of momentum behind the agreement, when key sections of the agreement, for realist political reasons, have yet to be implemented. A vivid example of a realist political compromise is the United States' failure to implement a key provision of the pact from Mexico's point of view, the provision which gives U.S. and Mexican trucks free access to each other's roads. The United States has refused to implement it for over seven years after the agreement was signed amid pressure from the Teamsters Union who insisted that Mexican trucks be safe and that the drivers be properly competent.

Tiring of talks that had gone nowhere for years, Mexico sued the United States under the NAFTA's dispute resolution process in September 1998. The United States countersued. A series of legal moves delayed any panel resolution. "We believe that reason is on our side and that this has little to do with technical concerns and more to do with politics," said Luis de la Calle, under secretary for international trade negotiations for Mexico's Ministry of Trade and Industry, early in January 2000.[2] "We would like to see that when two countries have an agreement, that the agreement is respected. And that's why we are upset."

While Canadian trucks have had access to the United States since 1982 and vice versa, the NAFTA accord was to have given trucks from the three countries unrestricted access to North American roads beginning in 1995. The Teamsters argue that Mexican trucks are unsafe but, writes the *L.A. Times*, Trade and State Department officials in the Clinton administration "say privately" that safety concerns "can be alleviated by a certification" program for Mexican trucks, which Mexican officials say is already in place consistent with U.S. standards. [3] The United States argued that since it has legitimate safety concerns causing the delay, Mexico's maintenance of restrictions on United States domiciled trucks was simply a unilateral act of retaliation and that unilateral acts are not permitted under NAFTA.

This dispute is a classic case of second image realist political postponement on the implementation of a part of the agreement in order to get any agreement at all back in 1992-93. This writer can remember when this postponement was made part of the NAFTA agreement since it was vital to the new Clinton administration, but it had to be agreed to by the Mexicans or there might have been no NAFTA, period

This issue shows not only the compromise behind full implementation but it shows NAFTA itself to be something less than a third image legal impediment to responding in the near future to a key hot political need the Democrats felt they had to satisfy. It is less serious though than the *Softwood Lumber* dispute of 1988 to 2001, because sooner or later the U.S. postponement on trucks access will end and the dispute settlement process will be underway and its workings can be observed. The dispute settlement mechanism on *Softwood* however has a well-studied history and can be assessed. A chronological review of the three *Softwood* disputes is included here because it provides a key case-study of the worse that can happen under panel review when political deadlock causes it. These are extreme "full court press" examples of the interaction of third image panel disciplines with second image political gamesmanship.

Softwood Lumber Disputes under the FTA and NAFTA

In 2001, the *Softwood Lumber* impasse reopened. As we have seen, the most difficult issue between the United States and Canada under the FTA. was the *Softwood Lumber* dispute. In early 2001, the United States lumber industry launched a request to President George W. Bush to more strictly enforce American trade laws to deal with the ten billion dollar Canadian lumber exports to the U.S. As the last agreement expired March 31, 2001, the American industry enlisted nearly half the United States Senate to write to the President contending Canada's low provincial lumber-cutting fees and restrictions on exports of unprocessed logs amount to a huge illegal subsidy.

This dispute has already seen remands on injury and two on subsidy. It even saw an extraordinary challenge committee (ECC) decision on the legitimacy of one panel's personnel! On *Softwood*, every twist and turn the FTA process of dispute resolution could take seems to have been taken. (A chronology is in Appendix C of this book). Above all else, it is an instructive "worst-case" or perhaps most "prolonged case" study. Some lessons could be learned from this story which tested almost all of the outer limits of the dispute settlement process. The FTA's successor, NAFTA, now helps to close one defect in the process. This closure will be explained. The definition of a "subsidy" under GATT and NAFTA has since been clarified as well. Even so, in the early dialectic from 1988 to 1993 as a minister often answering for this in Parliament, it was evident to this writer that the *Softwood* issue had become so abstruse and technical that front-page political attention had almost disappeared. The issue was shunted to a nearly indecipherable note in the business pages. Neither Canadian ministers nor the U.S. trade representative were encouraged to comment much on the grinding away of the processes of panel and ECC review. On each particular case these processes were meant to work their will without political interference. As a result, a thorny subject fraught with potential political tension had been removed for over six years from direct political glare. In Kenneth Waltz's terms, it had been removed from the hot first and second image coals of contention to the cooler, more opaque processes of "third image legal momentum" resolution. Put more crudely, the hunt had changed from "politics" to natural justice and somewhat more objective evaluation. This was the result for a time on *Softwood*, but not too long a time. All said and done, it was better to have a process to defuse a charged political issue for a short time than to have no political game-plan at all.

Jean Anderson, a former head negotiator for trade law, for the United States and now a partner of Weil, Gotshal & Manges LLP in Washington, D.C. has represented Canada on *Softwood Lumber* before FTA panels. She delivered a nuanced report card [4] on the potency of the FTA and NAFTA dispute settlement panels on *Softwood Lumber I, II,* and *III* at a Conference June 5, 1999. First she reminded us that the push to the process itself in the fall of 1987 in the FTA negotiations was prompted by the Canadians who wanted something that could improve objectivity of U.S. agencies based on its experience with *Softwood I*. So let us not forget *Softwood I* acted as a catalyst for the FTA itself.

Second, she reminded us that the decision of the panel in *Softwood I* was not split along national lines when it found the U.S. Department of Commerce determination was "not in accord with U.S. law." This reinforces the premise of the process which was to decide on whether adherence to (in this case) U.S. law had occurred. The finding found both Americans and Canadians panelists agreeing, which indicates that even on a fairly major "politically visible" issue the national origin of panelists didn't dictate the result.

As for *Softwood II* she explains the astonishing split in the panel *along national lines* on the illogical change of the American panelist "who took a position 180 degrees different from the first panel. This doesn't so much prove the process doesn't ever work, but that it can falter," she said.[5]

Nor can the panel process be described as a failure, she said, in the case of *Softwood III* under Chapter 19 of the FTA because in the settlement of this issue "It did not take six court cases and over nine years as some of my cases outside the panel process do." She reminds us 'the case is no longer being litigated. The countervail duties have been returned. The process was over in less than two years." [6]

Most insightfully, she notes, as other observers have, that the best of both worlds would be to make agencies think carefully so as to avoid issues becoming politicized when they make determinations. This care increasingly is happening because of FTA, NAFTA and WTO panels. Carefree thinking happened in *Softwood*. Neither the agency nor Commerce "tempered" their determinations. But one case doesn't invalidate the panel process's overall ameliorative tempering effect.[7]

She also concludes, as have most observers, that the relevant Chapters of the Uruguay WTO Agreement is leading to greater codification and harmonization of antidumping and countervail proceedings. "The WTO is more clear on what is a subsidy now and there are new WTO constraints on how antidumping duties can be applied."[8] All this may be a result to some degree of the *Softwood* story.

The *Softwood Lumber* cases show no panel process can happily settle *all* major "geographically specific" visible political issues (e.g., Oregon and British Columbia). These may have to be solved by a method other "than the standard application of domestic law" says Anderson. In other words, realist second image politics may have to be deployed on some of these issues when voluntarist third image legal momentum is superseded. To say this, however, is not to say that this third image paradigm has no value even on highly visible political issues.

The First Softwood Lumber Dispute 1982-83: Pre-FTA and Pre-NAFTA

Preliminary Injury Investigation

From 1975 to 1978, the Canadian share of the U.S. softwood lumber market increased from 18.6 percent to 28.1 percent. A high-point of 30 percent market share was reached in 1980 by the Canadian softwood lumber producers.[9] On October 7, 1982, the U.S. Coalition for Fair Canadian Lumber Imports filed a countervailing duty petition against Canadian softwood lumber products. The United States International Trade Commission (ITC) determined whether a foreign product imported into the United States is, or could be, injurious to the domestic industry for a like product.

The basic issue was new chip-n-saw technology that migrated from British Columbia to eastern Canada. As a result, eastern pulp and paper producers stopped pulping whole logs and, instead, produced lumber from the logs and pulped only the residual chips and sawdust. This increased by 10 percentage points the Canadian supply of exports to the United States. In fact, at all material times, British Columbia exports decreased in terms of percentage of lumber exports to the U.S. market.

However, at that time British Columbia still represented some 70 percent of all Canadian lumber exports to the U.S. market, meaning British Columbia had to be the target, no matter how spurious the "subsidy" case. The focus was on "stumpage" which is that residual fee charged by the woodlot owner – in this case the Crown (or the government) to the company cutting down the tree after certain deductions. Some say by definition, this cannot embody a subsidy – if the wood derives from a natural growth forest. But this stumpage matter revitted the DOC and ITC.

In its preliminary investigation, the ITC looks to see whether there is a reasonable indication that the import has seriously hurt or threatened the profits of domestic industry. In its final determination, the Commission sees whether the Department of Commerce International Trade Agency (ITA) has made a final determination of subsidy. If it has, the ITC makes a determination of whether there was in fact an injury. If a final determination of injury is found, a countervailing duty in the form of a tax is slapped on the imported product until the effect of the injurious subsidy is eliminated.[10]

A preliminary injury inquiry determines whether a specific product from the other country poses the menace of negative economic impact on the domestic industry. Material injury means harm which is clearly consequential, material or important.[11] On November 17, 1982, the ITC made a preliminary affirmative injury determination against Canadian softwood lumber imports to the United States.[12]

Preliminary Subsidy Investigation

When determining whether a foreign importer is exploiting a subsidy the Department of Commerce's International Trade Agency (ITA) considers whether the industry has been subsidized "preferentially" and whether the subsidy was somehow "specific" to that industry. Stumpage fees (for cutting and removing timber from Crown land) were deemed "non-specific," as they applied to all industries using softwood timber. Even if stumpage prices had been specific, the ITA found that they had not been set at preferential rates. The ITA maintained that the Crown had used discretion in favor of lumber procedures by license requirements linked to targeting, but that the discretion was only relevant if it led to the exclusion of other users, which was not the case.[13] The conclusion of the ITA was that stumpage was being used by key companies operating in three groups of industries, namely softwood lumber, pulp and paper, and furniture, consisting of a total of twenty-seven separate industries.[14] With this in mind, no finding of preliminary subsidy was found and the investigation ended.

The Second Softwood Lumber Dispute 1986

Preliminary Injury Investigation

In January 1986, discussions on softwood lumber imports became an issue again as a part of overall bilateral trade negotiations. On May 19, 1986, members of the American Coalition for Fair Lumber Imports filed a countervailing duty petition with the ITC alleging that Canadian timber pricing and allocation policies were injuring American lumber producers. Their demand: a 27 percent duty.[15]

On June 26, 1986, the ITC found in its preliminary investigation that there was a reasonable indication that the domestic softwood lumber industry was being materially injured by Canada. The ITC found that the U.S. lumber industry was being materially injured by an increase in Canadian lumber imports. The ITC however did not consider other important factors. These other factors included the value of the U.S. dollar, market forces and a series of judicial decisions cutting back softwood supply based on argued reasons including the preservation of the spotted-owl environmental case. This spotted-owl matter became a classic example of using an environmental argument to limit imports. The American dollar had appreciated relative to the Canadian dollar during Canada's market share upswing. Clearly, the rises and falls in the Canadian share of the U.S. market mirrored the fluctuating value of the U.S. dollar vis-à-vis the Canadian.[16] Another factor hindering the U.S. lumber industry was its poor productivity relative to the Canadian industry. Canadian employees produced about 100 board feet per hour more than U.S. employees. The differences in productivity were mostly due to economies of scale of the larger Canadian operations and modernized production facilities.[17]

A third factor not considered by the ITC was the different forest management practices of Canada and the United States. While 95 percent of Canada's forest land was Crown land (i.e., owned by federal and provincial governments), only 28 percent of U.S. forest land were state property. British Columbia, the province which exported the most softwood lumber, used a residual value appraisal method developed by an American forestry economist (Rothery) to calculate the stumpage fees. From the market price of the end product, the costs an average operator would incur in harvesting and a profit and risk allowance was subtracted. The remaining amount was the stumpage rate, the economic rent payable to the timber owner. In the United States, regardless of whether the forest land is privately or publicly held, the stumpage rate is determined by auction. On top of that, American lumber producers often had to bid on lumber to be harvested five years hence with all the attendant uncertainties. Canadian stumpage prices were lower, but arguably because a different (and arguably more fair) system was being used.[18]

The Preliminary Subsidy Investigation 1986

The preliminary determination of subsidy held that Canadian timber was being subsidized because the stumpage rates discriminated in favor of a specific industry, namely Canadian softwood lumber.[19] The ITA determined that Canada was using preferential pricing for a specific group of industries. After doing some math, the ITA further found that government costs *exceeded* provincial revenue from the land. By ITA calculations, the total subsidy amounted to 14.5 percent ad valorem on lumber products. As a factor in its decision, the ITA pointed to the discretion the provincial governments had to set the stumpage rates. [20]

The pulp and paper and softwood lumber industries did not share a common production technology; their products were and are dissimilar. Their workers belonged to two different unions. The employers adhered to different trade associations. Surely, one can question whether it is appropriate to justify lumping them together as one industry.[21] To repeat the arguments in an earlier chapter, this issue shows how differently developed capitalist states can fairly see things differently.

The "Memorandum of Understanding" in 1986

On September 30, 1986, Canada's International Trade Minister Pat Carney made a "final" offer of 10 percent more in stumpage fees, calling an export tax "unfair." The United States rejected the offer. On December 30, 1986, after further negotiations and the ITA preliminary determination of a 15 percent subsidy, a political agreement was reached for Canada to collect a 15 percent export tax for softwood lumber from the final subsidy determination's due date and to remit it rateably to the producer provinces. The second countervailing duty investigation of Canadian softwood lumber was terminated as a term of the Memorandum of Understanding (MOU).[22] This writer remember well the strenuous debate among ministers over that decision. Was the government of Canada admitting subsidy by doing this? Why collect from producers in some provinces and not others? It was a tortuous issue fraught with regional and nationalistic overtones. Still, the fact that Canada was to collect the duty and not the United States greatly decreased political tension. The government of Canada remitted proceeds from the tariff to the industry, tempering anger in British Columbia.

On December 16, 1987, the MOU was amended. The export for softwood lumber exports was eliminated, counterbalanced by new, provincially-enacted stumpage calculations. The export charge was dropped for softwood lumber first milled in British Columbia. The amendment exempted the four Atlantic provinces from the 15 percent export charge because they used market-determined stumpage rates. Quebec had implemented changes to its stumpage system. As a result, there was a phased reduction in export charges which would have been lowered to a 3 percent level by 1991.[23]

Canada conducted a study in 1991 showing that stumpage revenues were actually less than the costs of administering the system. This was one of the main pieces of evidence used by the ITA to argue after 1991 that the stumpage fees were nothing less than a subsidy. Canada decided that the MOU had served its purpose and (as was permitted under Article 9 of the MOU) terminated the Memorandum of Understanding, giving thirty days written notice on September 4, 1991. The MOU cancellation came into effect on October 4th, 1991.[24]

The Third Softwood Lumber Dispute 1991-94

FTA Chapter 19 Panel Subsidy Report
  The drama continued. The ITA initiated a *third* countervailing duty investigation for Canadian softwood lumber on October 31, 1991. Special circumstances justified the self-initiation: the second countervailing duty investigation had been withdrawn because of the existence of the MOU which had been terminated. On March 5, 1992, the preliminary determination of subsidy was set at 14.48 percent. The final determination of subsidy of 6.51 percent was handed down by the ITA on May 28, 1992. Canada asked for a review of the decision by a FTA Binational Panel.[25] On May 6, 1993, the Chapter 19 Binational Subsidy Panel (Subsidy Panel) voted 3-2, with two partial dissents, to remand the ITA subsidy determination. Why? There are four elements that the ITA was directed to consider when determining specificity of a subsidy, namely: government action, number of users, dominant or disproportionate use and government discretion.[26] The Canadian industry argued that the ITA had only considered one of the four factors required

to find specificity in the charges of unfair subsidy; meanwhile, only the number of users had been considered when the ruling was made.

The ITA responded that proving a subsidy to be specific did not require all four factors to be considered if at least one was found positive.[27] The Subsidy Panel deferred to ITA expertise in judging whether specificity existed. However, the issue was remanded to the ITA, requiring it to make another determination using all four factors and any other applicable evidence.[28]

If on remand the ITA did find there was specificity, the Panel held that the ITA would still have to authenticate the existence of a subsidy.[29] The panel concluded that the ITA had made a fundamental legal mistake in determining that it couldn't measure the benefits of stumpage programs because of market distortion analysis. (An example of market distortion analysis would be the effect of stumpage prices on output.[30]) The panel remanded the matter back to the ITA to consider market distortion analysis and the effect of the alleged subsidy on the operation of normal competitive markets.[31]

A new subsidy pounced on by the ITA, but not included in the previous two countervailing duty determinations was log export restraint by the government of British Columbia. The ITA held that restrictions on the number of logs that could be exported from British Columbia meant that B.C. log prices were held down. The specificity of the claim was held to be de jure instead of de facto.[32] The Panel concluded that there was no evidence recorded that showed that there was de jure or de facto specificity.[33]

However, the panel did not preclude the ITA from defining export restrictions as a subsidy. There was a 3-2 split in favor of log export restrictions qualifying as a possible subsidy. Another interesting fact was that the ITA had used market distortion analysis in the log restraint export subsidy, though they had claimed it could not be used for the stumpage fees subsidy.[34] There were also some other remands on relatively minor issues.

This writer remembers getting the news of the determination on remand filed by the ITA on September 17, 1993, in our office as minister of international trade for Canada. We discovered that United States agencies can be stubborn, even defiant, when faced with a remand from an FTA panel. The finding by the ITA asserted there was that there was still a subsidy. So the ITA repeated its original arguments of the final determination of subsidy of May 28, 1992, refusing to change its conclusions and in fact increasing the amount of countervailable duty. For log export restrictions, the ITA again looked only at the number of users in concluding specificity. One change was that the log export restrictions were held to be de facto instead of de jure specific. The panel had already rejected log export restrictions as de facto specific.[35]

On December 17, 1993, the Subsidy Panel remanded the ITA determination for the second time. On January 6, 1994, the ITA once again answered the remand order of the Subsidy Panel without changing its position. Even this did not debar the American-based producers. A few days later, an extraordinary challenge committee was requested by the American producers to challenge the legitimacy of the 1993 Subsidy Panel makeup.[36]

ITC Final Injury Determination

The ITC decided that the voice of one particular domestic group needed to be heard amid the chorus of industrial complaints: the mill operators'. It noted that United States softwood lumber producers' capacity had increased by 12 percent from 1986 to 1991, but that there had been a decline in production from 1987 to 1991 to below 1986 levels. Workers had been laid off and wages had increased less than 2 percent per year during this period. The first "required factor" to be judged by the ITC was the volume of Canadian softwood lumber imports. It was deemed to be significant in absolute terms and relative to U.S. production/consumption.[37]

The required factor for "injury" determination included such manifestations as: a decline in domestic output; lower domestic prices; lower employment; and lower wages.[38] From 1987 to 1991, the Canadian market share of softwood lumber imports in the U.S. market fell from 28.9 percent to 27.5 percent but the ITC noted that the market share in terms of value rose from 26.9 percent to 28.3 percent in the same time period. Again, the ITC conclusion was that there was enough volume to cause injury.[39]

Negligible third country import competition was regarded as an important factor in its own right, making market prices fundamentally sensitive to Canadian prices. Still, if there had been more international competition one would have to assume that prices would have at best stayed the same – and perhaps fallen even further. Prices for spruce pine fir dimension lumber were viewed as a bellwether in the market. From 1986 to 1991, the Canadian share of the spruce pine fir market was 75 percent.[40] The final conclusion was that there was a material injury caused by the stumpage subsidy determined in the ITA Final Subsidy Determination and the rate of countervailing duty would be 6.51 percent.

In the dissent to this conclusion, critics argued that stumpage fees were held to be so low a part of the price that they did not have any real effect on the U.S. market. Transportation costs accounted for between 5 and 20 percent of the cost also, it was argued. The injury to timber producers and designated domestic industry mill operators diffused the whole effect of the subsidy.[41] It was argued in dissent that the Canadian market share had been stable from 1988 to 1991, and one of the commissioners thought this capacity was not likely to increase. He argued further that subsidies were found to be domestic rather than export subsidies,[42] and that the drop in U.S. mill operator productivity had to be considered in light of the dramatic fall in new housing starts (from 1.5 million units in 1988 to 1.0 million units in 1991). In summary, the decline of American production had to be viewed in the light of the shrinking new housing market, even though the effect of Canadian imports on softwood lumber was cushioned by demand in the renovation and remodeling markets.[43]

FTA Chapter 19 Injury Panel Report

On July 24, 1992, it was evident to the Canadian government that it was in the provinces' best interest to join with the federal government on the softwood issue. The Canadian federal and provincial governments hooked up with the Canadian softwood lumber producers in requesting a review of the June 25, final affirmative determination of injury. A year later, the Injury Panel *unanimously* remanded the ITC determination for further action.[44] The panel found that the ITC had correctly determined that Canadian and U.S. softwood lumber were substitutable. The question of causation of the injury was held to be something which could not be proven by volume alone as the ITC had done. The panel disagreed with the ITC report and concluded that there was no evidence demonstrating that imports of Canadian softwood lumber significantly depressed U.S. softwood lumber prices during the period of investigation. The panel even went so far as to rule that spruce pine fir as a bellwether price indicator had yet to be proven.[45]

As noted, the Canadian complainants had claimed the ITC erred in not considering the drop in lumber demand during the investigation.[46] The panel remanded the ITC final determination and stated that the ITC could make a determination about causation of material injury by reason of imports of subsidized softwood lumber from Canada as long as it took into account all of the relevant factors. The panel also held that the ITC should indicate the actual price suppressing effect of the products if a price suppression analysis was used.[47] (Returning from the G7 Summit where the four Quad trade ministers were able to achieve important consensus on zero rate lower tariffs and other matters, this minister had an extra reason not to comment when this good news from the panel came in, as we were soon to open negotiations with the USTR and Mexican trade minister on the NAFTA side accords. No one wanted to antagonize the other, especially the USTR on the opening of those touchy negotiations.)

Returning to *Softwood* a year later, on August 4, 1994, the proceedings of the Subsidy Panel were stayed after a motion to dismiss. The motion to dismiss was made by the U.S. trade representatives after the extraordinary challenge committee (ECC) affirmed the panel's decision on remand on August 31, 1994. A Notice of Completion was filed by the U.S. trade representative. Part of the subsidy determination was now over.

The ECC split, unfortunately, 2-1 along national lines. Both sides in the dispute agreed that the ECC was the final tribunal to which the United States could appeal the decisions of the binational panels in the *Softwood Lumber* dispute. The Canadian majority held that although the two Canadian panelists, who had been charged with the appearance of bias, technically failed to meet the Code of Conduct, their bias had not been willful. The Americans had claimed that two of the Canadian panelists of the Subsidy Panel had partners in their firms who had clients in the softwood lumber industry. The majority held that failing to note this association was insufficient proof of gross misconduct, bias or serious conflict of interest. Justices Hart and Morgan held that even if the two Canadian panelists had disclosed their respective firms' interest in the softwood lumber industry, they would not have been rejected by the United States as panelists.[48]

In his dissent, retired U.S. Circuit Court Judge Malcolm Wilkie called for a vacating of the subsidy panel decision. He found that there was a bias, or appearance of bias, on the subsidy panel and that the two Canadian panelists in question had broken the Code of Conduct by not disclosing the softwood lumber dealings in their firms. Judge Wilkie called for a new subsidy panel to be convened and a revised decision issued.[49]

The ECC judges seemed to be concentrating more on the merits of the case and their own experience than their responsibility as a judicial review committee. The problem may have been that the retired judges on the ECC were more habituated to appeals than judicial reviews. The majority seemed to gloss over the so-called infraction by the Canadian panelists in violating the Code of Conduct. Of course, this may have more to do with their nationality than with familiarity with judicial review. (Although FTA decisions are seldom made along national lines in panels, the problem of decisions being made on national lines might be alleviated if NAFTA allowed another nondisputant NAFTA country's representative to be inserted as the third ECC panelist).

Finally, on September 30, 1994, the U.S. challenge to softwood lumber imports from Canada was abandoned by the U.S. Coalition for

Fair Lumber Imports. Eight hundred million dollars (U.S.) in duties collected by the Americans on softwood lumber were to be paid back to Canada, but that had to wait for a strategic threshold: the passing of GATT 1994 through a reluctant U.S. Congress.[50]

Comparison of the 1986 and 1991-94 Disputes

Clearly, the dispute went on too long and ended on an acrid note as a result of Judge Wilkie's dissent in the ECC and the Canadians' failure to disclose a conflict of interest, which, however minor, ought to have been disclosed before any appointment to the panel was accepted. For the sake of clarity, let us examine the length and the effectiveness of the second and third countervailing duty investigations for softwood lumber. The second investigation lasted eight months, from May 19, 1986, to December 30, 1986. The third countervailing duty investigation lasted from October 31, 1991 (when the ITA self-initiated an investigation on Canadian softwood lumber) until December 19, 1994 (at which point the U.S. officially agreed to repay $800 million in softwood lumber duties).

The disadvantage of the pre-FTA 1986 process was that *if it had occurred under the FTA* it could have lasted a maximum of 270 days with its strict time limits. Without the FTA Canada was left with few options but to agree to the export tax in 1986. Imposing this tax avoided a final subsidy determination, which may well have led to the United States collecting the money through a countervailing duty.

In fact, had there been no agreed settlement (MOU), the ITC final determination in 1986 would have concluded the second countervailing duty investigation, since it could not have been appealed to a Binational Panel (the Free Trade Agreement not coming into force until 1989). Without a FTA, Canada could have taken its grievance to the American judicial system by applying for a review of the decision to the U.S. Court of International Trade. If Canada had been dissatisfied with that ruling, it could have gone one step further on appeal through the U.S. appellate system. Nevertheless, it is questionable how much success Canada would have had in the United States court system. The Free Trade Agreement replaced court procedures for review in both Canada and the United States with the Binational Panels.[51] This writer believes the Canadian government was right to do what it did in 1986. The vindication of the Canadian argument by the panels under the FTA process helps in retrospect to advance the argument for a FTA dispute settlement process.

It is true that even under the FTA the 1991-94 process was a long and arduous one for the Canadian softwood lumber industry. Even though each ITC and ITA decision was twice remanded by the Binational Panels and ruled against by the extraordinary challenge committee, duties were still being collected. What is more striking is that even before the preliminary subsidy report, as an interim measure, the USTR directed the secretary of the treasury to impose bonding requirements for those products not covered by replacement measures instituted by the provincial governments. It was not until the preliminary and final subsidy reports were released that this was finally rectified.[52]

NAFTA

Under the Canada-U.S. Free Trade Agreement, final reviews of domestic agencies would be done through a binational panel. The panel would apply domestic law where the dispute took place and be mindful of the domestic standard of judicial review. The first review had to be done within 315 days; NAFTA panels have the same requirements. The panel review process was supposed to be a temporary one, enforced for a total of seven years or until the two sides agreed on a substitute system for subsidies and anti-dumping duties. The NAFTA permits each party to retain its own countervailing laws and use them accordingly (subject to minimum standards, of course). NAFTA panels consist of two members from each disputant party and a fifth panelist to be selected by the consensus of the two parties.[53]

Extraordinary challenge committees (ECC) under NAFTA are basically the same as those under the Free Trade Agreement. The ECC may review panel decisions if there is an allegation of gross misconduct: the panel seriously departed from a fundamental rule of procedure or the panel manifestly exceeded its powers, authority, or jurisdiction in some way, such as failing to apply the appropriate standard of review.

One of the problems with one of the chapters of NAFTA is that there is potential for a war of attrition. Article 1904 paragraph 8 states:

> The panel may uphold a decision or remand it for action not inconsistent with the panel's decision. . . . If review of the action taken by the competent investigating authority on remand is needed, such review shall be made before the same panel.[54]

In the third *Softwood Lumber* dispute, both the subsidy and injury final determinations were remanded twice. In each investigation the U.S. competent authority insisted that its interpretation of U.S. law was correct. The United States challenged the FTA Subsidy Panel under the extraordinary challenge committee (ECC) and agreed with Canada that it was the last employable avenue in the *Softwood Lumber* dispute. As we have seen, after the Americans were unsuccessful at the ECC, they made a motion to dismiss the third countervailing process for *Softwood Lumber* once and for all.

However, the ITC and the ITA never agreed to use the remand criteria imposed by the binational panels. Paragraph 8 of Article 1904 only mentions one review of a determination on remand ordered by the competent investigating authority (in this case, either the ITC or ITA). Moreover, it does not address what happens when the investigating authority twice does not answer the remand adequately.

Therefore, there is a potential for gridlock in future decisions hinging on Chapter 19 decisions in the future. If the United States had not agreed that the *Softwood Lumber* dispute was over, there just might be ITC and ITA decisions on remand which had not addressed the panel review of the remands. Article 1904 does not seem to allow a series of panel reviews of decisions of investigating authorities on remand. If it did, the process might seem interminable. If the U.S. president had not agreed to dismiss the case the final decision could once again have been political as it was in 1986. However, since NAFTA seems to be on the verge of expanding with the addition of countries such as Chile, the United States would be unlikely to discredit Chapter 19. Perhaps "trust building" is starting to replace second image "politics."

GATT and the 1986 Dispute

On May 8, 1986, U.S. President Reagan threatened to use Section 301 of the *1974 Trade Act* to take unilateral action in stopping Canada's "unfair" trade practices in softwood lumber. He was acting within his rights: Section 301 of the *1974 Trade Act*, as amended in 1979, authorizes the U.S. president to retaliate against a foreign trade practice that is "unjustifiable, unreasonable or discriminatory and burdens or restricts U.S. commerce."[55]

On May 22, 1986, Canada charged that the United States countervailing duty investigation on softwood violated the GATT Subsidies Code. On June 4, Canada asked for the consultations provided for under that same code. Canada maintained that the subsidy claimed by the U.S. lumber producers was not linked to softwood lumber.[56] If Canada had lodged a complaint to the GATT Council concerning the U.S. countervailing duty proceedings, the effort certainly would not have led to any magic solutions. Back then GATT consultations were known to stretch well into the three-year range, providing a moral victory at best. The proceedings would not have acted as appeals of the ITC and

ITA countervailing duty decisions. The best Canada could hope for would have been for a GATT-sanctioning of Canadian retaliation against the United States, and even if this retaliation were followed up, it surely would have poisoned the atmosphere for bilateral trade negotiations.[57]

Let us ask this question: where should the United States or Canada lodge future actions in the softwood lumber area? Canada was successful under the FTA. Moreover, NAFTA has not significantly changed Chapter 19 subsidy cases. The problem with using NAFTA for Canada is that the definition of a subsidy used is the American definition. The ITA is again likely to find that stumpage fees are a subsidy leading to yet another Chapter 19 panel. This panel is made distinct by one crucial quality: its functioning under the new NAFTA, with an American chair, the split could easily be 3-2 against Canada.

Bringing the complaint under GATT 1994 might help Canada more than the United States in a *Softwood Lumber* dispute, seeing as how a GATT definition of subsidy would be used. As shown above, Canada would have a good chance of avoiding the identification of stumpage as "specific" subsidies. Indeed, the United States or Canada would have much less control of the process because it would not have members on the panel as under NAFTA.

Conclusion

The 1986 *Softwood Lumber* dispute lasted for just under eight months. The third countervailing duty softwood lumber determination lasted from October 31, 1991, to December 19, 1994 – a total of thirty-eight months. In 1986, Canada imposed a 15 percent export tax on itself to avoid a possible final determination of subsidy and injury. On the other hand, Canada was successful in avoiding countervailing duties in the third dispute by having the binational panels twice remand the ITC and ITA when they came down against Canada for final injury and subsidy determination. Canada clearly benefited from careful consideration of reviews from the binational panels for trade disputes. Still, an industry with less resources than the softwood lumber industry might not have the fiscal firepower to fight a countervailing duty case for thirty-eight months.

Here's the rub: NAFTA has still not defined clearly what constitutes a subsidy. While so-called "Special Committees" are a new NAFTA option for panels, there is no real relief for the long panel process. The "new and improved" definition of subsidy offered by the World Trade Organization could potentially help untangle knots as tortuous as this *Softwood Lumber* case *if* reference is made to the WTO. If the improvements are made to any future bilateral/trilateral agreements, bilateral dispute over lumber may become less compelling as a predictor for other sets of conflicts. At present, most Canadian observers unfairly overlook the successful resolution of most disputes under the FTA and NAFTA, claiming the *Softwood Lumber* case typical of what goes on.

As a result of what was learned in the *Softwood Lumber* case the Canadian government in early August 2000, filed a complaint against the United States to constrain the way the United States might use its trade penalties if it decides to impose countervailing duties on Canadian lumber to retard imports after the expiry of Canada's voluntary limited export agreements. The case of *Softwood Lumber* is a generic concern in that Ottawa says Washington "casts its net too broadly so it can threaten counter-veiling duties, to boost the price of imports on a wider range of products."[58] Because the United States considers any kind of voluntary export restraints, such as the lumber quotas, "to be equivalent to import subsidies because they materially can force up the price to U.S. importers by restricting quantities," the United States argues Canada's complaint is without merit because of the American perceived definition of what it deems to be an import subsidy.

The *Softwood Lumber* drama in a way is not yet over but if the WTO clearly settles this question its impact on the definition of "subsidy" will be clear and this will be a major advance for the WTO.

Notes

1. S. Clarkson, 23rd paper University of Toronto, *International Relations Series*, Toronto, 1999.
2. *LA Times*, 7 January 2000, 16.
3. Op. cit.
4. McGill Conference, 5 June 1999, Montreal, Canada.
5. Op. cit.
6. Op. cit.
7. Op. cit.
8. Op. cit.
9. Charles F. Doran, *U.S.-Canadian Softwood Lumber: Trade Dispute Negotiations*. (Washington, D.C.: Foreign Policy Institute School of Advanced International Studies, The Johns Hopkins University, 1987), 2.
10. Philippe B. Venesoen, *The U.S. Trade Remedy System and the 1986 Softwood Lumber Dispute Between Canada and the United States, a New Era of Protectionist Trade Policy* (London, Ontario: Faculty of Graduate Studies, University of Western Ontario, 1989), 32.
11. Venesoen, 35.
12. Michael B. Percy and Christian Yoder, *The Softwood Lumber Dispute and Canada-U.S. Trade in Natural Resources* (Halifax: The Institute for Research on Public Policy, 1987), 143.

13. Percy, 48-51.

14. *In the Matter of Certain Softwood Lumber Products from Canada* (3 August 1994), ECC-94-1904-01 USA Article 1904.13 Extraordinary Challenge Committee, United States-Canada Free Trade Agreement, 3.

15. Percy, 147.

16. Venesoen, 73-75.

17. Venesoen, 76.

18. Venesoen, 81-82.

19. Venesoen, 89-91.

20. Venesoen, 91-93.

21. Venesoen, 95.

22. Percy, 148-9.

23. *Industry Profile, Lumber* (Ottawa: Business Centre Communications Branch, Industry, Science and Technology Canada, 1990-91), 3.

24. *In the Matter of Certain Softwood Lumber Products from Canada* (6 May 1993) U.S.A.-92-1904-01, Article 1904 Binational Panel Review, 4-5.

25. FTA Subsidy Panel, 6 May 1993, 5-11.

26. Extraordinary Challenge Committee, 7.

27. FTA Subsidy Panel, 6 May 1993, 35.

28. FTA Subsidy Panel, 6 May 1993, 39.

29. FTA Subsidy Panel, 6 May 1993, 44.

30. FTA Subsidy Panel, 6 May 1993, 52.

31. FTA Subsidy Panel, 6 May 1993, 59.

32. FTA Subsidy Panel, 6 May 1993, 61.

33. FTA Subsidy Panel, 6 May 1993, 76.

34. Extraordinary Challenge Committee, 9.

35. *In the Matter of Certain Softwood Lumber Products from Canada* (17 December 1993) U.S.A.-92-1904-01, Article 1904 Binational Panel Review, Decision of the Panel on Remand, 76.

36. *NAFTA WATCH*, (Chicago: CCH Incorporated, 19 January 1994), 3.

37. *Softwood Lumber from Canada*, (July 1992) Determination of the Commission in Investigation No. 701-TA-312 (Final) United States International Trade Commission, 11-18.

38. ITC Final Injury Report, July 1992, 23.

39. ITC Final Injury Report, 16.

40. ITC Final Injury Report, July 1992, 26-31.

41. ITC Final Injury Report, July 1992, 37-41.

42. ITC Final Injury Report, July 1992, 81-82.

43. ITC Final Injury Report, July 1992, 57.

44. *NAFTA WATCH*, 19 January 1994, 3.

45. *In the Matter of Certain Softwood Lumber from Canada* (26 July 1993), U.S.A.-92-1904-02, Article 1904 Binational Panel Review, 28-44.

46. FTA Injury Panel, 26 July 1993, 47.

47. FTA Injury Panel, 26 July 1993, 77.

48. *NAFTA WATCH*, 11 August 1994, 1.

49. *NAFTA WATCH*, 11 August 1994, 1.

50. *NAFTA WATCH*, 29 December 1994, 3.

51. Extraordinary Challenge Committee, 6.

52. ITC Final Injury Report, July 1992, 17.

53. Barry Appleton, *Navigating NAFTA: A Concise User's Guide to the North American Free Trade Agreement.* (Scarborough, Ontario: Carswell, 1994), 135-9.

54. *North American Free Trade Agreement Text,* including supplemental agreements. (Chicago: CCH Incorporated, 1994), 349.

55. Venesoen, 118-19.

56. Doran, 20.

57. "General Agreement on Tariffs and Trade: The Results of the Uruguay Round of Multilateral Trade Negotiations," *Multilateral Agreements on Trade in Goods* (Geneva: GATT, 1994), Annex 1A.

58. *National Post,* 5 August, 2000 , 5(A).

Chapter Ten

The Environmental and Labor Side Accords to NAFTA:
A Possible Solution for the WTO?

On the first page of our first chapter we contrasted the World Economic Forum and the World Social Forum.

At the inauguration of the World Social Forum at Porto Alegre, Brazil in early 2001, the conference itself (according to one press report), "took political correctness to the point of totalitarianism," yet Roberto Savio, founder of the Interpress News Agency, 'distanced himself' from this to suggest in a forum on the future of the nation state to move away from inflamed rhetoric to "give substance to institutions which are there and there for the protection of those in whose name we claim to speak . . . . The ideas we have are often in our countries constitutions, we must animate them." [1]

We began this book by recognizing the environmental, labor and often civil society pragmatists' insistence that their concerns be somehow grafted onto free trade agreements. Let us not forget that when before Bill Clinton defeated George Bush in the 1992 presidential election, he vowed in his campaign to add labor and environmental accords to NAFTA so that it could be expected to force all three countries to enforce their labor and environmental laws. The negotiations over the Side Accords occurred in the mid-summer months of 1993, early in Clinton's presidency, but late in the Canadian government's term in office. The key public issue in the side accords seemed to boil down to whether trade sanctions should be imposed if a NAFTA contracting party fails to pay a fine (or "monetary assessment," to use the dealings' lingo) for ignoring NAFTA panel rulings on environmental or labor cases.

These accords are directly relevant to the answer to be worked out as a result of the "civil society" protesters to the WTO. The accords maintain sovereignty to make environmental and labor laws but, in the case of one country at least, the accords do not involve trade sanctions. The side accords shift the burden to national governments to enhance environmental and labor laws through political pressures in each country without impeding trade liberalization. The accords shift to a multilateral agency the task, if challenged through proper procedures, to determine if that country is enforcing its own sovereignly-made law.

Assessments of the environmental accords performance appears in the last part to this chapter.

At the time of the original NAFTA side accord negotiations in 1993, arguments for demanding top-notch, strongly-worded side agreements were clear. It was evident in opinion polls that a significant number of U.S. and Canadians citizens were demanding that their governments take concrete steps to address such "big issues of the nineties" as recession-reduced wages and environmental challenges such as in high-profile logging sites like British Columbia's Clayoquot Sound. Canada's government and many in the United States Congress realized that well-conceived side agreements could create a historic precedent in terms of multinational North American cooperation in the crucial spheres of labor rights and ecological protection.

The critical voices calling for social justice in NAFTA dealings were colorful and diverse. In response to the ideas being advanced by these critics and other groups, both the United States and the Canadian governments, in 1993, argued that strong side-agreements for NAFTA would place North America in a position of leadership, well ahead of any international policy consensus on how to link environment and labor interests with trade and investment objectives. This "consensus" was destined to take on an even more controversial – and unworkable – form during the term of the next (Liberal) government on the Multilateral Agreement on Investment. Above all, we in Ottawa clearly needed the public on side with NAFTA; allowing the deal to pass without side-agreements was clearly not the way to win over a significant number of Canadians. President Clinton sensed a similar sentiment among Americans.

The challenge in creating protections for issues like labor rights, environmental protection and air/water pollution was the interior opposition to "trade sanctions" being written into a so-called "free trade" pact. Canadian business groups and many provincial leaders spoke out against this "sanctions" idea, calling it a contradiction. Newspaper editorials decried the very notion of "caving" on this, potentially affording *less* market access which would be the opposite of what NAFTA was set up to address. Even worse, trade sanctions would create disincentives to raise environmental and labor laws and standards and could actually encourage standards to lower them – a recipe for weakening progressive side agreements. Furthermore, trade sanctions could discourage investors and lead to the smaller economies of Canada and Mexico being bullied by some loophole-hungry multinational corporations.

After a series of preliminary meetings, the United States tabled its first concrete bargaining position in May of 1993. Comprised of six general points, the text of the initial U.S. offer would have been pleasing to environmentalists who were concerned by the weak wording of the NAFTA. The United States proposed: 1) the establishment of a commission composed of a ministerial council, an independent executive director and a secretariat vested with fact-finding capacities; (2) that privileges and immunities be granted to the commission to the extent necessary for its independence and freedom in applying the agreement; (3) that private nongovernmental groups could submit a complaint to the secretariat if they were of the opinion that a party had failed to enforce its domestic environmental laws; (4) that the standard for initiating dispute settlement was that another Party was guilty of a "persistent and unjustifiable pattern of non-enforcement" of its domestic environmental laws; (5) that the proposed agreement would apply to the domestic environmental laws of all parties; and, (6) that if a dispute could not be resolved, "a complaining party may suspend an appropriate level of benefits under the NAFTA."[2] Implicit in this last point was the empowerment of parties to impose trade sanctions, such as a steep import tariff, in order to punish another party that consistently abused its domestic environmental laws. Herein lay the "real teeth" to the U.S. position.[3]

While there were subtle differences between the initial Canadian and Mexican positions, they were both directed at the drafting of a less forceful agreement on environmental cooperation.[4] Both countries focussed upon the establishment of a weaker commission than did the Americans. The Mexican standard for initiating dispute settlement proceedings provided for a much higher threshold than that of the United States; it proposed that only when a party had "unjustifiably, persistently and systematically failed to enforce its domestic environmental law in order to attract or retain investment" could another party request dispute settlement. On this issue, the Canadian negotiating team was much less confrontational, calling for the creation of an inquiry committee that could examine those occurrences where parties were unable to reach "a mutually satisfactory resolution of differences concerning a consistent pattern of violations of the agreement by a party." Most notably, neither proposal spoke to the issue of employing trade sanctions in response to the noncompliance of a party with its domestic environmental laws. This issue would become the major sticking point of the negotiations.

For the most part, the parties to the NAAEC found a common ground on most of the issues that were broached in initial bargaining positions.

The administrative structure of the Council for Environmental Cooperation under the final agreement has aspects of all parties' proposals. The council is not as independent as the United States had originally hoped, for its main function is to "serve as a forum for the discussion of environmental matters" and to provide recommendations on a wide spectrum of issues.[5] Moreover, it is only provided with the power to "address the questions and differences that arise between the Parties."[6] The secretariat is to consider submissions from non-governmental organizations or persons "asserting that a party is failing to effectively enforce its environmental law."[7] Article 15(1) permits the secretariat to inform the council if it feels any submission "warrants a factual record" and it is to prepare such a record if the council instructs it to do so.

Only when the dispute settlement procedure of the final text of the NAAEC is examined do the effects of heated debate over the issue of trade sanctions come to light. The power to impose trade sanctions was ultimately included in the agreement, but the condition under which their use is permitted makes them a most unlikely and impractical option.

The standard for the commencement of dispute settlement is that a party displays a "persistent pattern of failure . . . . to effectively enforce its environmental law."[8] This is a lower threshold than any that had been proposed in the initial bargaining positions. However, viewed in the context of the cooperative dispute settlement procedure, it cannot be considered as a provision that will drastically alter the rights of a party. After the noting of a "persistent pattern of failure," disputing parties must hold consultations in an attempt to arrive at "a mutually satisfactory resolution of the matter."[9] If within sixty days the parties fail to resolve the matter, a special session of the council may be requested under Article 23(1).[10] After sixty more days, if the matter is still not resolved, a party may request that an arbitral panel be assembled to consider the dispute.[11] Within 180 days after the commencement of this proceeding the panel must present an initial report concluding whether or not there has been a "persistent pattern of failure" by the party that had been complained against.[12] Written comments may be submitted by disputing parties followed by a presentation of the final report by the arbitral panel within sixty days of that of the initial report.[13]

The issuance of the final report commences a new stage in the dispute settlement process. Under Article 33, parties are to agree on a mutually satisfactory action plan which is to conform with the recommendations of the panel. However, if the disputing parties have not agreed upon a plan within sixty days of receiving the final report, or if they cannot agree upon whether the party complained against is fully implementing the Article 33 action plan, the arbitral panel may then be reconvened.[14]

Upon examining these allegations the reconvened panel may impose a monetary enforcement assessment against a party who is not adhering to the terms of a sufficient or an approved action plan.[15]

Finally, after navigating through the procedure of the NAAEC, trade sanctions are permitted where a party fails to pay a monetary enforcement within 180 days after it is imposed by a panel.[16] As we shall see later, Canada staunchly avoided the possibility of having trade sanctions imposed against it by insisting that a fine issued against its government can be enforced in the Federal Court of Canada. This was an issue of considerable contention during the last weeks of negotiation, for the United States does not have the unique court structure of Canada; it was therefore forced to accept the possibility of trade sanctions as a final consequence for noncompliance with domestic environmental law. The monetary assessment could have been enforced in the judicial system of Mexico, but in the words of one Mexican official, the imposition of a fine "attacks the concept of sovereignty and is, as such, inadmissible."[17]

The resort to trade sanctions has found its way into other international environmental agreements such as the *Montreal Protocol on Substances that Deplete the Ozone Layer*.[18] This begs the question, "How and why have trade sanctions become an acceptable response to environmental degradation such as through ozone depletion?"

Hailed as the "forerunner of an evolving global diplomacy,"[19] the Montreal Protocol encourages and compels speedy ratification of and compliance with its requirements from all nations, primarily through the use of trade-restricting measures. Article 4 of the protocol provides for a three step import control program to compel nations into lowering the volume of ozone depleting substances that they emit into the atmosphere. First, a ban can be imposed upon the import of controlled substances under the protocol from *non-parties* to the protocol. Second, parties are able to draft a list of products containing controlled substances and the import of these products must be subsequently banned by all Parties in the future. Finally, the parties are to determine the feasibility of extending trade restrictions to non-parties on products that are manufactured with, but that do not contain, controlled substances.[20]

From the vantage point of a trade minister deep in the fray of negotiations with Mexico and the United States, one was able to see and suggest a number of alternatives to trade sanctions. State-to-state monetary assessments were a possible "other option." USTR Mickey Kantor said this is an option only if these assessments were backed up with trade sanctions (the very knots Canada was aiming to avoid!) if a country refuses to pay its "fine."

On the ecology front, one spoke out on several Canadian concerns as the side accords took shape. First of all, the United States and Mexico recognized that Canada had absolutely zero interest in being seen to be "buying" U.S. congressional support for NAFTA. It was also unclear – though not altogether unpromising – as to what the long-term opportunities would be for Canadian, not only American, environmental technology and services companies cashing in on a decade of major North American eco-clean-up projects. Our hope was that side deals would contribute to greater cooperation and information-sharing among the signatories of NAFTA regardless of our national political differences, a cooperation that could only lead to improvement of environmental standards and working conditions from the Arctic Circle to the Guatemalan border. We stressed that NAFTA itself already contained valuable environmental and labor measures that were reenforced by the side agreements. In the year 2000, one might now ask, could this happen on a global scale if the principles of the NAFTA side accords were universalized globally?

As of August 1993, several issues remained to be resolved in our ongoing negotiations for the side agreements. The first of these issues involved the poorest of NAFTA's three signatories, the state of Mexico. Mexico had some modest negotiating room with the United States and our government in Canada, but its expectations for labor standards could never be met while keeping favor with the labor groups in Canada and the United States who were calling for side-agreement clauses to grow Mexican wages in step with gains in economic productivity.

Many labor critics and their allies were also working to make the environmental side-agreement protections an outstanding issue that summer. Opportunities for Canadian environmental technology companies were at risk as well. This writer's (as Canada's trade minister) optimism about the prospects of the NAFTA side agreements working positively for ecology were tempered by critics in the media who charged that their governments had sold out to an agenda that sacrificed environmental protection for greater trade in goods and services.

Since bureaucracies can develop a life and priorities of their own, there was also some controversy over the secretariat appointment to run the side accord provisions. At the time, this minister felt that a reasonable prospect was the creation of a new, modest secretariat with appropriate structure and crucially ministerial oversight. However, the secretariat was far from a reality. It could not be established or agreed upon until *all* the side-accords were agreed upon.

The harsh media attention on this issue of "sanctions" as "the back-breaker" of the negotiation obscured the accords' actual content. The new mechanisms for information-sharing among the three NAFTA economies and the laborious process of ever reaching, let alone applying, sanctions were never fully understood by the public or reported on with any detail. Let us always remember politics.

This delicacy of combining civil society needs with trade liberalization is magnified if it promises to be a potentially pivotal issue in a nationwide election. This writer's government was on the cusp of calling a federal election under the leadership of the new Prime Minister Kim Campbell. The "crunch" in these August 1993 negotiations riveted media attention to trade politics since they sparkled about three months before the election. As trade minister, one felt that our government could never agree on an environmental and labor agreement that included trade sanctions. A failure to pay a fine would be unacceptable in Canada from both a third and second image perspective. The third image could not stomach the insertion of a new 'trade protectionist' opportunity to the United States or Mexico in NAFTA. As this writer saw it, this move would compromise a trade agreement created to *decrease* and *remove* trade sanctions and protectionism, not the opposite. Sanctions were, in our view, an anathema to "free" trade. And of course we could count on the Canadian political opposition portraying it this way. Agreeing with economic sanctions would first be viewed as a craven "caving in to the United States" by the Canadian government on the eve of a federal election. This would be political suicide. The *Toronto Star*, *Ottawa Citizen*, the Canadian Broadcasting Corporation and the *New York Times*, gave this issue continual prominence. This minister's negotiating team, led by John Weekes, fully concurred from a trade policy perspective.

Few things can top being told by one's prime minister, colleagues and key advisors that one's political reading was correct. It was a cathartic feeling to say, "we never, ever, will agree to trade sanctions." Yet deep down, one recognized this was putting our American and Mexican counterparts in an unenviable position. Even though this minister sensed his Mexican counterpart and his deputy agreed with us, we feared the agreement might collapse because of Canada's absolute opposition. Both the Mexicans and the Americans were right to see the actual implementation in practice of a trade sanction for failure to pay a fine as a nightmare so remote it could likely never occur. They could easily have seen the Canadian minister as grandstanding on a nonissue. There were many steps an environmental or labor dispute would have to climb before a "monetary assessment" would ever be imposed, let alone trade sanctions. They could be forgiven justifiable second image concerns (i.e., a recalcitrant offending NAFTA country keying its opposition off a remote eventuality) endangering the NAFTA edifice. Still, they never articulated this publicly, for which one can always respect them. Perhaps Canada was too much a side bar to these powerbrokers to warrant attracting huge attention. Whatever the reason, the example serves as a valuable reminder of how a parenthetical issue can complicate life for the United States, and how "carefully silent" American negotiators can be publicly when public complaint is not worthwhile. This is admirable from a long-term bilateral perspective.

The "trade sanctions" tempest brewing in our NAFTA teapot points to a key reality in political terms. It is also a lurker in any multinational trade agreement that attracts close political attention: symbolism is as important as content. There was little practical trade consequence linked to this remote "trade sanction" conclusion, but political costs were huge. When negotiating with the elephantine neighbor to the south, it is far easier for a Canadian government to pride itself in being "difficult" with the United States or even "anti-U.S." if it wants to escape censure by Canadian public opinion. Every foreign government will be tempted to be "difficult." The price for being difficult however is real. If good relations with American administrations are therefore severely jeopardized, it can be difficult for the prime minister and president to break bureaucratic log-jams as was successfully done in the Bush-Mulroney Acid Rain Accord and the Reagan-Mulroney FTA dispute settlement mechanism solution.

The fact that the Mulroney government was pragmatic, even *reasonable* in its negotiations with the United States over the FTA or NAFTA was viewed as suspect by a host of Canadian academic observers and media critics. As noted in this book, the Canadian government's successes in gaining American concessions were seldom acknowledged. Nearing what was clearly going to be a difficult election, opening our government to such a reflexive savaging by domestic audiences was clearly not an option.

The most stunning turn of events in this struggle of symbols against this writer's practical reality was the startling admission of Mickey Kantor, the United States trade representative. Rather than arguing that Canada's position was based on unreality and remote possibilities, he argued instead that the United States needed "trade sanctions" in the agreement for a symbolic reason. In one late night, six- person dinners in the Madison, we asked "what symbolism?" "Frankly," some administration Democrats said, "We need some 'red meat' to throw to these skeptics and anti-NAFTA people in Congress. This 'threat of trade sanctions' will go down well with these people. They will make less noise about NAFTA and then these Accords will pass." Essentially, they explained a need for "red meat" as shark bait even though it would probably be meaningless in policy terms. We did not doubt some Republicans as well as Democrats needed the bait.

Political symbolism, then, was the reason for the impasse. After Seattle, one regrets that thoughtful public discussion of how the accords creatively built on NAFTA while serving as a laboratory for GATT and the WTO never took place.

But it did privately! Every morning we would "park" the sanctions issue for our daytime dealings: we negotiated instead on all the accord details that had nothing to do with sanctions. It was this sense of the history and the imaginative content of what we were trying to do that propelled the three delegations to the negotiating table each morning at the Madison Hotel. Nevertheless, the huge media crowd at the hotel's front door insisted on harping on one issue to the public: sanctions.

As most of the key accord elements were agreed to (except sanctions) the accords could not be signed. This minister announced after over a week of negotiations that for him the negotiations were over. (This minister said he was going back to Ottawa the next day to brief the prime minister and cabinet. This minister was then flying to his London, Ontario constituency to try to run for his party's renomination for Parliament, determined not to return to the Madison until the Americans and Mexicans changed their tune on sanctions. This minister added a parting comment to the effect that if we agreed to sanctions, this parliamentarian might never be nominated – let alone win the election!).

After a productive day of negotiations (again on everything but the dread "trade sanctions") Mickey Kantor moved us into the American negotiating room where he and a few aides were watching TV for a roll call vote on President Clinton's first budget. It passed by one vote. He turned to us after the vote and said "Do you see what the President and I are dealing with? This is one tough Congress." This negotiator has always been an admirer of him after that. He, as well as us, were prisoners of politics, regardless of what "civil society" protesters, economists and ideologists like to think should dictate trade negotiations.

Jonathon Fried (our legal counsel) and John Weekes (our deputy) had approached this minister the next evening prior to another excruciating dinner of the ministers and deputies at the Madison about getting Canada to back off our veto of "trade sanctions". ("Excruciating" not because of the company or the food, but because at the end of the day we were all a bit fatigued and dinner conversation always, it seemed, was about getting Canada to back down on sanctions.) Mickey was often humorous, playing what he called the "arrogant S.O.B. American" with a leer. Jamie Serra Puche, our Mexican counterpart, was the consummate gentleman, more academic in tone than a negotiator.

Quietly, just before dinner, Fried, our deliberate and admirable legal expert looked nervously at Weekes. He made a suggestion: "We might have a way out of this impasse." This Minister replied a bit testily. "Politically; symbolically we have thought of everything." He responded: "This is a legal solution, minister. May I brief you?" he replied.

To this day, one resists being told that lawyers have all the answers. Skepticism is understandable because political life does not wait for lawyers to pull rabbits out of a hat. Political life is too often charged, too public, to move off stage for legal slicing and dicing. As it happened, Fried said something not unlike the following: "As you are aware, Minister, our Federal Court will, without rehearing the evidence, validate any 'International obligation' and order payment immediately. This means 'trade sanctions' would never be brought against Canada under this agreement. An officer of NAFTA would present the order for a 'monetary payment against Canada,' the Court would identify its paternity. That would be it." The fine would be paid. May I humbly suggest we suggest this in place of "trade sanctions" for Canada."

"Are you legally confident that your description of the Canadian legal context is accurate?" "Yes" Fried replied. Later during dinner this minister quietly suggested this as a "way out" to Mickey Kantor and Jaime Serra Puche. Both blinked and consulted their deputies.

"We Americans don't have one of those 'Federal Court things,'" said Mickey. "You mean you don't have an equivalent to our Federal Court?" we asked. "No, we have something under the Currency Act but no court as you describe it." "Too bad", we replied. Our Mexican counterpart allowed "we have a Court like that, "but there is no way we would let, what the Mexican media might call, 'Gringos' dressed in a NAFTA uniform come before our sovereign equivalent court and exact payment of some NAFTA fine. That would be political hell." "Too bad," we replied.

A few days later, we Canadians returned to Ottawa a few minutes short of midnight, charged for further cabinet meetings to enforce our withdrawal from negotiations if sanctions against Canada remained. Near midnight, we received in our office a call from both my opposing negotiators. As we flicked on our conference phone, part of their conference call was prematurely open. We heard them both agree to concede. Then they tried one last time to get us to change Canada's position. We refused. They reluctantly gave in. The result was a real achievement: no sanctions would ever be imposed on Canada because of the automaticity of payment by our Federal Court even though the United States and Mexico would remain open for trade sanctions for nonpayment of any monetary assessment. The staff celebrated briefly in the ministerial office. The agreement was warmly received by the Canadian media. Our prime minister was hailed and given credit for the so-called "concession" by the United States and Mexico. This surprising concession was hardly noticed by their media as their newspapers rushed to report that the side accords impasse had broken.

In burying the importance of this concession in the American trade representative and Mexican trade minister's press release, both the U.S. and Mexican governments were essentially ready to applaud the accord. Our government received the clear victory we had sought. What is more, all three national legislatures later approved the side agreements with little adverse publicity.

This author remains proud of Canada's negotiating team and their diligent homework. Canadians can remain proud of this achievement by the too brief Campbell ministry. Still, one is less confident that the public was ever able to follow the contours of the agreement in any of its intricacy. It is received wisdom in Canada that NAFTA and its side accords were somehow capitulations to the United States. In fact, on this occasion and even earlier during the Reagan administration, it was the Americans who conceded to bring Canada back. Canadians have an inferiority complex with the United States. Indeed, if the United States has ever conceded on a point there is reluctance in Canada to agree it has ever happened. The essential dynamic is clear. In any international trade negotiation, one must sustain political support even if it involves political symbolism. This irritates economists who know the economic answer. It irritates policy experts who need not worry about politics. One can argue from the political actors' point of view that this is a lucid example of the "political calculus" feeding realist "second image" impediments. These obstacles must be navigated and dealt with if a successful "legal momentum third- image" structure is ever to prevail. One cannot make foreign or trade policy by preaching only "third image" objectives. One must deal with other realities, many of them local and highly symbolic.

Far more important is the lasting example of this as a solution to the Seattle impasse for the WTO. If nations developed an equivalent to Canada's Federal Court, regional and WTO trade agreements could include side accords on nontrade issues beyond those already implicit in the WTO now. Without giving rise to a new excuse for trade sanctions through environmental or labor issues, national sovereignty to make such laws would also be respected.

To point to "winners or losers" in this "NAFTA side accord" drama would be infantile, even if politically potent. The side accords to NAFTA are a material step forward for those who care about environmental degradation and labor justice in trade agreements. There can be no doubt the NAFTA process negotiated is convoluted and strenuous. Still, it has its sting. The scorebook to date is not encyclopedic, but sprouts of activity are visible. Six environmental disputes have been dealt with and three labor by mid-1999. One can wish there had been more. But one can ask how many potential disputes have been dissolved quietly because of the necessary processes requiring information sharing and consultation before formal dispute settlement is needed? Let us follow John Kirton's close look at this in more detail in his work published in the *American Review of Canadian Studies*. Kirton has perhaps been the closest follower of the impact of the accords.

The North American Agreement on Environmental Cooperation created a Commission for Environmental Cooperation (CEC), consisting of a council (cabinet-level officials making decisions by consensus) and a secretariat. The Environmental Side Agreement contains dispute settlement processes for two types of controversies: allegations that a government has failed to enforce its environmental laws, called enforcement matters, and other, nonenforcement matters. The latter category is covered by Article 13, which provides that the secretariat may investigate a controversy and prepare a report that may be disclosed to the public. The council can preclude the investigation altogether or decline to make a report public.

For enforcement matters, two dispute resolution systems exist. First, Articles 14 and 15 apply when a government does not effectively enforce its environmental law. Any NGO or person may submit a petition to the secretariat alleging that a NAFTA country is offending. The secretariat then considers whether the matter merits developing a factual record. If it answers in the affirmative, a two-thirds vote of the council is required to proceed and another two-thirds vote is necessary for making the final record public.

Under the second system, Articles 22 through 36 apply if a government has engaged in a "persistent pattern" of failed environmental enforcement, defined as a "sustained or recurring course of action or inaction." In such situations, any party may request consultations with the offending party. If the consulting parties fail to reach a resolution within sixty days, any disputant may request a special session of the council. The council is to meet within twenty days and, if it fails to settle the matter within sixty days after convening, shall, upon the request of any consulting party, and by a two-thirds vote, convene an arbitral panel. Within 180 days after the final panelist is selected, the panel must produce an initial report. A thirty-day window for written comments then occurs, followed by the issuance of a final report thirty days after that. The final report is published five days after it is transmitted to the council. The final stage, if necessary, is the implementation of a decision finding that a party has persistently failed to enforce its environmental laws. If a mutually satisfactory action plan is agreed, the offending party has 180 days to implement it. After this date, the complaining party may request that the panel reconvene. Within sixty days after it is reconvened, the panel shall determine whether the action plan is being implemented and, if not, shall impose a "monetary enforcement assessment" upon the offending party. This may be "no greater than 0.007 percent of total trade goods between the Parties during the most recent year for which data are available" ($26.8 million in 1996), an amount paid into a special fund to be used for environmental improvements in the territory of the offending party. If an action plan is not agreed, the panel is reconvened and given the task of devising such a plan, if the complaining party so requests. Ultimately, noncompliance with an action plan and/or nonpayment of the monetary enforcement assessment may lead to the suspension of trade benefits.

There are a number of important differences between the environmental dispute settlement process and the framework in Chapter 20 of NAFTA. An environmental panel cannot be formed absent a majority vote of the council, the length of time allocated for resolving disputes is double that permitted under Chapter 20, the council has no discretion to withhold the publication of a panel's final report, and monetary penalties may be imposed on a noncompliant party without having a resort to the full-fledged suspension of trade benefits.

As of December 1996, the secretariat had formally reviewed a few matters pursuant to Article 13 and over ten matters pursuant to Articles 14 and 15.

Dispute Resolution under the Labor Side Agreement (applied provincially in December 1996 only to Alberta)

The NAFTA parties created a Commission for Labor Cooperation (CLC) consisting of a council (of labor ministers) and secretariat, and National Administrative Offices (NAOs) in each country. The Labor Side Agreement creates a four-step dispute settlement process consisting of: initial consultations between NAOs; ministerial consultations; expert evaluations; and further consultations that may lead to nonbinding arbitration. Article 16 of the agreement authorizes each NAO to receive submissions from the public concerning labor law matters arising in the territory of another NAFTA party. Within sixty days after a submission is filed, an NAO is required to determine whether to accept it for review. Ordinarily, the NAO should hold a public hearing and can request consultations with another NAO. Within 120 days after the submission is accepted, a public report should be issued. If Article 21 NAO consultations fail to resolve the controversy satisfactorily, an NAO may recommend advancement to the second stage of dispute resolution – ministerial consultations. Under Article 22, any NAFTA country may likewise request ministerial consultations regarding any matter within the scope of the Labor Side Agreement. If ministerial consultations fail to resolve the dispute, any consulting party may request that an Evaluation Committee of Experts (ECE) be convened. The subject matter authority of an ECE is much narrower than that of an NAO, as the ECE is limited to reviewing matters that relate to the enforcement of "occupational safety and health or other technical labor standards." The ECE conducts a nonadversarial analysis of how each NAFTA country deals with the matter at issue and, within 120 days of its establishment, presents a draft report for consideration by the council. Sixty days after this, the ECE is to present a final report, unless the council decides otherwise.

A labor dispute may advance to the fourth stage of dispute resolution (consultations that may lead to nonbinding arbitration) only if it falls within a narrow band of cases. The particular dispute must be the subject of an ECE final report presented to the council. It must involve one of three issues: occupational safety and health; child labor; or minimum wage. The ECE analysis must reveal a "persistent pattern" of failure by the country complained against to enforce its laws effectively. If all of these conditions are met, a complaining party may then request consultations with the offending party. Council involvement and arbitration ensue if necessary.

As of 2001, a number of controversies were formally submitted to the NAOs. All of these began as Article 16 submissions by private groups, were accepted for review, and advanced to the NAO consultations stage. In three cases concerning American companies' labor practices in Mexico, the disputes were terminated upon NAO consultations. Twice, the NAO dismissed the submissions because the workers concerned had accepted severance pay. On the third occasion, the American union complainant withdrew its submission, stating its belief that the NAO would conduct only a "whitewash" investigation.

Two of the seven disputes progressed to the level of ministerial consultations. In one, four human rights groups filed a submission with the U.S. NAO alleging that Sony Corporation fired union activists at a plant in Nuevo Laredo, Mexico, and that the Mexican government had failed to enforce the worker's constitutional rights to free association. In October 1994, the NAO accepted the case, noting that its analysis would be confined to whether Mexico enforced its labor laws effectively, and would not extend to whether Sony acted illegally. In April 1995, after public hearings, the U.S. NAO issued a report highly critical of the Mexican government. It recommended that ministerial consultations take place. In June, following consultations between the labor ministers of Mexico and the United States, Mexico announced that it would review its laws respecting the registration of independent labor unions. In March

1996, union leaders called on the U.S. labor secretary to reopen ministerial consultations with Mexico to bring it into compliance. The secretary decided not to reopen consultations, but instructed the NAO to monitor Mexico's labor laws for signs of improvement. In its December follow-up report, the NAO surveyed recent legislative proposals and Supreme Court decisions in Mexico that had the potential to liberalize the registration of independent trade unions. The NAO concluded its report with the reservation that the impact these developments will have in Mexico "remains to be seen."

Principal Lessons from the Early Experience

Do the NAFTA dispute settlement systems generate final outcomes? Under Chapter 20, only three of eight disputes were resolved. The five others lingered at the consultations stage for several reasons. First, there is no requirement that a party escalate a dispute to a Free Trade Commission meeting if consultations prove futile. Second, political considerations played a role, including Mexico's and Canada's sensitivity to the Clinton administration's preelection position and to the danger of escalating disputes in an atmosphere of American populist protectionism.

In contrast, Chapter 19's dispute-resolution process proved far more successful. Of the twenty-four antidumping controversies reviewed, twenty-two were resolved. Eight were terminated at the request of the parties and fourteen were resolved by panel decisions. The two pending cases were too recent to suggest any inability to generate outcomes.

The biggest success story for dispute resolution during NAFTA's first three years is found in the environmental sector. The Silva Reservoir submission led to tangible improvements in the way the three NAFTA countries protect migratory waterfowl. The Cozumel cruiseship pier submission led to a confrontation between the secretariat and Mexico that was politically uncomfortable for the Mexican government. Even though the secretariat terminated three controversies without recommending that a factual record be developed, it rendered prompt, clear and conclusive decisions for these terminations.

The Labor Side Agreement has led to results in the form of public reports, but the problems underlying the cases remained. Labor controversies appear to be more intensely and unavoidably political than environmental disputes. In the United States, organized labor has been far more critical and eager to point out purported shortcomings of the Labor Side Agreement than have environmental groups with respect to the Environmental Side Agreement. In addition, the U.S. Department of

Labor has chosen to define the role of its NAO in dispute settlement very narrowly (to assess only whether another NAFTA country has failed effectively to enforce its labor law). This precludes the NAO from attacking the root of many labor disputes – a private employer's abuse of workers. By contrast, the environmental secretariat is not constrained in this way under Article 13, nor are Chapter 19 panels or NAFTA parties under Chapter 20.

Compliance for the cases discussed in this chapter was complete. Precedent does exist for U.S. noncompliance with binational panel rulings in pre-NAFTA trade disputes with Canada. As of December 1996, the number of formal rulings for and against each of the three governments has been more or less balanced, a statistic conducive to the maintenance of each country's commitment to NAFTA dispute resolution.

Adherence to Chapter 20 time limits has been inconsistent. Despite the fact that Article 2007 envisions a consultation period of thirty days, some cases have remained at this stage for more that a year. Since any party "may," rather than must, request a Free Trade Commission meeting after thirty unsuccessful days of consultation, there is no imperative requiring progression of the dispute to a second stage. In theory, the agricultural products dispute between Canada and the United States should have been resolved in about 220 days from the request for consultations. In the event, over 660 days elapsed between the request and the presentation for the panel's final report. For some Chapter 19 cases, limits were also missed. Article 1904 (14) envisions that Chapter 19 panels should issue final decisions within 315 days of the request for a panel. This time frame was observed by six of fourteen panels. Two others issued opinions about fifty days late. In the six remaining disputes, however, decisions were rendered more than 110 days late, with one taking 620 days and another 769 days. Both cases pending at the end of 1996 were overdue. The records for environmental and labor disputes' timely resolution are considerable better, with efficient dispositions being characteristic.

Early events demonstrate that the NAFTA parties will violate the agreement under sufficient pressure from domestic political forces. This is the case for the U.S.-Mexico trucking dispute (the product of pressure by the U.S. trucking industry) and the *Helms-Burton Act* (the result of legislation designed to satisfy the demands of Cuban-Americans in an election year). Yet the NAFTA parties have displayed tremendous sensitivity to the domestic electoral pressures faced by their fellow trading partners.

Chapter 19 has emerged as more important than Chapter 20 to NAFTA's success. An antidumping dispute resolution mechanism keeps trade irritants from escalating and also serves to balance the relative power relations between trading partners. Without Chapter 19 it is clear, as early chapters in this book show, that Canada would not have joined the FTA or NAFTA.

It is Kirton's[21] assessment that although the Environmental Commission was a United States initiated institution, accepted with reluctance by Canada and, especially, Mexico, it has in its early years survived formidable political and financial obstacles to emerge as a permanent, legitimate, comprehensively active and increasingly effective center of North American governance.

At the core of the agreement in Kirton's view is a well-crafted compromise over the critical issue of international enforcement. For in cases where one party is alleged to have a persistent pattern of failure to effectively enforce its domestic environmental laws over economic activity involved in or affecting North American trade, the CEC's ministerial-level council can establish an international arbitral panel to report, provide a remedial action plan and, if necessary, levy monetary fines. These fines are limited to US$20 million for any single assessment in the first year, and no more than .007 percent of the annual total trade in goods between the parties thereafter, with the fines being given to the commission for use in environmental remediation in the violating country.

"Civil Society" activists would be wise to recognize also that the agreement has injected significant additional environmental sensitivity and expertise into the trade dispute settlement mechanisms of the NAFTA itself. Article 10.6 directs that CEC's council "shall cooperate with the NAFTA Free Trade Commission" to achieve that agreement's environmental purposes, by receiving comments from NGOs, assisting in Article 1114 consultations over alleged "pollution-haven" investment encouragement, making recommendations and identifying experts from all NAFTA bodies and, most broadly, "considering on an on-going basis the environmental effects of the NAFTA." Although this is a formidable array of mandatory functions, the initiative for accomplishing such enhanced environmental activity in the trade arena "still rests substantially with the NAFTA Free Trade Commission (FTC), and the trade policy community that controls it."

Beyond environmental standards, the agreement, in Article 2, mandates the parties, with respect to their own territory, to report on the state of the environment; develop environmental emergency preparedness measures; promote education, scientific research, technology development and economic instruments; and assess environmental impacts. It specifies that the council "shall" promote and facilitate environmental cooperation, exchange of information, technical cooperation; and develop recommendations for public access to information, appropriate limits for specific pollutants and environmental impact assessment of projects with transborder effects (Article 10.3, 10-5, 10-7). It also specifies that the council "may" consider and develop recommendations on nineteen specific subjects, including those aimed at strengthening the role of environmental considerations in national and trilateral economic activity. Under Article 9 of the NAAEC, the council, as CEC's governing body, oversees all CEC operations. As Kirton concludes "this body was deliberately born as a minimum framework or platform, to be developed and shaped as environmental demands and political pressures evolved . . in its essential architecture the new body represented a major advance on previous, environmentally relevant institutions on the North American continent."[22]

As the Seattle WTO meetings opened in 1997, there remain little of the enthusiasm that surrounded the birth of the NAFTA side accord. The genuine innovations within the NAFTA-NAAEC-CEC architecture, in bringing trilateralism and regional international organization to North America and a more integrated, balanced trade environment regime to the world.

It is clear that during its first few years that the CEC has brought trilateralism in an intense and permanent way to North America and to Canada-U.S. environmental governance. The regular annual ministerial-level meetings of the council, the creation of dozens of intergovernmental working groups and experts groups and numerous consultations through JPAC and other contacts have, along with the secretariat and JPAC, according to Kirton;

> created a dense, multilayered web of new trilateral activity embracing national politicians, civil servants, influential societal actors, and individual citizens. In the realm of enforcement, the initiation and results of Article 13 and 14-15 investigations, and the absence of Article 23-24 intergovernmental enforcement actions and sanctions show that from the start, but with increasing force, the CEC has not been an instrument for the U.S. to single out Mexico and benefit from a poorer partner forced to pay the price for American political preferences and economic interests. And in the area of environmental cooperation, through the power of statistical comparison and publicity, the July 1997 NAPRI report, and the public reaction to it, suggest that it is the United States and Canada that are being singled out and constrained.[23]

Half a decade has done little to resolve the tensions that exist between the trade and environmental policy agendas, even as the need to do so has become increasingly apparent. Still, many of the necessary elements for achieving a productive relationship between these two vital disciplines were included in the rules and institutions of the NAFTA system. Ultimately, there is more reason to hope than to despair that the NAFTA model will ultimately prove its environmental worth.

As Kirton makes clear, environmentalists did not come to the trade and investment policy arena in search of new techniques for exercising political leverage, but rather with a set of concerns for how rapidly advancing liberalized trade would affect ecological values. They search for "second image" solutions (better *domestic* regulation) and "third image" solutions (better *multilateral* disciplines).

It is regrettable that the debate over "sanctions" became one of the most contentious parts of the NAFTA environmental dialogue. It is not uncommon for business leaders to remember virtually nothing else about the NAAEC, other than its granting the hated right to use trade sanctions. What gets forgotten is how unlikely it is that these sanctions will or would ever be imposed. The citizen's petition process (the so-called "Article 14" process) is another matter. So far, eighteen submissions have been filed, although only one has gone through a complete investigation process. This casts suspicious light on the power of this avenue as a real tool for addressing NAFTA's environmental impacts.

NAFTA was supposed to act as a prototype for the integration of trade and environmental policies in future regional market integration agreements. It has been a disappointment to some that this has not yet proven to be the case to any great extent. Still, as Kirton makes clear, the NAFTA/NAAEC system represents the most advanced experiment in the *pari passu* pursuit of the environmental policies needed for sustainable international commerce. In the end, it is the weakness of this parallel effort, and not the direct frictions between trade systems and environmental values, that is the deepest cause of remaining conflict between trade and environmental agendas.

Given all the linkages between environment and labor and trade alleged at Seattle, the actual experience of the side accords is instructive. It is far from clear that trade sanctions is the answer. There may be much that can be learned, however, about the enforcement of sovereign laws on the environment and labor. Short of sanctions, given the experience with NAFTA's side accords, one hopes the "Seattle mess" will hasten more advances in the International Labor Organization and toward more global environmental standards, all of which would push for the advance of enhanced sovereign national standards. This was the emphasis of Roberto Savio at the inaugural World Social Forum. Side accords to the

WTO or to an FTAA or to other regional trade agreements could be added to help hasten enforcement of sovereign national standards.

This result would trump first image political opportunists who rally behind national sovereignty when it comes to enforcing those standards. These opportunists would be open instead to examples of second image domestic law with regard to those matters. Finally, the development of the WTO as a transforming legal rules-based liberalizer of trade could continue.

In conclusion, we can now see that the simplistic ideological juxtaposition of the WTO and its myriad protesters continues in the media after the Seattle debacle, the Quebec summit and the Davos Porto Alegre "dialogue of the deaf." This juxtaposition makes the dilemma seem irreconcilable. Yet in fact both have more in common than is ever acknowledged. Ideological "performance art" by protesters or opportunistic trade ministers hurts, not helps, bridge the gap.

The fundamental dilemma is largely practical, not ideological. Let us assume that some world body is established to protect labor rights or the environment or culture or all of the above. Let's assume this body is somehow grafted on to the WTO as the environmental and labor commissions were to NAFTA. What would be the sanction, or punishment, if there was a violation of any world code on environmental or labor or cultural protection? One must decide on what sanctions or punishments would be exacted as a result of any future violations to any side agreements on labor and the environment. The Clinton administration wanted trade sanctions if fines were not paid. Canada, rightly in this writer's view, steadfastly rejected the proposal that trade sanctions be leveled against Canada if a fine (called a "monetary assessment" in NAFTA-speak) was not paid. For an environmental or labor violation one saw trade sanctions as a back-handed way to use environmental and labor considerations to allow protectionists to get their way.

It is inevitable that the imperatives of global environmental, cultural and labor protection be somehow a factor in our emerging globalized architecture. The real questions is: What are the sanctions to be? They should not be trade sanctions or these other worthy imperatives of a "civil society" will be misused by trade protectionists. Especially against developing countries. Let us hope that the many groups of protesters in Seattle and Quebec and the WTO and FTAA ministers will move to addressing the sanctions question. What sanctions other than trade sanctions would be potent? With an answer to this we might see the emergence of a synthesis between the growth of trade and the growth of these other imperatives.

Selected Reading on the Operation of the North American Agreement on Environmental Cooperation.

Audley, John J. 1997. *Green Politics and Global Trade: NAFTA and the Future of Environmental Politics.* Washington, D.C.: Georgetown University Press.

Commission for Environmental Cooperation,. *Four Year Review of the North American Agreement on Environmental Cooperation, Report of the Independent Review Committee*, June. http://www.cec.org

Economic Policy Institute, 1997. *The Failed Experiment: NAFTA at Three Years.* Washington D.C. http://www.epn.org/epi.

Johnson, Pierre Marc, and Andé Beaulieu, 1996. *The Environment and NAFTA: Understanding and Implementing the New Continental Law,* Washington, D.C: Island Press.

Kirton, J. 1997. "The Commission for Environmental Cooperation and Canada-U.S. Environmental Governance in the NAFTA Era," *The American Review of Canadian Studies*, autumn: 459-86 at 461.

———— 1997. "NAFTA's Trade-Environment Institutions: Regional Impact, Hemispheric Potential," Paper presented at the Conference of International Studies Association and the Mexican Association of International Studies, Manzanillo, Mexico, December 11-13.

Kirton, John J., and John J. Audley. 1997. "NAFTA's Commission for Environmental Cooperation: North American Performance, Hemispheric Promise," Paper prepared for a publication of the National Wildlife Federation, Washington, D.C.

Lustig, Nora Claudia. 1997. *NAFTA: Setting the Record Straight.* Washington, D.C. The Brookings Institution.

Public Citizen. 1995. *NAFTA's Broken Promises.* Washington, D.C.: Public Citizen.

Saunders, J. O. 1994. "NAFTA and the North American Agreement on Environmental Cooperation: A New Model for International Collaboration on Trade and the Environment," *Colorado Journal of International Environmental Law and Policy* 5(2): 273-304.

Spalding Mark J. 1997. "Lessons of NAFTA for APEC," *Journal of Environment and Development* 6(3}: 252-75.

Spalding, Mark, and John Audley. 1997. "Promising Potential for the US-Mexico Border and for the Future: An Assessment of the BECC/NADBank

Institutions." Report Issued as a result of meetings between the authors and those involved in the BECC and NAD Bank activities.

White House, The. 1997. *Study on the Operation and Effect of the North American Free Trade Agreement.* Report submitted to Congress by President William J. Clinton, July.

Notes

1. John Lloyd "Attack on Planet Davos", Financial Magazine, *Financial Times,* Feb 24, 25, 2001.
2. For the draft text of the initial U.S. position see "U.S. Draft Legal Text for NAFTA Environmental Pact" reprinted in *Inside U.S. Trade (Special Report)* 21 May 1993) at s-13.
3. The resolve of the U.S. negotiating team was evident in Mickey Kantor's words when he vowed, "We will not – I repeat, we will not send NAFTA to the Congress, unless we have effective side agreements." See "Kantor Insists on Sanctions," *The New York Times,* 13 July 1993, D2.
4. For complete copies of the draft texts of the initial Canadian and Mexican positions see "Confidential Canadian Proposal for NAFTA Environment Accord" in *Inside U.S. Trade (Special Report)* 14 May 1993 at s-2. See also "Mexican Draft Text for NAFTA Environmental Pact" in *Inside U.S. Trade (Special Report)* 21 May 1993 at s-14.
5. Article 10(1)(a) and Article 10(2).
6 Article 10(1)(d).
7. Article 14(1).
8. Article 22(1).
9. Article 22(4). Note that individuals have no right of action under the NAAEC. This precludes environmental protection groups, who have the best resources to establish a "persistent pattern of failure," from having access to the NAAEC instrument. Therefore, the traditional tactics of lobbying and publicity campaigns shall remain as the only resort for these organizations under the NAFTA.
10. Under Article 23(4) the council may then make recommendations or establish working groups to reach a resolution of the dispute.
11. Article 24.
12. Article 31(2)(b).
13. Article 32.
14. Article 34(1).
15. Articles 34(4) and 34(5). Annex 34 of the agreement provides that for the first year after date of the entry into force of the NAFTA, a fine shall be no greater than 20 million dollars (U.S.) or its equivalent in the currency of the party complained against. Thereafter, a fine shall be no great than.007 percent of total trade in goods between the disputing parties during the most recent year for which data is available.
16. Article 36. Annex 36B of the agreement delineates the limitations that are imposed upon the imposition of trade sanctions.
17. Clyde H. Farnsworth, "Now Canada Objects on Trade Pact," *The New York Times,* 13 August 1993, D1. The differential treatment of NAFTA partners on the issue of trade sanctions creates an unimportant distinction between the parties as the agreement goes to a painstaking extent to promote cooperation. Moreover, the likelihood of trade sanctions becoming a substantive measure under the NAAEC is elusive at best, given the

length, cost and complexity of the quasi-judicial process set out under the agreement. However, the exception created for Canada on the issue of sanctions is of great symbolic importance. One tenth the size and heavily trade dependent upon the United States, Canada could not agree to an arrangement that left open the possibility of U.S. imposed trade sanctions. This fate was not spared for Mexican Trade Minister Jaime Serra Puche who was condemned in Mexico for "caving in" to the inclusion of trade sanctions after having held out for so long. See Clyde Farnsworth, "A Gamble by Campbell Earns Praise and Points" *The New York Times,* 14 August 1993, 145.

18. U.N. Doc. UNEP/002565 (1987), reprinted in *26 International Legal Materials* 1550 (1987) [hereinafter Montreal Protocol]. Note that the evolution of the Montreal Protocol began with The *Vienna Convention for the Protection of the Ozone Layer* in March 1985. This led to the drafting of the 1987 Montreal Protocol which was amended somewhat by the *London Revisions to the Montreal Protocol* in June 1990.

19. Richard Bendick, *Ozone Diplomacy: New Directions in Safeguarding the Planet* (Cambridge: Harvard University Press, 1991), 211.

20. Note that this final provision is especially innovative for it essentially dictates to a country how it must produce its goods and as such imposes a considerable restriction on national sovereignty

21. John Kirton, *The American Review of Canadian Studies* (autumn 1997): 459-86

22. See Kirton, 459-86.

23. Ibid.

APPENDIX A

Arbitration Clauses Used in China[1]

At present, three common arbitration clauses are being used in China, namely:

1. Arbitration executed in China

Any dispute, controversy or claim arising out of or related to the contract, or the breach, termination or invalidity thereof, shall be settled amicably through negotiation. In the case no settlement can be reached through negotiation, the case shall then be submitted to the Foreign Economic and Trade Arbitration Commission of the China Council for the Promotion of International Trade, Beijing for arbitration in accordance with its Provisional Rules of Procedure. The arbitral award is final and binding upon all parties.

2. Arbitration executed in the defendant's country

Any dispute, controversy or claim arising out of or related to the contract, or the breach, termination or invalidity thereof, shall be settled amicably through negotiation. In the case no settlement can be reached through negotiation, the case shall then be submitted for arbitration. The location of arbitration shall be in the country of domicile for the defendant. If in China, the arbitration shall be conducted by the Council for the Promotion of International Trade, Beijing in accordance with its Provisional Rules of Procedure. If in _____ _____ (name of the defendant's country, the arbitration shall be conducted by _____ _____(arbitral organization in the defendant's country) in accordance with its rules of procedure. The arbitral award is final and binding upon both parties.

3. Arbitration executed by a third party

Any dispute, controversy or claim arising out of or related to the contract, or the breach, termination or invalidity thereof, shall be settled amicably through negotiation. In the case no settlement can be reached through negotiation, the case shall then be submitted to _____ _____ (arbitral organization of third party) for arbitration in accordance with its arbitral rules of procedure. The arbitral award is final and binding upon both parties.

Articles XXII and XXIII of the GATT[2]

Article XXII: Consultation

1. Each contracting party shall accord sympathetic consideration to, and shall afford adequate opportunity for consultation regarding, such representations as may be made by another contracting party with respect to any matter affecting the operation of this Agreement.

2. The contracting parties may, at the request of a contracting party, consult with any contracting party or parties in respect of any matter for which it has not been possible to find satisfactory solution through consultation under paragraph 1.

Article XXIII: Nullification or Impairment

1. If any contracting party should consider that any benefit accruing to it directly or indirectly under this agreement is being nullified or impaired or that the attainment if any objective of this agreement is being impeded as a result of

    a. The failure of another contracting party to carry out its obligations under this agreement, or
    b. The application by another contracting party of any measure, whether or not it conflicts with the provisions of this agreement, or
    c. The existence of any other situation,

    The contracting party may, with a view to the satisfactory adjustment of the matter, make written representations or proposals to the other contracting party or parties which it considers to be concerned. Any contracting party thus approached shall give sympathetic consideration to the representations or proposals made to it.

2. If no satisfactory adjustment is effected between the contracting parties concerned within a reasonable time, or if the difficulty is of the type described in paragraph 1 c) of this article, the matter may be referred to the contracting parties. The contracting parties shall promptly investigate any matter so referred to them and shall make the appropriate recommendations to the contracting parties which they consider to be concerned, or give a ruling on the matter, as appropriate. The contracting parties may consult with contracting parties, with the Economic and Social Council of the United Nations and with any appropriate intergovernmental organization in cases where they consider such consultation necessary. If the contracting parties consider that the circumstances are serious enough to justify such action, they may authorize a contracting party or parties of such concessions or other obligations under this agreement as they determine to be appropriate in the circumstances. If the application of any other contracting party of any other concession or obligation is in fact suspended, that contracting party shall then be free, not later than sixty days after such action is taken, to give written notice to the executive secretary to the contracting parties of its intention to withdraw from this agreement and such withdrawal shall take effect upon the sixtieth day following the day on which such notice is received by him.

Notes

1. Thomas C.W. Chiu, *China Trade Documents*, 2nd ed. (Philadelphia: Taylor & Francis, 1988), Section XI: Appendix.

2. *General Agreement on Tariffs and Trade*, 30 October 1947, Can. T.S. 1947 No. 27, 55 U.N.T.S. 187, T.I.A.S. No. 1700.

APPENDIX B

Appendix 1 of the *DSU*

Agreements Covered by the Understanding

(A)   Agreement Establishing the World Trade Organization

(B)   Multilateral Trade Agreements

    Annex 1A: Multilateral Agreements on Trade in Goods
    Annex 1B: General Agreement on Trade in Services
    Annex 1C: Agreement on Trade Related Aspects of
                  Intellectual Property Rights
    Annex 2:   Understanding on the Rules and Procedures
                  Governing the Settlement of Disputes

(C)   Plurilateral Trade Agreements

    Annex 4:   Agreement on Trade in Civil Aircraft
                  Agreement on Government Procurement
                  International Dairy Agreement
                  International Bovine Agreement

The applicability of this Understanding to the Plurilateral Trade Agreements shall be subject to the adoption of a decision by the parties to each agreement setting out the terms for the application of the Understanding to the individual agreement, including any special or additional rules or procedures for inclusion in Appendix 2, as notified to the DSB.

For authoritative up-to-date information on the WTO see:

1. *World Trade and Arbitration Materials* (Jacques Werner ed.: The Hague: Kluwer Law International, 1994-). Bimonthly journal which seems to be the most up-to date source for the full text of WTO panel discussions (Dispute Settlement Body (DSB) and Appellate Body (AB)) in paper/print format. Formed by the union of *World Trade Materials* and *Arbitration Materials* (Geneva, Switzerland: Werner Pub. Co.).

2. *Handbook of WTO/GATT Dispute Settlement* (Pierre Pescatore, William J. Davey & Andreas Lowenfeld eds., Transnational Publishers, 1991-) (ISBN: 1-57105-032-9). Includes full text of WTO/GATT panel reports. Kept up-to-date by looseleaf supplements.

3. *The International Trade Law Reports* (London:Cameron May,1996-) (ISSN: 1364-9205). Looseleaf including decisions of the World Trade Organization panels and the Appellate Body.

4. *Law and Practice of the World Trade Organization* (Joseph F. Dennin ed., New York: Oceana Publications, 1996-)(ISBN: 0379213583). Looseleaf service includes <u>Dispute Resolution</u> binders containing WTO panel reports.

5. World Trade Organization, *Basic Instruments and Selected Documents* (WTO BISD).

6. World Trade Organization, *World Trade Organization Dispute Settlement Decisions : Bernan's Annotated Reporter* (Lanham, Md.: Bernan Press, 1998-)(ISBN: 0890591067; 0890591059) (v. I. Decisions reported January 29, 1996- February 25, 1997 – v.2. Decisions reported February 26, 1997-May 31, 1997).

Perhaps the most extensive and masterful commentary on the GATT and the WTO panels is:

1. John Howard Jackson, *Jurisprudence of GATT and the WTO* (Cambridge: Cambridge University Press, 2000), 500p.

2. *WTO/GATT Research* (research guide by Jeanne Rehberg, New York University School of Law, October 15, 1999; includes links on dispute settlement).

APPENDIX C

Chronology

Softwood Lumber

1987-91	The United States conducts the first countervailing duty investigation of softwood lumber from Canada. The Department of Commerce (DOC) concludes that Canadian programs do not confer subsidies to Canadian lumber producers.
1986	The United States conducts the second countervailing duty investigation of softwood lumber from Canda. The DOC reverses itself and concludes that provincial stumpage programs confer subsidies of 15 percent to Canadian lumber producers.
December 30, 1986	Canada and the United States resolve the bitter and highly political trade dispute by entering into the softwood lumber Memorandum of Understanding (MOU). Canada agrees to impose an export charge of 15 percent on softwood lumber exports to the United States in return for the U.S. industry withdrawing its countervailing duty petition and the U.S. government terminating the investigation.
1987-91	The MOU is amended on several occasions to exempt the Atlantic Provinces from the Canadian export charge and to reduce the export charge for British Columbia and Quebec as a result of replacement measures implement by the provinces.

September 3, 1991   The government of Canada serves a Diplomatic Note on the government of the United States, advising of Canada's intent to terminate the 1986 softwood lumber Memorandum of Understanding, effective October 4, 1991.

October 4, 1991   Canada terminates the softwood lumber Memorandum of Understanding.

The United States announces its intention to self-initiate the third countervailing duty investigation and to impose interim bonding requirement on imports of Canadian softwood lumber.

October 31, 1991   The DOC self-initates the third countervailing duty investigation.

December 16, 1991   The U.S. International Trade Commission (ITC) makes affirmative Preliminary Determination of Injury.

At Canada's request, the GATT Subsidies Code Committee establishes a panel to examine whether the U.S. imposition of interim bonding measures and the self-initiation of the countervailing duty investigation violated U.S. trade obligations.

March 5, 1992   The DOC makes the Preliminary Determination of Subsidy – 14.48 percent.

May 28, 1992   The DOC makes the Final Determination of Subsidy – 6.51 percent.

The government of Canada, provincial governments and Canadian industry appeal the Final Subsidy Determination to binding binational panel review under Chapter 19 of the Canada-United States Free Trade Agreement.

June 25, 1992	The ITC makes a Final Determination of Injury – affirmative material injury.
July 24, 1992	The government of Canada, provincial governments and Canadian industry appeal the Final Injury Determination to binding binational panel review under FTA Chapter 19.
February 19, 1993	The GATT Subsidies Code panel distributes final report to the the Subsidies Code Committee. The panel concludes that the United States violated its trade obligations when its used Section 301 of the Trade Act to impose the bonding requirement, but that it possessed sufficient evidence to initiate the countervailing duty investigation.
May 6, 1993	The FTA Chapter 19 Subsidy Panel reports its findings, instructing the DOC to reexamine its original determination on each of the major issues.
July 26, 1993	The FTA Chapter 19 Injury Panel reports its findings, concluding that the ITC's determination of material injury was not supported by substantial evidence on the record.
September 17, 1993	The DOC makes a new subsidy determination on remand as a result of review by the FTA Chapter 19 Subsidy Panel.
October 25, 1993	The ITC is to make a new injury determination on remand as a result of review by the FTA Chapter 19 Injury Panel.

Index

About the Author

Thomas A. Hockin is a former parliamentarian and trade minister who brings practical "real world" experience to his academic background as a scholar in comparative government and international relations. He has taught at Harvard, York University and the Ivey School of Business, the University of Western Ontario. He has published three books and countless scholarly articles. As minister of state (finance) and trade minister he participated in the negotiations leading to the WTO and NAFTA and negotiated the environmental and labor side agreements to NAFA in 1993. He was a member of Canada's Parliament from 1984-1993 and is currently President of the Investment Funds Institute of Canada, and recently Visiting Professor of the University of Western Ontario, Faculty of Law.